THE GLOBAL DYNAMICS OF RACIAL AND ETHNIC MOBILIZATION

STUDIES IN
SOCIAL INEQUALITY

EDITORS

David B. Grusky, STANFORD UNIVERSITY

Paula England, STANFORD UNIVERSITY

OTHER BOOKS IN THE SERIES

THE GLOBAL DYNAMICS OF RACIAL AND ETHNIC MOBILIZATION

Susan Olzak

STANFORD UNIVERSITY PRESS

STANFORD, CALIFORNIA 2006

Stanford University Press
Stanford, California

Printed in the United States of America on acid-free, archival-quality paper

Library of Congress Cataloging-in-Publication Data

Olzak, Susan.

The global dynamics of racial and ethnic mobilization / Susan Olzak.

    p. cm.

Includes bibliographical references and index.

ISBN 0-8047-3998-6 (cloth : alk. paper)

1. Ethnicity–Political aspects. 2. Ethnic conflict.
3. Political violence. 4. Culture and globalization. 5. Social move-ments. 6. Social integration. I. Title.

GN495.6.O49 2006

305.8–dc22

                                  2005032416

Original Printing 2006
Last figure below indicates year of this printing:
15   16   13   12   11   10   09   08   07   06

THIS BOOK IS DEDICATED TO

Suzanne Shanahan

FOR HER PERSEVERANCE, INTELLIGENCE, AND COURAGE.

CONTENTS

LIST OF FIGURES AND TABLES

COW   Correlates of War (data set)
ELF   Ethnic Linguistic Fractionalization (index)
GDP   Gross Domestic Product
IGOs   International Governmental Organizations
INGOs   International Non-governmental Organizations
KEDS   Kansas Event Data System
MAR   *Minorities at Risk* (data set)
PANDA   Protocol for the Assessment of Nonviolent Direct Action
POS   Political Opportunity Structure (theory)

My purpose in undertaking this research is to offer an examination of theoretical arguments that focus on the global scope of racial and ethnic events as they have unfolded in the contemporary period. As most scholars know, the majority of research on ethnic movements has generated numerous case studies with rich historical detail, but it has not generated much in the ways of generalizable and testable propositions. Moreover, scholars have focused mainly on local factors of inequality, ethnic entrepreneurs, or failed state structures to explain outbreaks of violence or protest. Because relatively few theoretical arguments at the global level have been offered, country-level analysis has dominated the study of ethnic conflicts, protest, and violence. In this book I argue that there are specific advantages to moving away from a sole concern with local mechanisms that spark ethnic conflict and protest. By emphasizing global processes that link the fates of movements and the states they challenge, I find that country- and group-level factors are just part of the story.

My argument holds that to the degree that states participate in world organizations, ethnic mobilization will be more likely. Beyond this ethnic activation process, national economic and political factors further channel the form that mobilization will take. Thus, I seek to contribute to the existing literature, which has largely ignored the global context of ethnic movements. I explore two different data sets on ethnic conflict and protest to achieve this end. One source of information is the *Minorities at Risk* data set, painstakingly collected and updated by Ted Gurr and his associates. These data provide categorical information on ethnic mobilization that addresses questions about the magnitude and scope of ethnic protest and conflict. Because the data were collected at the ethnic-group level, they allow researchers the flexibility of moving from ethnic-group to national levels of analysis. My second data set on ethnic conflict and protest was provided to me by Doug Bond and his associates, as part of their larger effort of data collection using the PANDA parsing method for coding events directly from daily newspaper accounts published by Reuters news service. The PANDA data set yields information on the timing and location of ethnic events anywhere in the world recorded by this news organization. Together, these large and comprehensive data sets allowed me to ask several key research questions:

1. *What is the trajectory of ethnic and racial mobilization in recent decades?* Many scholarly treatments of ethnic violence, conflict, and activation of ethnic boundaries begin with the assumption that ethnic identity has provoked and sustained major group conflict since World War II, and many more warn that ethnicity threatens the foundation of the nation-state, and the division of geography and administrative units into state organizations. Because this assumption has been rarely examined empirically, this book takes on this task as its first goal.

2. *What is the relationship between ethnic conflict and protest? Are the causal factors the same or different, and if different, how?* This question focuses on theories and arguments relating nationalism, social movements, and peaceful forms of political claims-making to more contentious and violent forms of activity based on ethnic identity. At its most basic level, this book formulates an argument that links ethnic conflict and process to global economic, political, and social processes that have become increasingly important at the local level, activating (or re-activating) ethnic boundaries that now make claims on a world platform.

3. *Do links to the world economic and diplomatic network moderate ethnic tensions or exacerbate them and lead to ethnic and nationalist social movements?* A vast array of literature suggests that inequality and political opportunities vary across countries, shaping and channeling social-movement activity of all kinds. Yet few studies have considered whether global links among organizations expressly created for the purpose of affecting policy outcomes at the world level might interact with these national-level factors. This book offers an argument that global processes and links among international actors provide the motivation and means for ethnic actors within countries to motivate ethnic populations within and across national boundaries.

Guide to the Chapters

As is often the case, various chapters of this book will be more and less useful to readers with differing interests, tastes, and disciplinary backgrounds. In this section, I provide a few guidelines to different sections of the book. Chapters 1–3 are discursive and less technical, while Chapters 4–9 present quantitative estimates of the effects of group-, national-, and global-level factors associated with ethnic mobilization.

For readers seeking an overview, my main arguments are summarized in the introductory Chapter 1 and the concluding Chapter 10. Chapter 2 reviews a number of conceptual definitions and distinguishes my definitions from alternative formulations. For those readers who are familiar with the literature on ethnicity, ethnic identity, social movements, and nationalism, this chapter will be less relevant. Chapter 3 provides a general temporal overview of empirical data, and begins to sketch several alternative interpretations of these trends. Chapters 4, 5, and 6 examine sources of the magnitude and scope of ethnic protest and conflict. They present quantitative results using the *Minorities at Risk* data set on ethnic nonviolent protest and conflict, and the analyses distinguish between pre– and post–Cold War periods. Chapter 7 examines the temporal and spatial distribution of reports on ethnic activity since the end of the Cold War. In this chapter, I compare the effects of cultural, linguistic, and competition factors using data from the *Minorities at Risk* and the PANDA data sets. Chapter 8 uses data on ethnic violence, internal war, and international war to explore the influence of a number of political structures and opportunities on these outcomes. This chapter compares the effects of democracy, civil rights, and geographical contagion on ethnic violence with their effects on other types of warfare. Chapter 9 explores issues of two-way causation between state repression and ethnic conflict. It applies a number of methodological procedures that raise (but do not always solve) a number of questions about the endogeneity of the process, specifically trying to sort out whether fragile or undemocratic states create political opportunities for ethnic violence, or whether ethnic violence creates situations that make it difficult to sustain democracy.

Acknowledgments

This research monograph was partially funded by a fellowship-in-residence (2000–2001) provided by The Netherlands Institute for Advanced Study (NIAS). The author thanks Ted Gurr and Monty Marshall for providing the *Minorities at Risk* data set on the intensity of protest, violence, and rebellion. Ann Hironaka (2000, personal communication) shared her annual time-series of international governmental and non-governmental organizations. Doug Bond provided cross-national data on ethnic protest, conflict, and rebellion, from the *Protocol for the Assessment of Nonviolent Direct Action* (PANDA data set), in collaboration with the Program on Nonviolent Sanctions and Cultural Survival, Weatherhead Center for International Affairs, Harvard University. Excellent research assistance in assembling the PANDA data was provided by Sean Everton and Evan Schofer. Stanford colleagues James Fearon and David Laitin provided stimulating criticism, information and data, and support for this project. Many of the original ideas about the diffusion of human rights ideology come from John Meyer's brilliant work on the world polity, and I have drawn from this as well as from the work of many of his students, including John Boli, Chris Chase-Dunn, Ron Jepperson, Ann Hironaka, Francisco Ramirez, Evan Schofer, Suzanne Shanahan, Yasemin Soysal and George Thomas. I have had a large group of colleagues at Stanford and in the Netherlands who commented on my interpretations and pushed me to clarify my arguments. In particular, Al Bergesen, Daniel Chirot, Meindert Fennema, Michael Hannan, Jonathan Haynes, Michael Hechter, Ron Jepperson, Laura López-Sanders, John Meyer, Shushanik Makaryan, Emily Ryo, Suzanne Shanahan, Evan Schofer, and Sidney Tarrow provided excellent suggestions, criticisms, and encouragement, and I thank them all.

THE GLOBAL DYNAMICS
OF RACIAL AND ETHNIC
MOBILIZATION

CHAPTER ONE

World Integration and Centrifugal Forces

Ethnic movements appear worldwide in different guises. Ethnic mayhem by Sudanese Muslim soldiers, ethnic cleansing in Bosnia, nonviolent civil rights marches in the United States, Québécois separatism in Canada, Mexican-American protests in California for bilingual education, Protestant displays of patriotism in Northern Ireland, and regional autonomy movements in the Chiapas region of Mexico all provide challenges to social scientists attempting to explain the widespread occurrence of social movements based upon ethnic identity. While some of these movements have been peaceful, comparative research indicates that ethnic movements have contributed to the majority of violent conflicts among and within nation-states since World War II. Furthermore, some scholars warn that ethnic mobilization increasingly threatens the legitimacy and stability of the world's states.[1]

What accounts for ethnic conflict, rebellions, and protest? Up until recently, most academic and policy research has tended to rely on explanations of ethnic movements that focus on the internal characteristics of states (such as economic inequality, weakness of regimes, and the absence of democracy). Such perspectives have come under scrutiny recently because they tend to reify existing states as the key actors in world politics and they miss the relational aspect of states and nonstate organizations as a system of interconnected actors (Glick Schiller and Wimmer 2003). To begin to rectify these problems, I start by asking if global forces have contributed to ethnic political

---

[1]For instance, see Gurr (1993), Barber (1996), Strange (1996), Fearon and Laitin (2003), Fox (2002), Hegre, Gissinger, and Gleditsch (2003). In contrast, others emphasize more benign outcomes of ethnic politics, arguing that human rights have been expanded as a consequence of anti-discrimination movements (Risse-Kappen 1995; Räikkä 1996; Keck and Sikkink 1998; Risse, Ropp, and Sikkink 1999; Coicaud, Doyle, and Gardner 2003).

movements organized around distinctive features of culture, heritage, and identity.

In this book I offer and test a new approach to ethnic mobilization that considers the interplay between global forces of integration and the political mobilization of ethnicity. While it has become accepted wisdom that the fates of different polities have become more intertwined (Keohane and Nye 1972; Risse-Kappen 1995; Boli and Thomas 1999), there are few systematic treatments of globalization and ethnic politics. Here I explore whether globalization and ethnic social movements are causally connected.

Recent theoretical advances by a number of sociologists and political scientists inform my strategy of focusing on the world level of analysis.[2] Although there are differences and disagreements among scholarly studies on the impact of globalization, most researchers have emphasized the consequences of a densely connected system of economic and political links among states (Keohane and Milner 1996; J. Meyer, Boli, Thomas, and Ramirez 1997; Borstelmann 2001). These perspectives vary widely, from concern with world system position, to focus on impact of direct foreign investment, to interest in the legacy of the Cold War on international relations. Some scholars studying globalization take a political stand against globalization, while others are more analytically inclined. However, all of these perspectives share the growing recognition that international forces have produced a striking isomorphism among organizational forms found in institutions, constitutions, treaties, human rights, identity politics, and other social movements.[3]

My work expands on these theories of globalization, international networks, and transnational social movements by suggesting that processes associated with globalization have intensified at the same time that ethnic conflict appears increasingly divisive (Barber 1996; Gurr 2000; Yashar 1999, 2001; Sambanis 2001). These theories have considered the impact of global forces on the internal politics of nation-states, organizations, social

[2]The concepts of globalization, transnational politics, and internationalism are sometimes used interchangeably. For arguments documenting the importance of making distinctions between global market forces and transnational social movement outcomes, see Glick Schiller, Basch, and Blanc-Szanton (1992), O'Brien, Goetz, Scholte, and Williams (2000), della Porta and Tarrow (2005), and Tarrow (2005).

[3]For examples, see Roeder (1991), J. Meyer et al. (1997), Ramirez, Soysal, and Shanahan (1997), Gurowitz (1999), Barber (1996), Huntington (1996), Keck and Sikkink (1998), Risse et al. (1999), Frank, Hironaka, and Schofer (2000), O'Brien et al. (2000) Berkowitz (1999), and Borstelmann (2001).

movements, and other political actors (Tarrow 2005). Globalization processes include networks of diplomatic ties and treaties, formal and informal trade and economic links, international economic aid and agreements, and non-governmental organizations and transnational advocacy networks that coordinate activities in multiple regions simultaneously.[4]

By applying a global perspective here I theorize about the dynamics of forces that have repercussions across global, state, and local levels. Such forces exert pressure on political actors through economic trade networks, diplomatic ties, military interventions, and/or ideological/cultural institutions. World system theorists once proposed quite similar notions (see Wallerstein 1976; Boswell and Dixon 1990).[5] For instance, world system perspectives focus on the role of stratification of different territorial regions as a single force. Although the world system approach is useful to some kinds of analyses of economic cycles (Arrighi and Silver 1999), one of its shortcomings is its tendency to slight important country or cultural variations and contexts that also constrain and empower nation-states and actors (Tarrow 2001). Because of this limitation, the theory cannot explain differences in form and variation in goals, magnitude of violence, success, and other outcomes within world system categories. To counter this tendency, I build on recent work on transnational social movements, politics, and activism (e.g., Risse-Kappen 1995; J. Smith, Chatfield, and Pagnucco 1997; Keck and Sikkink 1998; Gurowitz 1999; O'Brien et al. 2000; della Porta and Tarrow 2005), by including empirical analyses of organizational, state, and global processes, in an effort to identify the mechanisms that shape different paths of ethnic mobilization. Globalization also includes transnational diffusion processes, which result in the ability of events occurring in one country to affect their distant as well as proximate neighbors (e.g., see J. Smith 2004).

Globalization has taken on a number of different meanings, including (1) actions by non-state actors (especially non-governmental organizations

[4]For reviews and research, see Keohane and Milner (1996), Keck and Sikkink (1998), Tarrow (2001, 2005), della Porta and Tarrow (2005), Hegre et al. (2003).

[5]Whether the plural label, "world systems theory," or the singular label, "world system theory" (indicating a single system), is more appropriate depends on whether the analytic frame assumes the existence of a more or less unified set of processes at the global level. Because my argument regarding its effects on ethnic mobilization rests on a unified conception, I use "world system theory" throughout this book. See www.sociology.emory.edu/globalization/theories01.html for further discussion.

and social movement actors) who organize across borders (Boli and Thomas 1999); (2) the diffusion of specific social movement organizations (e.g., the peace movement, the anti-globalization movement, the environmental movement, the human rights movement) that have organized across country borders (O'Brien et al. 2000; Zafarullah and Habibur Rahman 2002; J. Smith 2004); (3) transnational networks of organizations that aggregate and coordinate country-level organizations (Keck and Sikkink 1998); (4) diplomatic or trade associations between two or more countries, as in protected trade treaties or economic regional associations (Keohane and Milner 1996); (5) international ties or associations, which activists mobilize support for or against (e.g., social movement activism against dams or underground mines); and (6) trends that include the global reach and spread of economic capitalism, transnational corporations, and ideological forces that support world capitalism that justify economic policies in a number of countries (e.g., outsourcing) (McMichael 2004), which various anti-globalization movements strongly oppose. Some scholars combine analysis of these forces into a single phenomenon (e.g., Barber 1996). Yet others argue persuasively that it is more useful to consider these as quite different dimensions. For empirical purposes, it seems crucial to distinguish the economic and political forces from social movement outcomes.[6]

This research monograph offers and tests the argument that processes of globalization and internal features of states both incite ethnic mobilization (Figure 1.1, p. 27, displays the key processes). Ethnic mobilization is collective action based upon ethnic claims, protest, or intergroup hostility that makes reference to a group's demands based upon one or more cultural markers. Ethnic markers (such as skin pigmentation, language, religious

[6]For example, Tarrow and della Porta (2005: 235) and Tarrow (2005) make a distinction between international economic and diplomatic ties among nations ("globalization") and the expansion of international institutions, actors, and organizations that act on a distinctly global stage ("complex internationalism"). Others use the term "globalization" to refer to institutions (such as the World Trade Organization) that promote reduced trade barriers among nations (J. Smith and Johnston 2002). For my purposes, it is important to distinguish links among countries and international organizations from social movement outcomes. However, the majority of ethnic and nationalist movements that operate within national borders are not generally transnational in scope (but consider the counterexample of pan-Arab nationalism) (Russett, Oneal, and Cox 2000; O'Brien et al. 2000).

distinctions, dialect, cultural practices, or regional or homeland identification) delineate a potential membership pool, which may or may not become activated.[7]

Several research questions guide the analysis of the temporal and geographic diffusion of ethnic movements across a large set of countries. Can global-level factors help explain mobilization based upon ethnic identity, and can global processes help us understand which forms ethnic mobilization will take? Also, when and under what conditions will ethnic movements be relatively peaceful protests, and when will they turn violent? To answer these questions, I use information on the magnitude and occurrence of ethnic protest and conflict events in more than one hundred countries, followed over time since 1965. I use data from the *Minorities at Risk* and PANDA data sets on ethnic mobilization events to evaluate ideas about how international forces that integrate regions might influence ethnic movements. In doing so, I address some of the contemporary debates in the literature about the links among ethnicity, nationalism, and civil war.

Conventional Perspectives

Conventional treatments of ethnic mobilization find that inequality or the absence of democracy has systematically produced more ethnic conflict and protest.[8] So Collier and Hoeffler (2004) argue that "greedy entrepreneurs" cause civil war (see also Brown 1996), while Fearon and Laitin (2003) find that poverty and rough terrain matter more to most forms of civil unrest,

---

[7]While there is no shortage of definitions of ethnicity, there is growing consensus that focusing on ethnic boundaries provides useful insights for operationalizing ethnic identity (Barth 1969; Olzak 1992; Hechter 2000). Nevertheless, the process by which ethnic boundaries become transformed into active social movements has not been identified with precision. I pursue these concepts more thoroughly in Chapter 2. For examples of ethnic mobilization, see Gurr and Scarritt (1989); Gurr (1993, 2000), Olzak and Nagel (1986), Horowitz (1985, 2001), Lake and Rothchild (1998), Connor (1973, 1978), Fearon and Laitin (2003), Hegre et al. (2003). For reviews, see Brass (1991), Nielsen (1985), Olzak (1983), Brubaker and Laitin (1998), Yashar (2001).

[8]The tendency to rely on the nation-state as a core unit of analysis for studying social processes within states has been labeled "methodological nationalism." This approach can be contrasted with methodological transnationalism, which seeks to uncover the interactions and links between state, local, and international levels and flows of information, exchange, personnel, and resources (Glick Schiller and Wimmer 2003). For a review, see Tarrow (2001).

including ethnic ones. Petersen (2002) finds that resentment plays a role, whereas Horowitz (2001) finds that the presence of revenge motivations and strong emotions helps to predict when local feuds will end in deadly ethnic riots.

My analysis adds another layer of complexity to these arguments by examining the impact of key globalization processes. I do not claim that these intrasocietal forces are inconsequential; indeed, they undoubtedly shape the nature and timing of specific events and outbreaks of violence and protest. Rather, I am arguing that theories that emphasize internal factors capture only part of the story. Thus, my approach stresses both direct and indirect effects of measures that have impacts at the global level, in addition to the effects of poverty and inequality at the country level. Refuting my argument would imply that the globalization indicators are not systematically related to outbreaks of ethnic mobilization. Alternatively, supporting evidence must show that globalization forces have significant effects on ethnic movements, once internal features of ethnic inequality, poverty, and cultural diversity have been taken into account.

Prior empirical research has understated the possibility that ideological mechanisms underlie both nonviolent and violent ethnic mobilization. In applying a global perspective, I seek to redirect attention to transnational organizations that have encouraged widespread acceptance of ideologies of human rights and equality. My framework emphasizes the importance of diffusion of a worldwide human rights ideology, as it has been carried to remote regions by organizations that have established local connections in many countries.

In exploring these theoretical and methodological issues, my aim is to move the discussion about ethnic mobilization beyond discussions of intranational characteristics that spawn ethnic movements, by systematically analyzing the causes of movements that have roots in processes associated with world integration. This global perspective has proven extremely useful in the analysis of economics and international trade (e.g., Keohane and Nye 1972; Keohane and Milner 1996), international relations (Krasner 2001; Tarrow 2001), human rights (Risse-Kappen 1995; Gurowitz 1999), social movements and voluntary associations (Frank and McEneaney 1999; O'Brien et al. 2000; Schofer and Fourcade-Gourinchas 2001; J. Smith 2004; Khagram, Riker, and Sikkink 2002; Khagram 2004; Sikkink 2005), and international conflict (Hegre et al. 2003). My purpose here is to understand how a global perspective provides new insights on why different forms of ethnic mobilization might appear in different settings and historical periods.

World Integration and Ethnic Mobilization

The inclusion of arguments about the interplay between global and state-level forces in our analysis gives us more leverage over an increasingly interconnected world in which global forces affect internal politics. Economic and political crises that once affected only local areas now have repercussions in vastly different and formerly unconnected regions and states. Since the advent of the modern media, civil wars, terrorist acts, and acts by ethnic social movements have produced reactions across national borders. It seems reasonable to carry the implications of this fact one step further, to consider whether integrative processes have specific, centrifugal consequences for ethnic politics. Put differently, I first explore whether the magnitude of ethnic and nationalist movements varies systematically with integration into the world system.

Taking an international perspective helps clarify how economic interdependence among states may also foster rising ethnic subnational movements. Regional associations such as the EU, OPEC, NATO, and other supranational organizations promote interstate migration and decrease reliance of regions within states on the military and economic power of the nation-state. Multistate organizations also provide an audience for insurgent groups demanding new sovereignty rights (Olzak and Nagel 1986; Koopmans and Statham 1999, 2000). In this view, the growing network of international economic relations, exemplified by multinational corporations, growing trade and foreign investment, and supranational economic associations, will continue to produce more large-scale ethnic movements.

My strategy here offers arguments about forces of globalization that produce inequality, competition, and mobilization. My argument holds that *integration of a world economic and political system has encouraged ethnic fragmentation within states*. It does so by (1) increasing access of formerly disadvantaged groups to political resources, thus creating new political opportunities for mobilization, and (2) increasing levels of economic inequality in peripheral countries, which increases the potential for competition and conflict among groups within these states. This in turn encourages groups to make demands for redress of injustices or inequalities within states based

on ethnic identity. My argument further specifies that the process of integration of the world's states has varying effects on different sectors of the
world system. Thus, my argument builds on prior work showing the impact
of changing levels of economic and political access, but also considers various interaction effects between a country's position in the world system and
its economic and political characteristics. The goal of this project is to uncover some of the global causes of ethnic mobilization, while trying to sort
out those factors that shape ethnic and nationalist movements in different
settings and in different time periods.

I present three arguments linking interdependence among states in the
world economic and political system to internal sources of variation in rates
of ethnic mobilization. First, I use world-systems inequality theory to suggest that *patterns of ethnic violence ought to differ in peripheral and non-
peripheral countries.* In particular, I expect more ethnic violence (and more
state repression) in countries that are most dependent on the world economic
and diplomatic system.[9] Peripheral countries are those that are dependent,
economically, politically, and militarily, on more central and dominant countries. Dominance in the world system, though associated with wealth and
democratic regimes, is not conceptually equivalent with these other characteristics. It refers specifically to the number and coherence of ties to the
center of world economic and political activity.

A second line of argument relates globalization to the emergence of
a worldwide ideology supporting the expansion of broad civil rights to
various deserving groups, including ethnic minorities (Appadurai 1996).
The legitimation of this ideology across states has produced reactive local rebellions based on these claims.[10] Research findings by scholars studying transnational movements have added insights about the organizational
mechanisms of international non-governmental networks and associations
that transmit this ideology.[11] Following these scholars, I argue that one (un-
intended) consequence of the global diffusion of an ideology supporting

[9] For empirical support regarding collective violence see Boswell and Dixon 1990.

[10] At first glance, there seems to be some similarity between this literature and other
popular arguments linking processes of economic globalization to various forms of
insurgency, as in *Jihad vs. McWorld* (Barber 1996), or to a "clash of civilizations"
(Huntington 1996). While these arguments have wide appeal, they have not received
much support when investigated systematically (Oneal and Russett 1997).

[11] For instance, see Keck and Sikkink (1998), Risse et al. (1999), and Tarrow
(2005).

minority rights and rights of sovereignty is the mobilization of ethnic movements at the local level. My point is that a distinctly global ideology validating human rights mobilizes groups to make claims to acquire resources, attain parity with other groups or expanded civil liberties, or gain rights of governance over homeland territories. To the extent that local reactions to a world culture of guaranteeing human rights also intensifies competition for power among interacting ethnic groups, ethnic mobilization will arise (Barth 1969; Hannan 1979; Olzak 1992). These ideological frames legitimate powerful claims against injustice and provide strong motivation for activating local ethnic group identities. Conflict may escalate as other local groups mobilize in reaction to these forces, in order to resist coming under the power and control of oppressor groups. According to this argument, the spread of a world culture legitimating human rights for minorities and oppressed groups *increases political opportunities for minorities, raises the likelihood of ethnic protest, and exacerbates ethnic tensions within states.*

A third argument relates these international ideological forces to the internal characteristics of countries. It states that, although an international culture supporting human rights has diffused broadly, this culture is likely to have divergent effects on local regions, depending on varying levels of inequality, resources, and political opportunities (Keck and Sikkink 1998; della Porta and Tarrow 2005; Sikkink 2005). The literature on transnational social movements suggests that while a global human rights ideology has delivered a crucial message about the sovereign rights of groups, this message is refracted and reshaped by a number of cultural factors and opposition movements at the country level (Tarrow 2001). These country-level characteristics provide the cultural and historical context for defining ethnic claims for expanded rights within particular ethnic movements.

I argue that the diffusion of an international culture favoring human rights will produce systematically different forms of ethnic mobilization in different settings. Violent ethnic movements ought to be strongest in regions where ethnic rights are denied by the political system, and nonviolent ethnic protest will arise where ethnic group rights have institutional standing. Thus, I argue that while there has been widespread diffusion of an ideology championing the rights and protection of minorities, this ideology will produce different types of ethnic mobilization within different countries. In particular, *core countries and countries granting more inclusionary rights to minorities will exhibit ethnic mobilization that is less violent, while more exclusionary states will experience significantly more violent outbreaks.*

Status in the World System and Inequality

Although it is seldom applied to ethnic movements, the notion that world-level forces affect internal economies and polities is not new. For many decades, world system theory has offered a coherent analytic framework that provides a theoretical context for understanding global integration processes and their consequences.[12] According to a world system theory of stratification, the economic integration of the world system has linked together various regions, polities, and markets into a dense and interdependent system. Wallerstein (1976) emphasized that over the past 300 years, the integration of a world economy created a hierarchy of more and less powerful countries.

World system theory rests on the historical argument that the world's states were gradually transformed into economically and politically dominant "core" nations, a less-developed "semi-periphery," and increasingly dependent "peripheral" nations. Core states can be defined as having (1) centrality in trade and military interventions; (2) maintained dominance through the use (or threat) of a superior armed force; and (3) centrality in a network of diplomatic information and exchange, specifically in their role of sending diplomats and authoring treaties (see Snyder and Kick 1979). Peripheral states are those that score lowest on centrality and dominance. Other researchers have argued that the middle, in-between category of "semi-periphery" is perhaps more relevant to understanding outbreaks of conflict, because this category includes many countries moving from the periphery to the core. Such countries are also likely to be in flux, experiencing various economic and political transitions. This makes them especially interesting and relevant to arguments regarding the role of increasing and decreasing political freedom and economic inequality. Thus, it makes sense to explore the impact of semi-peripheral status on ethnic mobilization in the empirical analysis chapters that follow. Wallerstein and his colleagues have suggested that the addition of this intermediate category advances the theory because

---

[12]See Wallerstein (1976), Bornschier and Chase-Dunn (1985), Strang (1990), McMichael (2004), and Arrighi and Silver (1999).

it carries the implication that dependency can be viewed on a continuum, rather than as a dichotomous variable (Wallerstein 1976).

POVERTY AND INCOME INEQUALITY

According to the world system perspective, the diffusion of a world capitalist system has increasingly reinforced the dependence of the peripheral nations on core nations. The consequence is that the persistence of inequality among nations retards political and economic development in the peripheral countries, including the diffusion of minority rights (see Strang 1990; Alderson and Nielsen 2002). From a world-system/dependency theory perspective, peripheral nations ought to have a different political dynamic with respect to existing group inequalities than do core nations. This is due to the fact that peripheral nations by definition hold a relatively dependent position in the world stratification system. In this view, dependency intensifies the effects of all types of internal conflict. The analogy here is with a local environment of shrinking or limited resources, in which groups find themselves increasingly in competition over fewer political and economic resources. The processes of change within peripheral nations will have more immediate and more intensified consequences in more dependent settings, where there are fewer degrees of freedom. According to this view, the triumph of an integrated world economic and political system widened even small gaps that existed between richer and poorer regions within and between countries.

In contrast, several leading social movement perspectives have claimed that declining gaps in resources mobilize challengers against authorities. Thus, resource mobilization perspectives suggest that increasing access to resources among disadvantaged groups offers new opportunities for mobilizing at the grassroots level (e.g., McCarthy and Zald 1977; McAdam, McCarthy, and Zald 1988). To the extent that embeddedness in a world system encourages economic development, *increasing equality among regions (or groups) within a country releases forces of competitive exclusion and conflict*. This is because advantaged groups perceiving a growing threat from upwardly mobile groups will react by suppressing opportunities and closing off means for advancement. Ethnic aggression can occur as dominant groups attempt to reassert their dominance over newly competing groups. At the same time, protest rates rise as formerly disadvantaged ethnic groups gain access to resources and challenge the existing power structure. The changing economic leverage among ethnic groups provides the impetus for mobilization by newly empowered subordinate groups and by dominant groups whose position becomes threatened. This argument suggests the hypothesis that countries with higher levels of income inequality will experience more disruptive ethnic violence.[13]

Furthermore, these economic effects are likely to depend upon the degree of embeddedness of a country in an international organizational network. Highly dependent peripheral countries without external links to international organizations are likely to be the most vulnerable to ethnic aggression. Conversely, peripheral countries that are embedded in the world system of organizations may be shielded from disruptive internal ethnic aggression. In countries more embedded in the global community, internal strife is more likely to invite external intervention (diplomatic, military, and otherwise) (Keck and Sikkink 1998; Boli and Thomas 1999). This argument implies an interaction effect between peripheral status and the number of memberships in international non-governmental organizations. Following this logic, peripheral countries that also have a large number of links to the international network of organizations would have lower levels of ethnic aggression, when compared to peripheral countries without such links.

The threshold for mobilizing nonviolent ethnic protest is likely to be higher in the periphery than in core countries. In peripheral countries where there are authoritarian regimes, mild forms of collective protest will be suppressed and human rights activists less able to form local networks (Olivier 1990; Francisco 1995; Rasler 1996; Olzak, Beasley, and Olivier 2003). This suggests that, on average, peripheral countries would experience less ethnic protest. At the same time, because the cost of protest is high, protest levels remain relatively low. However, when protest does erupt in less

---

[13] Recent empirical evidence suggests that income inequality among nations is declining (Firebaugh and Goesling 2004; Goesling 2001). Does this evidence run counter to my hypothesis regarding the impact of inequality? Not necessarily. This is because my argument states that the spread of human rights ideologies implies that the persistence of any gap in human rights, income, well-being, minority treatment, etc., among ethnic groups has rendered ethnic identity more salient. Existing evidence shows that the rhetoric, demands, and claims of ethnic movements are more likely to be based on claims of economic inequality and civil rights, when compared to earlier periods when these comparisons were less global in scope. Furthermore, resource mobilization theories of social movements find that ethnic groups mobilize when formerly disadvantaged groups experience economic gains. Taken together, these findings suggest that recent declines in income inequality among all nations will not necessarily eradicate ethnic movements.

democratic states, it is likely to have achieved some momentum and support. In this view, protest is more likely to be violent, secessionist, and confrontational in more repressive countries compared to more democratic and open ones (Koopmans 1995; Kriesi, Koopmans, Duyvendak, and Guigni 1995; Olzak and Tsutsui 1998; but see Fearon and Laitin 2003).

VARIATION IN MEMBERSHIPS IN INTERNATIONAL ORGANIZATIONS

At the global level of analysis, I expect that international links have a galvanizing effect on ethnic alliances and hostilities within states. As the evidence from the Cold War period suggests, even the threat of an outbreak of international conflict provided a structure for building new alliances, coalitions, and interdependent relations between countries that can generate new opportunities for local mobilization efforts (Borstelmann 2001). With each new realignment of nation-states comes a new set of regulations for political asylum, immigration laws regarding citizenship, welfare rights, and deportation. As scholars in the international relations field argue, the recent demise of the Cold War demonstrates that new and different sets of network alliances can emerge among former enemy camps. My argument is that international organizations have produced additional forces of realignment within countries.[14]

To examine this argument empirically, it is crucial to distinguish nongovernmental organizations from ethnic social movements. Tarrow (2001) and Keck and Sikkink (1998) have defined international non-governmental organizations (INGOs) as organizations that include members from more than one nation-state, operate independently from authorities in any given nation-state, and engage in routine activities that include interacting with local residents to influence the organization's goals (e.g., human rights, world health, AIDS research, etc.). Although social movements generally include goals of broad social change as part of their mission, *ethnic social movements* are contentious social actors, because they incite conflict against other ethnic groups, make claims to authorities demanding the end of discrimination, or make demands for expanded rights of geographical autonomy, separatism, or statehood that are not being met. Thus, as Tarrow (2001: 12) indicates,

---

[14]Refugee flows can be analyzed as both causes and consequences of these same historical processes. International wars as well as internal conflicts provide a steady stream of political refugees seeking safety (Jenkins and Schmeidl 1995). In Chapter 8, I investigate the impact of ethnic conflict on civil war and international wars.

although both INGOs and ethnic social movements may seem to share common goals, their behaviors are (usually) quite distinct.[15]

The extent to which a country is tied to the international network will determine its response to the forces of globalization (Keck and Sikkink 1998; O'Brien et al. 2000; Tsutsui 2004). I pursue the argument that a country's number of connections to INGOs will amplify forces of political and economic stratification in the world system. Conversely, the absence of ties to INGOs implies that global culture and ideology will have weaker effects in more isolated states. Thus, I expect that ethnic movements in peripheral states will be most affected by membership in international organizations that have been established, dominated, and run by core countries. Because core countries are more deeply embedded in the transnational organization network, I expect that the global integration of human rights ideology will facilitate more nonviolent protest in these countries, and that these same forces of integration will constrain outbreaks of violent ethnic demands.

I am not arguing that international organizations produce more protest because groups in subordinate countries attempt to imitate social movements in the core. Instead, I am proposing that international networks are themselves a major vehicle for transporting ideology, behavior, and institutions supporting human rights. Consequently, countries with a greater number of links to these agencies should be most influenced by pressures that are both ideological (e.g., J. Meyer et al. 1997) and material (Tarrow 2001). Conversely, those countries that are most isolated from the international system of government organization should experience the lowest amount of protest.

The Diffusion of Human Rights Ideology

Recent analysis of the diffusion of world culture and ideology has shifted the emphasis of world system theory to consider the ideological implications of the integration of the world system (J. Smith 1995; Keohane and Milner 1996; J. Meyer et al. 1997; Ramirez et al. 1997). According to the world polity perspective, the diffusion of human rights has become a key motivation

[15] For some scholars, the key distinction between INGOs and social movements is that the latter engage in contentious politics, with state authorities, power holders, or other groups competing for power, whereas INGOs engage in fewer confrontational tactics and strategies (D. Meyer and Tarrow 1998). Since the Seattle anti–World Trade Organization protests and participation of INGOs and IGOs (international governmental organizations) in the annual meetings of the World Social Forum, these distinctions have become less useful (Caniglia 2002).

underlying modern social movements, including ethnic ones (Soysal 1994; O'Brien et al. 2000; della Porta and Tarrow 2005). Growth in number of memberships in human rights organizations and associations has led to the expansion of group rights in states that declared independence since 1945 (Ramirez et al. 1997). Countries that are richer, participate more in world trade, have more educated populations, and are larger participate more in this world culture (Boli and Thomas 1999: 68). Research from this tradition also finds that since 1960, all newly independent states have formally guaranteed human rights in their constitutions. This evidence has led some scholars to claim that there is an emerging international culture (Soysal 1994; Boli and Thomas 1999).

The world polity perspective suggests several ways to link the outbreak of ethnic movements in the contemporary period with processes associated with the diffusion of nationalism in earlier periods. In this perspective, modern citizenship has been conceptualized in terms of two concepts: rights and identity. Because human rights are formulated in terms of rights to self-determination that are increasingly guaranteed (and regulated) at the global level, identity politics make demands for recognition of groups in terms of national identity, separatist rights, or administrative self-rule (Soysal 1994: 159). Accordingly, nationalist and ethnic movements share common ideological roots that legitimate demands that "a people" deserve specific rights, and that some of these rights include claims of "sovereignty." Seen in this way, nationalist and ethnic social movements can be analyzed as consequences of a (more or less) cohesive world culture of democratic principles linked together by an interdependent world system of economic and diplomatic exchanges. Thus, nationalism increasingly spawns new claims-making activity, based upon a gradual escalation and diffusion of human rights to any deserving group. Identity social movements (those based on gender, sexual orientation, ethnic, and religious identities) proliferate as a result of this diffusion (Frank and McEneaney 1999).

In this view, legitimate identities in liberal state polities accrue first to individuals or groups, who become viewed as actors in their own right, entitled to (or excluded from) guarantees of religious and ethnic rights and of freedom of expression.[16] Programs and policies guaranteeing civil rights now reach a variety of local communities, but there is considerable variation

---

[16]For examples, see J. Meyer et al. (1997), Boli and Thomas (1999), Frank and McEneaney (1999), and Frank et al. (2000).

in the extent to which immigrants, refugees, and diasporas are deemed eligible to receive these rights.[17] Expanding on these global perspectives of social movements, it seems likely that increasing forces of world integration also influence the content of internal policies of ethnic rights of inclusion and exclusion within states. I suggest that as nation-states have become linked together by membership in transnational organizations, attempts by renegade states to limit minority rights are increasingly viewed as illegitimate. As a result, violations of minority rights have become an issue for international debate (Risse et al. 1999). In this way, a combination of forces related to globalization have reframed minority rights (once considered purely local issues) as key international concerns.

Global diffusion processes that spread nationalism as a legitimating ideology and stimulated independence movements have parallels with anti-colonialism movements, human rights movements, and ethnic mobilization (Strang 1990). With respect to human rights, this process has been labeled a type of "boomerang" effect, in which demands for expanded human rights in one country create the demand for parallel movements in other countries (Keck and Sikkink 1998: 13, fig. 1). This boomerang process is activated when a domestic organization exerts pressure on states to conform to existing laws and guaranteed rights, but a state ignores (or denies) these rights (for example, against child labor, domestic abuse, etc.). According to Keck and Sikkink (1998), these organizations turn to support from transnational networks of advocacy organizations, whose members can pressure their own states and/or other third-party organizations to exert pressure in turn upon the recalcitrant states. Furthermore, international institutions look more favorably upon human rights campaigns than they did previously. According to Sikkink, international associations became more open than transnational economic organizations were to international social movements related to human rights by the 1990s, in contrast to the 1960s (Sikkink 2005).

Analyzed from this perspective, international organizations might also promote mobilization for ethnic rights, as a result of this same boomerang process.[18] In this way, ethnic resurgence can be analyzed as a by-product of

[17] For examples of this research, see Soysal (1994) Keck and Sikkink (1998), Risse et al. (1999), della Porta and Tarrow (2005), Tarrow (2005).

[18] Sikkink (2005: 157) argues that the opening of international opportunity structures for groups located within closed domestic opportunity structures produces this boomerang effect, in which international organizations become the critical support network for local social movements. See also Risse et al. (1999).

the global interplay between these domestic and international social movement networks, demands, and information flows. Here my argument suggests that global movements will have an independent effect on local insurgencies, net of the effects of local grievances and mobilization capacities.

Processes of ethnic resurgence are not new, but they might be intensifying as economic and political organizations gain influence in multiple countries. In particular, as political associations (such as the EU, NATO, the UN) expand their authority over activities once controlled *only* by state authorities, international organizations become the target of new claims and demands, providing career paths and experience for human rights activists. International associations, anti-globalization conferences, and regional associations provide a forum for debate over ethnic rights (Nagel and Olzak 1982; J. Smith 2004). Such expansion of authority over larger territorial units has implications for the scale of subnational movements and their aims. For example, ethnic populations that span borders are now more likely to express nationalist demands for statehood, rather than demands for expanded rights within the states where they reside (Brass 1991; Horowitz 1985). As military, economic, trade, and other international associations grow in number, the actions of individual nation-states will become less salient relative to those of regions, politicians, or other powerful actors within states. As states become more enmeshed in a world system of diplomats, economics, and financial and military obligations, state actions become more constrained by the density of ties. At the same time that states are more constrained by world integrative processes, ethnic groups within states become less constrained by their own state authorities (Strange 1996). This is because highly integrated nation-states cannot simply repress, jail, or torture the ethnic challengers without risking international condemnation. World-level sanctions are regularly employed to induce recalcitrant states to conform to international norms, as are military forces, advisers, and other external pressures.[19] As state authority becomes challenged by external control, internal cleavages gain at least some new opportunities to challenge the state. My point is that the rise in the political authority of transnational

[19]This argument does not imply that international sanctions will be successful in achieving their aims. Rather, I am arguing that, in the contemporary period, the imposition of sanctions is increasingly likely to be debated at the international level, as reducing human rights violations has become part of the goals of human rights organizations (Räikkä 1996).

associations ought to coincide with an increasing number of movements based on ethnicity.

This second globalization argument suggests that as principles of sovereignty, self-determination, and human rights have become increasingly accepted and legitimate in institutions that span national borders, ethnic movements will become more numerous. In other words, demands and protests concerning standards of living, amenities, public services, discrimination, and violation of human rights that were once limited to local comparisons now take on wider scope (Keck and Sikkink 1998). As others have commented, residents of regions lagging behind in development or family income can become mobilized in response to the dissemination of information about economic disparities (Gurr and Moore 1997). While it is difficult to identify precisely when this process became more intense, the years between 1960 and 1965 show a sharp increase in United Nations attention to ethnic and racial rights.[20]

In the core, support for the expansion of human rights provides a clearly articulated and legitimate ideology to frame new demands for economic and political rights among ethnic groups (Boli 2001). Furthermore, institutionalization of ethnic demands for inclusion is likely to be underdeveloped and less openly sanctioned in peripheral countries. Following this logic, levels of ethnic protest will be significantly lower in peripheral countries compared to levels of protest in core countries.

THE POLITICS OF ETHNIC INCORPORATION AND IDENTITY MOBILIZATION

Arguments about the political consequences of incorporation rules for immigrants and ethnic minorities suggest several important implications for theories of ethnic social movements.[21] For instance, Levitt and de la Dehesa (2003) argue that national rules of political incorporation (such as the formal rights of groups, immigration policies, or racial discrimination policies)

---

[20] See Räikkä (1996) for a record of UN member histories of ratification of a set of declarations regarding minority ethnic and racial rights. For a history of participation and ratification of the UN International Convention on the Elimination of All Forms of Racial Discrimination (from its introduction in 1965 to the present), see www.civicwebs.com/cwvlib/constitutions/un/e_un_conv_racial_discrimination.htm (accessed November 19, 2004).

[21] See Soysal (1994), Jepperson (1992), J. Meyer and Jepperson (2000), and Levitt (2001).

TABLE I.I

Location of Authority and Basis of Social Interests in Polities

Basis of Social Interests	LOCATION OF SOCIAL AUTHORITY	
	Civil Society	*State*
Functional/Class	Social Corporateness (Sweden)	State Corporateness (Japan)
Ethnic Group	Consociationalism (Canada)	Apartheid (South Africa)
Individualistic	Liberal-State (United States)	State-Nationalist (France)

and the degree of centralization of authority within states inform us about which types of political identities will be more and less effective in different systems. This theoretical tradition rests on the notion that polities empower and legitimate either groups or individuals with certain rights and duties.[22] As Soysal (1994) describes, immigrants in Western Europe have confronted vastly different state policies regarding membership, access, and rights. The degree to which immigration policies absorb newcomers into the polity has implications for ethnic mobilization within states.

In Table 1.1 I build on the world polity perspective's four-fold typology regarding the centralization and corporateness of polities (Jepperson 1992; Soysal 1994; Nagel 1995).[23] One implication is that ethnic politics will predominate if group (rather than individual) and ethnicity (rather than class) are the dominant modes of political incorporation. Table 1.1 suggests that states that incorporate citizenship rights and obligations based on formal class or occupational position (as in Sweden), or in terms of

[22] Jepperson (1992, 2000) refers to a set of legitimate "scripts" that are activated during the process of making political claims. These cultural scripts shape the political identities of individuals and groups that are recognized (by both the state and its challengers) as efficacious.

[23] Jepperson (1992, 2000) proposes two contrasting dimensions of organizational authority and the basis of social interests in a political system. The first dimension, labeled "statism," refers to the degree of centralization of the state apparatus. In Table 1.1, countries that locate social authority in the state are high on this "statism" dimension. The second dimension refers to variation in levels of "corporateness," of which "high" refers to the degree to which states grant rights of incorporation and citizenship to groups, and "low" refers to a more individualist, market orientation. In this table, I add an ethnic component to the world polity argument about how states authorize citizenship based upon a specific type of group identity. Jepperson applies this typology to explain underlying institutional changes among states in post–World War II Europe.

production work teams (as in Japan) will have relatively less ethnic conflict than will states that strongly reinforce the significance of ethnic identity
in the political sphere.[24]

It seems likely that political opportunities for ethnic groups are more
and less open in states depending on the degree to which the states may be
classified along the dimensions of statism and corporateness. Incorporation
may be fundamentally along ethnic, class, or some other cleavage. It may
be organized at the group level (as in occupational or class categories) or
by a highly individualist identity (as independent citizens). According to this
view, if states implement more corporatist (or group-oriented) as compared
to individualist strategies, we might expect mobilization along group identity
lines to rise in response (Soysal 1994; Risse et al. 1999; Jepperson 2000;
J. Meyer and Jepperson 2000).

This incorporation argument has additional implications for the impact
of immigration on ethnic conflict. Using Table 1.1 as a rough guideline, if a
country's mode of incorporation facilitates mobilization around particular
identities, we might expect that states that incorporate newcomers on the
basis of ethnic group status will experience more ethnic tensions over citizenship, identity, and human rights. Alternatively, states that incorporate
newcomers into the polity in terms of class or labor union status ought to
have higher rates of labor unrest but lower rates of ethnic mobilization. Race
and ethnic categories play a pivotal role in most countries in defining eligi-
bility for citizenship (Soysal 1994). For example, in countries where national
citizenship rests upon assumptions of a single ethnic or racial identity (as in
Germany), the divergent definitions of national and ethnic identity can easily
become problematic. In countries where ethnic and religious divisions cross-
cut one another, ethnic mobilization is likely to be subdued (Mazrui 2000).
Using this same "group incorporation" argument, we might also expect hostilities to peak when ethnic and religious boundaries directly coincide (Fox
2002).

Political party structures can be arrayed along a continuum indicating
the extent to which ethnic identity is directly incorporated into the party

---

[24]It is important to distinguish "corporateness" from "corporatism." The former
refers to group incorporation of routines, laws, and polities, while the latter refers
to government coordination of large-scale collective bodies, such as business or labor (Jepperson personal communication; see also Schofer and Fourcade-Gourinchas
2001).

structure (in terms of the degree to which the constituent support, representation, or leaders overlap with ethnic interests).[25] The political incorporation argument suggests that by formalizing ethnic group identity in party structures or other institutions (e.g., cabinet posts), states reinforce ethnic solidarity and increase the potential for ethnic conflict.[26] Recent empirical evidence supports this hypothesis. For instance, Wilkinson's (2004) analysis of ethnic conflict in India finds that the participation of ethnic parties in highly competitive elections evidently intensifies the process of ethnic competition and incites violence. In particular, Wilkinson finds that when political party contests are most evenly divided in local settings across India, ethnic violence erupts in a systematically patterned way. Because ethnic incorporation is part of the structure of the political system in India, local politics invariably generate ethnic confrontations. Wilkinson reports that even innocuous "national day" marches in India can be transformed into violent clashes between Hindus and Muslims. Not surprisingly, as in Northern Ireland, symbols of ethnic loyalty that begin in celebration can mobilize movements and countermovements that can erupt into violence.

Processes of transition and change also affect the likelihood of mobilization along one or more of these levels of identity. For example, in countries undergoing state building, efforts of unification can become the basis of ethnic insurgency especially when state builders attempt to impose a *single* national ethnic identity where many existed previously. Similarly, efforts of state building imposed from external authorities (e.g., colonialism, empires, or occupation forces) may only temporarily decrease the likelihood of ethnic mobilization, but increase its resurgence in the long run. Furthermore, shifts among different levels of identity arranged in concentric circles can take place, as coalition politics render some identities more salient than others.

[25] This general argument is suggested by Jepperson (2000). In his view, high corporateness and low statist structures maximize the degree of empowerment of group identity in state systems which allow easy access and regularized participation. See also Schofer and Fourcade-Gourinchas (2001) for an examination of this thesis with respect to corporateness and participation in voluntary associations.

[26] If a country's dominant mode of incorporation along ethnic lines facilitates ethnic mobilization, then Table 1.1 suggests that the failure of consociationalism to provide a peaceful solution to ethnic strife is structurally induced (see also Varshney 2002). Consociationalism legitimates ethnic political parties by creating systems of ethnic regional representation or by instituting formulas of proportional representation in the polity. Chapter 2 reviews some relevant research on consociationalism and ethnic mobilization.

Examples such as Bosnia or Chechnya, which were once parts of the former (nonwarring) regions of Yugoslavia and the Soviet Union, illustrate these points dramatically (Toft 2003).

POLITICAL EXCLUSION AND ETHNIC MOBILIZATION

State policies that exclude ethnic groups have equally strong implications for what types of identities become mobilized against the state or against other groups. Whether or not ethnic protest continues to challenge state authorities depends on a number of other factors, including the centralization dimension ("statism") of state authority. Prior to 1994, South Africa offered an extreme example of a state that ranked extremely high on ethnic corporateness, exclusion, and statist dimensions. In the case of apartheid in South Africa, race and ethnic identity governed economic, social, and political options. Political opportunities were accordingly open (or closed) to any individual in this state dominated by a powerful administrative center. The implication is that political conflicts are more likely to occur along race and ethnic lines in countries where these divisions have been institutionalized as official categories, compared to countries that do not incorporate group rights on the basis of racial or ethnic identity.[27]

In states that exclude ethnic groups it is likely that forms of ethnic mobilization will adopt more violent tactics than in states where ethnic groups have regularized access to the polity. Whether or not ethnic movements will turn violent also depends upon the level of state centralization, the state's use of repression, and the dynamics between movement violence and state-sponsored violence (Olivier 1990). Weaker and decentralized states (which are low on the statist dimension) encourage collective violence, and this effect is likely to be stronger in states where access to political institutions has been eroded (Hironaka 2005).

The application of repressive force in centralized states as compared to in less centralized states also plays a role in shaping ethnic movements. Such differences are likely to emerge as important when states confront challenges from internal insurgent movements and from external ideological pressures to expand human rights. We might expect violent ethnic movements to characterize states weakened by internal insurgency and civil unrest. Conversely,

---

[27]For an analysis of the consequences of official categories of race on different levels of anti-apartheid protest in South Africa, see Olzak et al. (2003).

states with institutionalized ethnic group rights are more likely to experience nonviolent protest based upon ethnic and national identities.

The Global Diffusion of Social Movements

Temporal and spatial diffusion properties of social movements increase the rate of social mobilization (Strang and Soule 1998). To the extent that diffusion has intensified in recent decades, diffusion processes might also assist us in understanding the spread of ethnic movements. Studies analyzing the diffusion of movements, tactics, and ideologies have directed attention toward the ability of similar social movements to be imitated and adopted successfully in many countries.[28] Diffusion theories have found empirical support from case studies reporting that democracy movements, independence movements, anti-globalization protests, Islamic fundamentalist movements, student movements, and other goal-oriented social movements seem to cluster in time.[29]

Many researchers have noticed that collective action seems to occur in periodic surges of activity, growth, and decline (e.g., Tilly 1978; Tarrow 1998; Koopmans 1995). These "cycles of protest" perspectives direct attention to specific historical periods that elevate the risk of contentious and public protest. For example, the cycles of protest model suggests that peaks and troughs in collective events produce distinctive regularities in protest activity. Other scholars have focused on the fact that it seems that regions that have experienced civil unrest are somehow more vulnerable to subsequent eruptions. For instance, in research on race riots in the United States, Spilerman (1976) found that cities that have experienced at least one race riot have a higher risk of experiencing a second or third one. There is also evidence of an independent effect of the recentness of an event. For instance, the probability of another race riot occurring is highest in the twenty-four hours after a riot has occurred (Olzak, Shanahan, and McEneaney 1996). A wide variety of studies found that occurrence of and participation in racial unrest affected the spread of race riots across (mostly urban) America (Spilerman

---

[28]For reviews of the literature on transnational social movements, see Tarrow (2001), J. Smith and Johnston (2002), and J. Smith (2004).

[29]For empirical research and reviews, see Strang (1990), Strang and Meyer (1993), Strang and Tuma (1993), Strang and Soule (1998), Soule (2004), and Tarrow and McAdam (2005).

1970a, 1970b, 1971, 1976; Boskin 1976; McPhail and Wohlstein 1983; Olzak 1983; Olzak et al. 1996; Myers 1997; but see Myers and Caniglia 2004).

Following Tarrow's (1998) pioneering theoretical ideas, research also suggests that during the height of a protest cycle, the *salience* of a particular type of event spreads to other groups, countries, or settings. Examples have included the diffusion of airplane hijackings, bombings, terrorist attacks, race riots, and other dramatic events (Strang and Soule 1998). In this view, an event produces initially potent ripple effects that eventually dissipate over time (Strang 1990).

But what are the mechanisms of contagion? Most researchers have reasoned that strategies, claims, and grievances are more easily imitated soon after an event has occurred. For example, studies of race riots in the United States suggest that looting provokes similar behavior in nearby counties soon after the initial race riot.[30] In practical terms, this implies that the rate of protest rises up to some optimal point, at which point activity, mobilization, and imitation become much harder to sustain. Thus, the very existence of a growing upsurge in protest activity acts as an inducement to others to engage in collective action. The downward cycle is analogous to dissipation of contagion, as motivation, energy, and resources become exhausted.[31]

There is also empirical evidence in support of worldwide diffusion mechanisms that have spread ideas and tactics related to various civil rights movements. While the legitimacy of protest has diffused broadly, state reactions to specific tactics vary widely, depending on the repressive nature of given regimes. For example, the classification of protest as contentious behavior depends heavily on the institutional context of political freedom and civil liberties within countries, as the civil rights "sit-in" tactical history suggests (McAdam 1983). Internal political structures of access and inclusion may

[30] For evidence on diffusion and race riots, see McPhail and Wohlstein (1983), Baldassare (1994), Myers (1997), Myers and Caniglia (2004).

[31] Fearon (1998) provides another explanation for exhaustion, related to game-theoretic notions that over time the payoffs to continuing cycles of violence are self-limiting, and both sides (in a two-person game) eventually realize this fact. However, as Sambanis (2001) notes, most ethnic conflicts involve more than two parties, and escalate when third parties enter the conflict. On the other hand, Wilkinson (2004) has found that, in India, when the political payoffs attached to nonviolence are greater than those attached to violence, local police have successfully undermined the escalation of ethnic riots.

also depend on world-level differences among countries, in which the diffusion of human rights ideology spreads from more democratic settings to less democratic ones.

There is some evidence in favor of this argument, especially in the literature on Western European protest. Indeed, one characteristic of the so-called "New Social Movements" is that nonviolent tactics have become more common. In this tradition, identity movements, which would include ethnic protest movements and movements for expanded civil rights, are characteristically less violent and more likely to engage in institutionally sanctioned claims-making (Koopmans 1995). Kriesi et al. have added that protest movements in the nations granting many civil liberties will commonly involve conventional party politics or conventional nonviolent protest, such as marches, vigils, and petitioning (Kriesi et al. 1995: 176–78).

These endeavors have benefited from the emergence of new theories and methods for tracking the process of diffusion (Strang and Tuma 1993; Bremer, Regan, and Clark 2003). Such methods appear relevant for testing claims that ethnic movements diffuse rapidly in the current world system and that spatial and temporal proximity affects diffusion. These theories have been applied successfully to the study of the breakdown of colonial regimes (Strang 1990) and to the study of race riots (Myers 1997). Analysis of the connections between cycles of protest in different countries begins to make more transparent some of the consequences of the globalization of ethnicity.

Diffusion encourages instability both directly and indirectly by providing networks of social movement actors organizing and financing campaigns of instability. For example, such movements move across country borders to recruit political refugees or exiles as mercenary soldiers, informants, or spies. Obstacles to analyzing this type of activity include the lack of reliable data and the difficulty of untangling the causal sequence of events. For instance, there is a classic endogeneity problem in trying to sort out whether it is weak state authorities or the infiltration of insurgents (or increasing supply of weapons) from neighboring countries that incites civil war (Sambanis 2001). Indeed, a number of scholars have found that a decline in the political authority of a state coincides with an increasing number of movements based on ethnic regionalism (e.g., Brown 1996; Hechter 2000). Another international process suggests that social movements such as ethnic cleansing or Islamic nationalism that occur in neighboring countries are highly likely to diffuse into contiguous countries. The presence of contentious neighbors also destabilizes nearby regimes (Sambanis 2001). Brown (1996), Collier and Hoeffler (2004), and Levine (1996) all argue that elite factions (or warlords) offering military and financial support from neighboring countries have played crucial roles in prolonging ethnic wars in Africa and Central Asia in recent years. Although this is very difficult to study (because many of the transactions are clandestine), it also seems increasingly important to scrutinize flows of arms, mercenaries, supporting organizations, and finances that have fueled ethnic wars (without state or international sanctions) in neighboring countries (See, e.g., Brown 1996).

Heuristic Model

Figure 1.1 highlights the main causal arguments explored in this book. It emphasizes how position within the world system, embeddedness in the world system of international organizations, inequality, poverty, and restrictions on minority civil rights all play roles in the generation of ethnic mobilization. For simplicity, I have omitted many feedback loops and other relationships, in order to highlight the key relationships between global and state-level forces. In later chapters I will argue that most of these processes interact in complicated ways (as shown, for example, by research examining the impact of ethnic conflict on inequality). The purpose of Figure 1.1 is to suggest a type of channeling effect of internal features of states, their relationship to three key global forces, and types of ethnic mobilization outcomes. The argument outlined above suggests ways that human rights movements facilitate ethnic nonviolence while global forces of dependence and inequality exacerbate violence.

While I have argued that global forces have generally increased the overall potential for ethnic mobilization, the mechanisms that propel social movements toward violence are likely to depend on internal characteristics of states. In particular, for nonviolent ethnic protest, the key intervening mechanism is an increase in opportunities for mobilization, which are in turn escalated by the widespread acceptance of a broad human rights ideology (Risse-Kappen 1995). As countries become more embedded in the world system, and as neighboring countries experience more cross-border ethnic mobilization, all forms of ethnic mobilization might be expected to increase.

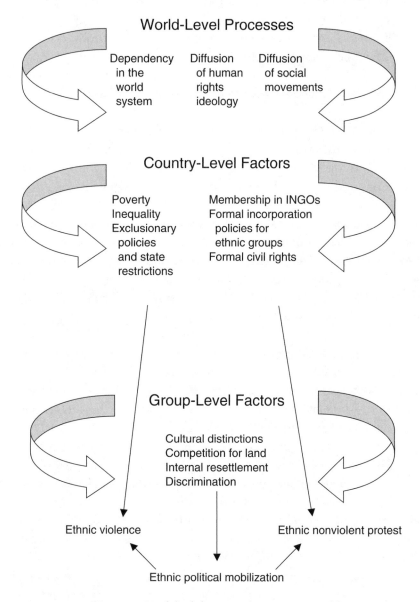

World-Level Processes

Dependency   Diffusion   Diffusion
in the   of human   of social
world   rights   movements
system   ideology

Country-Level Factors

Poverty   Membership in INGOs
Inequality   Formal incorporation
Exclusionary   policies for
  policies   ethnic groups
  and state   Formal civil rights
  restrictions

Group-Level Factors

Cultural distinctions
Competition for land
Internal resettlement
Discrimination

Ethnic violence   Ethnic nonviolent protest

Ethnic political mobilization

FIGURE 1.1 *Heuristic Model of the Interplay among World-, Country-, and Group-level Forces and Ethnic Mobilization.*

Factors that enhance the relative position of given ethnic groups so that they gain new leverage against competing groups, or in negotiations with state or international authorities, also expand opportunities for ethnic mobilization. Countries that both are dominant in the world system and grant civil liberties will therefore experience more protest that is nonviolent in character. In contrast, higher levels of inequality in peripheral countries encourage ethnic violence based upon claims of discrimination and victimization.

Figure 1.1 also suggests that ethnic mobilization shares many underlying causal features with other types of social movement activity. Diffusion of ethnic protest ought to be most potent across proximate regions; thus, nonviolent and violent ethnic mobilization ought to have strong spillover effects into neighboring countries.

There are also a number of countervailing forces at work. While authoritarian states and states with many restrictions on civil rights will have low rates of nonviolent protest, core states with restrictions on ethnic rights will have more nonviolence and less violence, all else being equal. Peripheral states that are more embedded in the world system will be less likely to experience violence than will peripheral countries that are relatively isolated from the diffusion of a world culture extending human rights.

As economic and political comparisons across ethnic groups become more common, ethnic grievances and claims are likely to become more violent. My argument is that dependence in the world system magnifies discontent with regional poverty and ethnic inequality, and that this discontent has been shaped by human rights ideologies that activate ethnic social movements aimed at reducing inequality. For this reason, we would expect poor and dependent countries to be significantly more prone to outbreaks of ethnic violence.[32] If a global human rights ideology has diffused as I have argued, existing inequalities within countries have become increasingly indefensible and are more likely to incite protest than in earlier periods. Thus, income inequality may have an independent effect on ethnic mobilization, net of the effect of total average income in a country.

According to this global argument, restrictions on civil liberties ought to increase grievances and comparisons with countries that grant more

---

[32] Poorer countries are also more likely to experience internal civil war—see Fearon and Laitin (2003) and Chapter 8 of this book.

liberties, thus facilitating ethnic violence. I also expect participation in world organizations and diffusion to produce more ethnic violence, as ethnic social movements become legitimate forms of nationalist claims-making. Finally, I expect that, in contrast to core countries, the more dependent peripheral countries will experience more ethnic violence, net of the effects of poverty and organizational involvement in the world system.

The Global Perspective

This book seeks to explain how different forms of ethnic mobilization share common causes that operate and interact with varying historical, economic, and political features within states. While worldwide trends have set in motion forces activating ethnic identities, not all movements turn violent, not all are successful, and many have different goals and purposes. Thus, I will explore the conditions under which global trends mobilize direct ethnic challenges to any given state's authority, rather than examining ethnic social movements that are relatively more peaceful celebrations of ethnic identity and culture (Horowitz 2001; Gurr 2000).

A global perspective has many advantages. First, an explicitly international perspective provides a context for understanding some of the key paradoxes in the empirical literature. For example, Collier and Hoeffler (2004) find that states that rely on a high level of primary commodity exports (such as oil) experience more insurgency and civil war. As a result, these authors conclude that economic viability (as measured by primary commodity exports) increases risks of rebellion and civil war, whereas Fearon and Laitin (2003) find no effect of primary commodity exports. Instead the latter scholars report that poor states and states weakened by political instability and ineffective bureaucracies matter most. While the debate over "greed" versus "grievance" versus "weak states" has not been resolved empirically, it is likely that the development of increasingly dense networks of trade and diplomacy affects all three measures. In particular, while world trade networks and exchange partners shape demand for primary exports, it seems equally reasonable that diplomatic ties and links to international organizations constrain and weaken the ability of states to counter insurgency within their borders (Hironaka 2005). Thus, it seems important to try to tease out the impact of global ties from the influence of internal forces (and their interaction) on ethnic mobilization.

A second advantage of using a global perspective is that we gain insights on the different layers of cultural difference expressed as ethnicity, in order to see patterns that might not be visible otherwise. For instance, there is little consensus about the labels used to describe the phenomena of ethnic movements. They can refer to specific religious, ethnic or racial, or regional differences, or they can involve various combinations of these identities—as in the various polymorph labels "ethnoreligious," "politically active communal groups," and "peripheral nationalism" (e.g., Hechter 1975; Gurr 1993; Fox 2002; Varshney 2002). By stepping back from each specific case history (which often carries its own historical label), we might uncover the core analytic causal mechanisms shared across cases.

Third, a global vantage point allows some distance from assumptions that ethnic movements are inevitably malevolent. By viewing all forms of ethnic mobilization as rooted in similar global processes but shaped by internal factors, we can begin to make sense out of the claim that ethnic identity appears to be a divisive force in nearly every region of the world. However, scholars who have argued that ethnic nationalist movements threaten the nation-state system have not provided a cohesive argument about why this should be the case. Furthermore, Gurr (2000) finds that ethnic violence has actually decreased over time. By examining two large data sets, and by controlling for a number of other factors, I will be able to evaluate these claims.

Fourth, a global view can help give a unifying perspective of most existing accounts of ethnic mobilization, which are driven by empirical analyses of state-level factors that have produced long and sometimes contradictory lists of factors. So studies variously emphasize the importance of issues such as increasing (or decreasing) economic inequality, intergroup competition, the absence of democratic institutions, transitions to democracy, gaps in cultural or linguistic differences, increasing acts of discrimination, weak states, political transitions, the collapse of state regimes, absence of civil liberties, changing demographic patterns, rapid modernization, and poverty (either separately or in combination).[33] Without theoretical guidelines, it becomes difficult to judge what sets of factors have priority. And if global factors also affect internal politics (as many suggest they do), then models restricted to internal characteristics of states are misspecified.

---

[33] For examples, see Bollen (1989), Brown (1996), Collier and Hoeffler (2004), Wimmer (2002), Fearon and Laitin (2003), Wilkes and Okamoto (2002).

Fifth, a global approach provides strategies for confronting the criticism that ethnic mobilization lacks a cumulative theoretical and empirical tradition. One explanation for this shortcoming is that scholars often use different indicators and statistical techniques, often analyzed over different time periods. Furthermore, the units of analysis used (country versus region versus event- or group-level analysis) differ so substantially that the creation of cumulative knowledge about these movements has been difficult.[34] Simply put, a distinctly global perspective opens up the potential for unifying a number of disciplinary findings.

This research seeks to contribute to theoretical efforts conducted at the macropolitical level. I believe that by examining the process of ethnic mobilization with a wide-angle lens we can begin to theorize about how ethnicity is affected by network connections of information, labor migration, political treaties, and refugee flows, as well as by distribution of international corporations and companies that span country borders. If these explanations make sense at the world level, then we will have gained more understanding of the rising importance of ethnicity as a political identity in the modern world.

Conclusion

This chapter began with the argument that world integration of state economies and politics has led to ethnic fragmentation and conflict. In particular, the chapter has introduced the notion that processes of economic and political integration in the world system have caused a rise in ethnic protest movements. In core nations ethnic protest may be relatively more frequent than in other countries, but in these core countries ethnic politics are more likely to be routinized by institutional politics and open systems of ethnic inclusion. In contrast, in peripheral nations ethnic protest is likely to be more sporadic, but potentially more violent. Whether scattered nonviolent protests develop into armed rebellions also depends on internal processes related to political and economic opportunities for ethnic inclusion and economic mobility.

Since the end of the Cold War and the breakup of the Soviet Union, scholars have suggested that these forces have intensified, creating a cascading

[34]For examples, see Connor (1973, 1978), Nagel and Olzak (1982), Gurr (1993, 2000), Horowitz (1985, 2001), Lake and Rothchild (1998), and Wimmer (2002). For reviews, see Nielsen (1985), Olzak (1983), Brass (1991), Brubaker and Laitin (1998), and Koopmans and Olzak (2004).

process of discontent, separatism, and, all too often, violence in their wake (Gurr 1993, 2000). However, these claims have rarely been tested empirically. Moreover, few theories have been offered that would link the end of the Cold War to multiple episodes of ethnic violence in African, Middle Eastern, and Asian states. On a smaller scale, competitive forces may arise in states weakened by external wars and/or regime crises, independent of Cold War processes. These conditions make it favorable for small-scale ethnic entrepreneurs to mobilize. I argue that the integration of the world system facilitates these local-level processes because the ideologies, strategies, tactics, and leaders rapidly diffuse across geographical and administrative units. If the arguments presented here show evidence at this world level of analysis, then we will have gained more understanding of the rising importance of ethnicity as a political identity in the modern world.

CHAPTER TWO

Definitions and Dynamics of Racial/Ethnic Mobilization

Concepts of Race and Ethnicity

In studying race and ethnic identity, researchers confront a number of tricky and sensitive questions regarding the choice of labels, definitions, and assumptions surrounding these concepts. What terminology should be used? What are the advantages and disadvantages to using the all-inclusive term "ethnicity" to cover both race and ethnicity? Alternatively, should we distinguish racial *versus* ethnic social movements? How should we distinguish between ethnic conflicts among groups and state-sponsored genocide?

To begin to answer these questions, I briefly recount some of the difficulties that arise when trying to define (or distinguish) the two concepts of race and ethnicity. Many contemporary scholars use "ethnicity" to cover both concepts (see Bonacich 1972; Gurr 2000). For simplicity (and to avoid invoking unscientific assumptions about the genetic basis of racial characteristics), these researchers prefer the more generic labels of "ethnic mobilization" and "communal mobilization" (Olzak 2004; Varshney 2002; Laitin 2000; Barth 1969). Yet this decision has its critics, who have argued that subsuming race under the broader category of ethnicity necessarily ignores some of the historical specifics surrounding racial discrimination patterns in the United States and elsewhere (Winant 1994).

Conventional treatments of race and ethnicity often emphasize the importance of signifying cultural practices or identifying features, such as racial characteristics, believed to be inherited characteristics of a group and central to their identity. Barth's (1956, 1969) theoretical reformulation of ethnic group membership as activity indicating an organizational boundary raised important questions about the immutable nature of race and ethnic group

33

membership. This theoretical tradition has proved especially useful for studying the activation of race and ethnic boundaries in the form of collective action and social movements (Hechter 1975; Olzak 1992; Brubaker 1996). According to this view, behaviors surrounding and maintaining the ethnic boundary become relevant to identifying in-group and out-group identities. In this way, ethnicity does not inevitably lead to mobilization, nor does mobilization necessarily rely on some objective features of culture, such as language, skin pigmentation, or historic label.

Despite the fact that social construction theories of ethnicity are useful, I do not wish to offer the view that ethnic and nationalist identities are simply instrumental constructions of modernization or state building. They are powerful identities because they are often based on historical legacies and accepted group characteristics. Thus, the persistence of ethnic mobilization in the contemporary period raises important questions about the process that activates group identities and generates collective action along ethnic lines. Because ethnic movements seem to be associated with group ties that hold sway over emotions and behavior in fundamental ways that cannot easily be put aside, histories of prior violence and hatred appear to be strong motivating factors, especially when compared to more rational calculations of the consequences and costs of ethnic violence (Horowitz 2001; Petersen 2002). Indeed, some scholars claim that ethnic movements are expressions of deeply held primordial or biologically linked identities (van den Berghe 1967; Isaacs 1975). Rather than fight the battle over whether ethnicity is primordial or instrumental (or whether or not race is "real"), I take the position that it is more useful to consider how racial and ethnic movements have revived ancient traditions, dialects, or practices, and how they have made use of historical myths in mobilizing sentiments and loyalties against ethnic enemies (Horowitz 1985; Nagel 1995).

Other scholars question the concept of ethnicity as standing apart from other mobilizing identities. Is ethnicity just localism or kinship, or regional politics that has been relabeled in a modern context? Or are there specific attributes of ethnicity and ethnic movements that render this form of political identity unique, in terms of goals, degrees of loyalties, and activities? Part of the confusion that arises in answering these questions is that the literature has often defined the terms "ethnicity," "ethnic mobilization," and "nationalism" interchangeably. In many ways, this confusion is understandable, since ethnic identities are often voiced in the same sort of rhetoric of nationalist identities, legends, and shared cultures and histories.

The relationship between ethnicity and collective action is undoubtedly mutually reinforcing. Rather than try to identify a "first cause," it might be more useful to explore how collective action validates, recruits, and reinforces loyalties based upon ethnic markers. This is because individuals express ethnicity through participation in social interaction, which may include festivals, cultural events, civil war, or support for terrorists. Like all forms of identity, claims about ethnicity are subject to social validation. Members (and nonmembers) point to specific, often visible, ethnic markers that indicate that they possess some (unspecified) number of shared characteristics, including physical characteristics such as skin pigmentation or body type, as well as social characteristics of shared language or dialect, religion, dress, or other cultural features. A key feature of ethnicity is a sense of in-group identification that distinguishes a group's members from some specified group of others who do not share these features.

This discussion implies that social constructionists view ethnicity as having at least some voluntary qualities, the assumption being that individuals and groups can choose to emphasize (or de-emphasize) some subset of markers, as in the case of persons "passing" as white or black or Jewish or Irish Protestant. Based on this insight, the constructionist perspective provides an important counterpoint to essentialist views of ethnicity and race as being inherited and immutable. But there are other complications. There are limits to someone being able to claim to be, say, a "Chinese American," without some reference to valid family ties. Thus, without some other validation, these cultural labels fail to be compelling, at least for most audiences familiar with the labels. So it is often said that ethnic and racial group membership "is believed to be" an ascribed characteristic, in the sense that membership is not a matter of choice. In this view, ethnicity or racial group membership can be contrasted with ideological commitment or voluntary group membership, which is a matter of choice. In Barth's (1969) framework, ethnicity is an imperative, but the imperative is social, not biological. Moreover, in the absence of objective indicators, historical claims of kinship and ethnic ties take precedence. Thus, ethnic and racial identities have qualities that are distinct from other types of identity that become visible only when a racial or ethnic boundary is socially constructed and accepted by members from both inside and outside the boundary.

The Mobilization of Ethnic Identity

Ethnic mobilization expressed through group conflict and protest requires commitment to a particular identity over some extended time period (and costs may rise with levels of commitment). We can array a variety of expressions of ethnicity along a commitment and risk continuum. However, because it involves some degree of contentious political behavior, ethnic mobilization is a particularly dramatic way of activating ethnic boundaries. By what mechanisms are cultural expressions of ethnic identity transformed into more active and politically mobilized expressions of race and ethnicity? The degree to which individuals act on the basis of ethnicity varies substantially over time and place. By examining sources of ethnic solidarity, we may begin to understand some of the causal factors producing variation in ethnic mobilization among groups and over time. Ethnic solidarity is characterized as the conscious identification with (and loyalty to) a particular race or ethnic population. It is commonly measured along a continuum of willingness to engage in ethnic activities, such as joining organizations and engaging in group monitoring behaviors. Measures of ethnic solidarity generally also include some indicators of group cohesion. Thus, studies of ethnic solidarity measure strong versus weak networks of ethnic interaction and/or organizations and institutions that socialize new members and reinforce social obligations. By keeping the definition of solidarity distinct from the definition of mobilization, we can examine the conditions under which ethnic mobilization facilitates solidarity, as well as the reverse.[1]

Mobilization is commonly defined as the capacity to harness resources (including loyalty, organizations, and material resources) in an effort to reach some collective goal (Tilly 1978). *Ethnic mobilization* is collective action in pursuit of collective ends by groups organized around some ethnic or racial marker that distinguishes members from nonmembers. Using this definition, some scholars have argued that ethnic claims have become increasingly

---

[1] More theoretical power can be gained from turning these definitions into empirical questions. Arguments from resource mobilization can then be examined by asking: Under what conditions will solidarity lead to mobilization? This strategy contrasts with those that assume that an association between mobilization and solidarity always exists. Without making the distinction between solidarity and mobilization, this proposition becomes tautological. Not everyone agrees with this distinction, however. For example, Hechter (1987b) makes exactly the opposite claim in his article titled "Nationalism as Group Solidarity."

numerous because ethnic boundaries are elastic, ambiguous, and difficult to verify (Nagel and Olzak 1982; Nielsen 1985). Because there is little consensus about what set (or what proportion of the set) of ethnic and racial characteristics confers ethnic group membership, ethnic ties tend to rely on outward manifestations and behaviors that validate membership.

A key identifying feature of ethnic mobilization (as compared to mobilization along class, regional, occupational, or some other lines) is that claims are made based upon particular identity or boundary, defined by the presence of racial or ethnic markers, as described above. Ethnic *political* mobilization also implies that a group engages in some form of claims-making, conflict, or hostility directed against a state authority or against another group.

I apply these definitions to a number of leading social movement perspectives in order to advance our understanding of the connections between ethnic identity and social movement activity in a number of ways. I begin with a working definition of social movements as (a) sustained collective actions by an identifiable group, (b) in interaction with opponents (countermovements), authorities, or both (McCarthy and Zald 1977; Tarrow 1998; Tilly 1978). Others have added the requirements that social movements also (c) involve some degree of organization and that (d) they use at least some extra-institutional tactics, beyond lobbying and everyday legal political behavior such as campaigning, voting, and so on (Snow, Soule, and Kriesi 2004).

Scholars have analyzed the transformation of group identity into political movements by emphasizing how waves of protest excite populations, provide templates for action, and models for claims-making activity (Tarrow 1998; McAdam, Tarrow, and Tilly 2001; Beissinger 2002). Moreover, during peak periods of social movement activity, ethnic politics of various kinds become salient, as formerly inert groups find new allies and issues. During peak cycles, various groups find templates for tactics, ideology, and recruitment that spin off from various successful initiator social movements. The classic example of this process is the United States' civil rights movement (which itself employed tactics of nonviolent disobedience adapted from India's movement for independence under Gandhi). Thus, social movement perspectives regarding the impact of "cycles of protest" provide some insights on why movements generated by different ethnic groups arise simultaneously in different parts of the world.

Much theoretical ground can be gained by reversing the conventional argument that the persistence (or strength) of ethnic identification causes mobilization. So Tilly (2003), Kalyvas (2003) and McAdam et al. (2001) have suggested instead that ethnic identity can be (perhaps more plausibly) analyzed as an *outcome* of collective action instead of as its cause. While this notion is useful, the premise that identity is a function of collective action drives the question back one step further: Why do the same ethnic cleavages produce contention in some (but not all) settings? What are the underlying mechanisms encouraging mobilization along lines of ethnic identity instead of class, locality, religion, etc.? Recent theoretical analysis in social movement theory suggests that group identity can be analyzed as both an important precursor and a consequence of mobilization. In particular, movements articulate demands and pursue social movement "frames" (Snow 2004) that invoke one or more cultural themes of nationalism, rights of self-determination, expansion of human rights, and basic rights of sovereignty (see also Smith 1979, 1981, 1986; Hechter 1987b; Nagel 1995; Brubaker and Laitin 1998). Sovereignty claims usually refer to shared experiences of "a people," which need not be based on objective facts (Anderson 1991). In this view, ethnic identity is a key outcome of collective action that is socially constructed, maintained, and dissolved.

The position taken in this book reflects a similarly constructionist view that ethnic markers—especially language, self-identification, and other cultural markers—cannot simply be assumed to be static characteristics of individuals or groups. They do not automatically generate ethnic social movements and they are not the sole basis of nationalism. Rather, the extent to which ethnic groups become solidary, mobilized in pursuit of some goal, or transformed into nationalist movements are all empirical questions that deserve more scrutiny.

Ethnicity and Nationalism

Following the lead of Calhoun (1993), Hechter (2000), and Tilly (2003), it seems useful to sharpen the difference between nationalism and expressions of ethnicity. While ethnicity can be designated as a recognized set of cultural markers, outward expressions of loyalty and self-identification, and/or phenotypic features of race, nationalism is a social movement making a territorial claim. Thus, Hechter (2000: 7) defines nationalism as a process of "collective action designed to render the boundaries of a nation congruent with those of its governance unit." Gellner (1983: 1) adds that nationalism is "primarily a political principle," in which a governing unit should neither cut across nor exclude members who share a common cultural boundary.

Brubaker (1996: 6–12) finds that nationalism tends to reflect three major categories of collective action mobilized by national minorities, nationalizing states, and external national homelands. The most familiar of these forms include claims by national minorities (within or against existing state structures), nationalizing states (sometimes emerging from fragmented federations, as occurred after the dissolution of the Soviet Union), and claims by external national homelands for a new state (Beissinger 2002). These variants of nationalism evoke demands for expanded cultural or political rights, but diverge with respect to the degree to which they claim full sovereignty rights as a state. This perspective illustrates the advantage of treating sovereignty claims as a varying dimension, rather than a defining feature, of social movements.

These definitions have the advantage of treating the outcomes of nationalist movements as contingent upon the behavior of a nationalizing group in contest with an existing regime, empire, colonial power, or host nation. Put differently, ethnicity becomes transformed into nationalism when it makes specific historical claims and attempts to administer the group as a political community (Calhoun 1993: 224). The advantage of this conceptualization of nationalism allows us to analyze different claims, goals, and tactics that invoke claims of legitimacy that are based upon a single ethnic identity.

To what extent do ethnic markers (especially linguistic ones) facilitate nationalist movements? In order to examine the argument that ethnic distinctions foster nationalist social movements, we have to observe variation in the range of ethnic movements, violence, and demands. Practically speaking, this means that if ethnicity and nationalism were defined as the same phenomenon, the causal link between ethnic characteristics and mobilization outcomes could not be examined empirically. Thus, it is useful to distinguish ethnicity from the concept of nationalism, as others have done, based upon the scope of a group's political goals, territorial range, and demands for sovereignty.[2]

Ethnicity refers to a common set of traits that generate different levels of affiliation, solidarity, and identification among individuals and groups.

---

[2] Not all scholars make this distinction. For example, Varshney (2002: 86) argues that when discussing most ethnic conflicts, the terms "ethnicity" and "nationalism" can be used interchangeably.

In contrast, *nationalist movements* are social movements (which may or may not be based on ethnic distinctions) invoking claims for territorial sovereignty.[3] Yet nationalist movements will often adopt claims to ethnic integrity, in efforts to build historical legends or myths that render the group distinct, in terms of language, heritage, shared culture, or other features. Claims of nationalist movements vary from demands for regional autonomy or special status within a federation (often involving linguistic rights), to full-scale separation from multinational states, regimes, or empires. Like ethnicity, demands for territorial sovereignty are often based upon historical narratives or claims of ethnic heritage that do not require objective verification. Thus many nationalist movements invoke claims based upon ethnic identity.[4]

Alternatively, nationalist movements may claim sovereign rights by invoking other types of identities, such as pan-religious identities that cross-cut various other identities (Fox 2002; Varshney 2002; Snow and Marshall 1984). Other forms of nationalist movements are territorial in a different way, claiming forceful removal from an ancestral homeland, as in the case of some diasporic movements, including Armenian and Kurdish movements based on settlements in a variety of different countries. Members of nationalist movements may also share a territory that lies under another jurisdiction (e.g., Québécois nationalism), or they may be spread across multiple regions (e.g., pan-Islamic nationalism).

A more conventional form of nationalism might be termed nation strengthening, or nation building, in which a single identity (often ethnic or linguistic in character) has been forged (or imposed externally) from many different, smaller identities. The formation of Yugoslavian identity after World War II under President Tito is one example, while an effort to establish

[3] A fertile debate exists over whether or not nationalism inevitably refers to common ethnicity, culture, and fate (e.g., Brubaker and Laitin 1998; Varshney 2002; Hechter 2000). For the most part, scholars find that nationalist movements situated within one country will be coterminous with expressions of ethnicity. But, as Hechter (2000) notes, this is not always the case. Furthermore, defining the two concepts as coterminous would ignore many cases of diasporic movements (which cross state boundaries), pan-ethnic movements, movements such as "Cherokee Nation" and "Pan-Arab Identity," and other cases that defy simple one-to-one correspondence with a single ethnicity.

[4] The distinctions made between ethnicity and nationalism in this section draw on a similar discussion published in Olzak (2004).

a legitimate government authority in post-Taliban Afghanistan is another. The Russification of the republics of the Soviet Union is another case in point.

The key distinction between ethnic and nationalist movements is that the latter reflect claims to authority over territory and self-determination that are currently unsatisfied (Hechter 2000). This discussion prompts us to consider a continuum of nationalist movements that reflect the extent to which a movement expresses goals of self-determination and sovereignty apart from an existing state. Movements can then be analyzed chronologically with respect to movement along this dimension. Nationalism, in other words, is a variable (Hechter 2000). Such a perspective is flexible because it allows movements to shift their scope over time, as in the case of a separatist movement emerging from a civil rights movement or from a cultural identity movement. Despite the fact that ethnic movements can become nationalist movements, most research shows that ethnic movements (at least initially) tend to express relatively modest goals or reforms that involve negotiation within an existing political structure. These are likely to include demands for increasing use of a minority language, expanded citizenship rights, or legitimation of a group's cultural practices. In contrast, nationalist movements focus on obtaining legitimate rights to territory (Hechter 2000; A. Smith 1991). Ethnic movements that demand improvement in civil or economic rights for a self-conscious group often direct these demands to institutional authorities or state officials. Antagonistic ethnic movements can be directed against other ethnic groups, or the state authorities, or they may be in conflict with both. In contrast, most nationalist movements aspire to become state authorities in their own right.

Based on these distinctions, it seems important to clarify how ethnic identity and boundaries can be analyzed apart from the contemporary constellation of nation-states. Claims (for statehood, expanded civil rights, linguistic rights, etc.) based on ethnic identity are not constrained by existing geographical boundaries, population concentrations, or any other feature of modern states. Precisely because ethnic identity can span or dissect national borders, mobilized ethnic movements are often viewed as a threat to the integrity of the state system (or to any given state that has ethnic groups with external ties). But because nationalism also usually invokes ethnic-like claims based upon historical, territorial, or cultural distinctions, ethnic social movements and nation-states depend on each other in a delicate balance of self-definition, political claims-making, and contests over power, authority, and legitimacy.

Nationalist movements are social movements that also seek to establish new (or recapture old) sovereignty rights (Rokkan 1970; Tilly 1975; Anderson 1991; A. Smith 2000). This last characteristic often brings nationalist and ethnic social movements into conflict with existing regimes. Such conflicts can remain quiescent for long periods of time, or they may erupt suddenly into full-blown ethnic civil wars, depending on a number of factors including regime stability, outside support, internal mobilization of resources, and reaction by state authorities to nationalist movements. While ethnic and nationalist movements can adopt different forms, they share a number of important social movement claims, ideological roots, and tactics. Thus it seems reasonable to begin by considering the characteristics of these movements.

Types of Ethnic and Nationalist Movements

Social movement theories assist us in distinguishing various types of ethnic collective action by empirically taking into account the duration, target, tactics, violence, audience, and content of the claims and demands of various movements. These distinctions yield four broad categories of ethnic and nationalist movements: (1) regional movements (including separatist, nationalist, and autonomy movements), which demand sovereignty over a particular territory (Hechter 2000); (2) civil rights movements, which demand expansion of a group's civil and economic rights or demand an end to discrimination (Morris 1984); (3) antagonist movements directed against specific ethnic targets, including collective attacks ranging from symbolic threats (swastikas, defamation of synagogues, etc.) to genocide, ethnic cleansing (Akbar 1995), mob violence, and ethnic riots (Horowitz 2001); (4) state-strengthening nationalism, which attempts to unify diverse cultures (state-building nationalism) or merge politically divided territories into one state (unification nationalism) or make claims for unifying statehood (e.g., by a diaspora group) (Hechter 2000). While studies of ethnic and nationalist movements traditionally analyze these forms separately (Horowitz 1985; Banton 1983), these forms often combine in complicated ways. It bears repeating that the same ethnic event can be alternatively described as genocide or as a liberation movement, depending on the actors defining the situation.

TABLE 2.1
Forms of Ethnic Mobilization

Ethnic Protest	*Ethnic Aggression*
Nonviolent	
Civil Rights Movements	Symbolic Attack or Vandalism
U.S. black movement	Attacks on Jewish gravestones in U.S.
Lapp civil rights	Epithets shouted at Muslims in France
Hispanic bilingualism rights	Swastika posters in Austria
Violent	
Autonomy Movements	Mob Attacks
Chechen rebels	Attacks on foreigners in Germany
East Timor in Indonesia	Anti-Muslim violence in Chinese villages
Chiapas rebellion in Mexico	Lynching of blacks in the U.S.
Separatist Movements	Genocide/Ethnic Cleansing
Basque Movement	Serbian-Muslim conflict in Bosnia
Tamils in Sri Lanka	Hutu-Tutsis in Rwanda

Table 2.1 distinguishes ethnic aggression from ethnic/racial protests against discrimination (Olzak 1992; Olzak and Olivier 1998). Ethnic aggression occurs when two or more persons collectively attack one or more members of an ethnic/racial group and this confrontation is reported as primarily motivated by the target's ethnic identity, language, or skin color (often accounts are coded from newspapers, or first-hand and survey accounts, or from police records). In *racial/ethnic aggression*, one group (or more than one) may be designated as the victim of the attack, or many groups may simultaneously confront each other in a conflict. Victims might also be involved symbolically, as in a cross burning in a predominantly white neighborhood threatened by racial integration.

In the case of an *ethnic protest*, a group expresses a racial or ethnic grievance, usually to government officials or the public at large. Examples include a sit-in against a discriminating store or restaurant, as happened frequently during the civil rights movement in the U.S. The "shantytown" protest tactic, used in anti-apartheid social movements, that spread across U.S. college campuses during the 1980s is another example (Soule 1997). Protests against anti-foreigner violence in Germany (and elsewhere) during the 1990s illustrate another form of countermovement activity. Researchers generally separate collective protest from regularly scheduled events and institutionalized events such as political speeches, conventional lobbying strategies, and interest group politics.[5]

Ordinary instances of interracial crime and violent ethnic attacks are often difficult to distinguish, as the concept of "hate crimes" suggests.[6] Most researchers of ethnic group conflict or racial violence have chosen strategies that err on the conservative side in the attempt to include only those incidents that show evidence that perpetrators had primarily ethnic/racial motives.[7]

The second conceptual distinction contrasts nonviolent ethnic events with ethnic aggression. Ethnic events turn violent if participants (or authorities) use weapons, take over buildings, deface property, or threaten or harm persons or property, and invoke ethnic identity as the key motivating factor for these behaviors. When accounting for ethnic violence, it is equally important (if possible) to distinguish state-sponsored violence (on the part of state police, soldiers, or armies) from instigator violence, as well as events in which both sides use violence.[8] As can be seen in Table 2.1, distinguishing ethnic protest from ethnic aggression allows for more flexibility for analyzing shifts in social movement tactics. By defining these concepts separately,

---

[5] Scholars interested in protest tend to analyze newspaper editorials, speeches and press conferences by politicians, and opinion-editorial columns about racial and ethnic issues separately from public protest events. This distinction (between events and editorial commentary) allows research to gauge the impact of the media on public demonstrations. The strategy has turned out to be useful in understanding how the public discourse in the printed and televised media shapes which groups become targets of ethnic violence (Koopmans and Olzak 2004).

[6] For a useful set of related definitions and operational measures on hate crimes in the United States, see Jenness and Grattet (2001), Green, Glaser, and Rich (1998), and Green, Wong, and Strolovitch (1998). Although hate crimes (defined differently in the U.S. at federal, state, and local levels of law enforcement) vary in forms, claims, and victims, most forms of ethnic and racial mob attack would be counted as one type of hate crime. However, most legal definitions of hate crime in the United States encompass a diverse set of crimes against victims based on a number of personal characteristics, including gender, sexual orientation, race, religion, nationality, and other characteristics.

[7] While these rates are interesting in their own right, in past research I have excluded interracial muggings, rapes, or robberies that constitute everyday crime events. I have also excluded pronouncements by public figures, political speeches, and editorials on racial issues (Olzak 1992, Olzak, Shanahan, and West 1994; Olzak et al. 1996).

[8] For an empirical analysis of state-sponsored violence, see Krain (1997).

we are able to analyze the conditions under which peaceful protests will turn violent.[9]

Most scholars also distinguish a continuum of violence, with riots and armed rebellions at one extreme, and sporadic use of threats against others at the other (Gurr 1993). *Riots* are generally distinguished from other kinds of ethnic/racial activity in that they involve more than scattered acts of sabotage or violence, are enacted by a large mob (hundreds or thousands of persons), and involve violent activity that lasts several hours or more (Olzak et al. 1996; Horowitz 2001). Although this definition is more or less used by the international media, there are differences among countries that are important. For example, the size of riots differs substantially, depending on the size of minority population at risk. Olzak and Olivier (1998) find that individual South African race riots mobilized thousands of participants, while in the United States race riots only rarely involve more than one thousand active participants in one city. While a given riot might mobilize thousands, the riots are typically short in duration, rarely lasting more than one or two days.[10]

In Table 2.1, the levels of violence and the scope of political demands escalate from the top to bottom of the table. At one end of the continuum are acts of vandalism or racial slurs and protests against discrimination that use mainly nonviolent tactics. At the other end of the continuum are separatist movements and genocide. In contrast to more sporadic activity and smaller-scale social movements, these movements can be conceptualized as more organized, politically motivated and ongoing movements, with identifiable goals and participants, and episodes that last months and years rather than days. Thus, ethnic aggression (on the right-hand side of Table 2.1) ranges from verbal slurs and vandalism to ethnic civil war.

In other words, at the high end of the ethnic aggression continuum, ethnic rebellions represent an escalation in the level of violence and political aims when compared to more sporadic attacks with fewer participants. But

[9]There are numerous problems in assuming that violence and ethnic conflict are always found together—ethnic conflict may or may not be violent (see Brubaker and Laitin [1998], Varshney [2003] for expanded discussions of this issue).
[10]My research suggests that in all cases of black race riots in South Africa and the United States, injuries and damage to property occurred, racial claims of injustice, discrimination, and/or racial demands for change were expressed, and in all cases the police were a visible and active presence.

when does an ethnic rebellion become a social movement? Answering this question is difficult because ethnic rebellions have different constituencies, as well as targets that depend upon a given political context. One needs only to consider all the possible ways to describe an IRA bombing in central London to see the political complexities involved. Criminal violence or heroism? Murder or martyrdom? The labels will likely vary considerably, depending on the source, context, and audience of any given report of the event. To be sure, historians and social scientists routinely confront sources of data with skepticism, and information about ethnic movements certainly deserves scrutiny. While keeping these caveats in mind, I suggest some basic categories of ethnic movements, distinguished by their claims and goals.

In contrast to isolated ethnic events, *ethnic rebellions and social movements* involve sustained efforts to effect major political changes, such as in policies regarding subordinate groups, redefinition of citizenship boundaries or rights, and/or efforts to exclude, subjugate, or control a subpopulation or a region. Ethnic movements tend to have broad goals of social change in institutions, especially political systems. Well-developed ethnic movements will have identifiable goals that seek to change the society so as to redistribute resources to disadvantaged minorities, obtain new political rights, change (or prevent) some public policy or law, or affect public opinion concerning an ethnic or racial population. More diffuse movements will involve claims of discrimination centered on an aggrieved group or region.

A subcategory of protest is an autonomy movement. These groups demand special attention from the state, but often stop short of demands for outright secession. They often seek to negotiate special regional status , but they do not aim at complete separation from the administrative state (at least initially). They may start out as nonviolent, but in the examples listed, many have ultimately used armed force and terrorist tactics (Hechter 1992; Wilkes and Okamoto 2002).

In the bottom-left corner of Table 2.1 we find examples of ethnic protests that seek to eradicate and replace existing geographical and administrative state boundaries, in the form of secession or separatist movements. They differ from other forms of ethnic movements in that they involve demands for "formal withdrawal from a central political authority by a member unit or units on the basis of a claim to independent sovereign status" (Hechter 1992: 267). Secessionists seek to establish a new state (or, in the case of irredentist movements, to separate and join another existing state). However, secession movements are usually difficult to sustain, because host states have (by definition) a monopoly over legitimate militia forces, treaty rights, and other ties with existing states. The power balance is usually, but not always, highly asymmetric. It usually tips in the direction of the state, but the ability to exploit this power depends on a number of factors, including the state's legitimacy, its implementation of rules of citizenship and other civil rights, and the openness of its civil society. Moreover, the use of repression by states against insurgents often has paradoxical implications. Thus, in some contexts, the repression of ethnic insurgents might be seen as a show of state strength, but resorting to violence also implies a crisis of legitimacy that could be perceived as state weakness on the international stage. As Tilly (1975) noted some time ago, repression is likely to be most effective when it is not used but remains a credible threat (see also Earl 2003).

Secession movements and their repression are dramatic but relatively rare events. Hechter (1992: 270) has argued that *successful* secession movements are relatively infrequent because they are extremely costly for smaller subregions and they require political organizations capable of mobilizing large numbers willing to confront state repression. Yet since the end of the Cold War, many separatist movements have occurred, especially in Eastern Europe. To explain these events, I argue below that the core/periphery status and the levels of ethnic inequality within countries together shape ethnic protest. In particular, I propose that core nations experiencing a decline in ethnic inequality will begin to see rising claims for autonomy and political rights for minorities, while patterns of ethnic violence will be more likely to occur in states that exclude ethnic minorities from the political process (A. Smith 1979: 35).

Nevertheless, even if ultimate success has often eluded secessionist groups, their claims can provoke widespread violence and long-term civil wars. Secession movements that invoke principles of self-determination as their anthem imply that domination of their region by another ethnic group is illegitimate. State organizations and bureaucracies that are dominated by one or more ethnic groups will forcefully resist the breakup of the state. In this case, further ethnic conflict might be generated as various groups respond to secessionist ethnic movements.

Anthony Smith (1979: 34) identifies a common set of events that encourage a separatist response over a more accommodationist position. These sequences begin with initial state building processes, including creation of a centralized bureaucracy and diffusion of national educational institutions. If ethnic elites find their mobility blocked, ethnic movements based on minority discrimination will arise. The resulting discontent commonly involves a sense of violated rights, distributive injustice, and devalued self-esteem (see also Horowitz 1985: 181). Ethnic conflict persists to the extent that one side maintains efforts at institutionalizing low status and economic valuations based on ethnic identity. Civil wars of the kind in Rwanda, Eritrea, Bangladesh, Biafra, and Sri Lanka are recent examples of this form of ethnic secessionist movements.

Ethnic autonomy movements are protest movements that claim special status for a territory but usually refrain from outright secession. Such movements share many characteristics of civil rights movements. Their claims use the language of discrimination and draw attention to unacceptable levels of ethnic or racial inequality, and they tend to employ standard social movement strategies (such as marches, referenda, sit-ins, ethnic symbols). As Horowitz (1985) notes, the rhetoric of ethnic autonomy movements strikes similar themes of injustice, whether in the Chiapas movement in Mexico, the Punjabi in India, Northern Ireland's Catholics, or the contemporary Chechen movement in the former Soviet Union. As many have claimed, ethnic disadvantages do not need to be objectively verifiable in order to have potent effects on social movements for autonomy. Advocates of regional autonomy tend to voice the rhetoric of economic and/or political subjugation, even in regions that are undergoing economic booms (Nielsen 1980; Olzak 1982).

An extreme form of ethnic aggression directed against a target population might be called "exaggerated nationalism" (but see Anderson 1991). In the past, these movements often voiced goals of ethnic or racial purity that required exclusion of some other group of undesirables. Most recently, this form of violence has arisen as former states (or modern empires) fragment or dissolve entirely and attempt to forge new and ethnically homogeneous identities (Jalali and Lipset 1992–93). The consequence is often a combination of disenfranchisement, pogroms, and terrorist movements, as well as other methods of physical attack, such as rape, civil war, and taking of hostages.

The dynamics of ethnic collective action obviously depend on the political context, including reactions to ethnic claims by competing ethnic groups, state authorities, or other institutional leaders and elites. To the extent that ethnic and nationalist social movements seek to eradicate and replace existing geographical and administrative state boundaries, they provoke reactions by state authorities that can escalate into violence. This escalation into ethnic violence or rebellion is particularly likely for separatist or secession movements that are claiming rights of withdrawal from formal state authority. Violence is also more likely to erupt when ethnic movements claim territorial sovereignty for formerly dispersed or resettled populations (Hechter 1992; Carment and James 1995). Thus, as the goals of ethnic mobilization challenge existing territories or political regimes, violence becomes more likely. It is also important to not confuse the language used to justify violence with the underlying causes of violence. Ethnic adherents justify violence in such movements as a necessary price paid in the struggle for liberation. Outsiders (who may include international, regional, or state authorities) reframe repression against such movements, claiming that violence is justified against terrorist or genocidal groups. As Kalyvas (2003) and Petersen (2002) warn, the causal sequence of events leading to ethnic conflict undergoes continuous redefinition and reframing, which renders ethnic conflict extremely difficult to evaluate.

Orienting Research Questions

What causes ethnic and nationalist movements to turn against host states? Answers to this question vary with disciplinary traditions, theoretical perspectives, and methodological strategies. For example, researchers using collective action perspectives tend to treat ethnic and nationalist movements as constituting a series of historically contingent events, rather than as series of predetermined stages in the nation-building process. Others prefer to examine macro-level political structures as forces that render ethnic identities more salient than other types of boundaries. This section outlines a set of core questions that have oriented the research literature on ethnic mobilization. Drawing on the definitions of concepts of ethnicity and its activation, I now review a set of explanations suggesting those factors that are instrumental in transforming ethnic identity in viable ethnic movements.

THE ROLE OF CULTURAL DISTINCTIONS

Under what conditions will ethnic diversity promote mobilization? Recent analysis in social movement theory suggests that group identity is both an important mobilizing strategy and a consequence of mobilization. In particular, movements articulate demands and pursue social movement "frames" (Snow, Rochford, Worden, and Benford 1986; Snow 2004) that invoke one or more cultural themes of nationalism, rights of self-determination, expansion of human rights, and basic rights of sovereignty (see also A. Smith 1979, 1984; Hechter 1987b; Nagel 1995; Brubaker and Laitin 1998). Sovereignty claims usually refer to shared experiences of "a people," which need not be based on objective facts (Anderson 1991; Krasner 2001). In this view, ethnic identity is a key outcome of collective action and is socially constructed, maintained, and dissolved.

However, empirical investigations of the role of ethnic diversity, cultural differences, linguistic diversity, and other measures of cultural differences have not always supported the claim that cultural distinctions cause ethnic conflict or protest.[11] The empirical literature reports ambiguous results, leading many scholars to suggest that the salience of ethnic differences may result from conflict, rather than the reverse.

So, in contrast to theories that rely on (mainly static) cultural group differences, constructionist perspectives track the dynamics of the rising and falling salience of particular ethnic boundaries (Cornell and Hartmann 1998). This perspective allows researchers to study how social mechanisms of contact, conflict, borrowing, and other forms of interaction might influence the emergence of new ethnic or racial categories. Over time, as ethnic conflicts recur along increasingly recognizable cleavages, more fluid identities become hardened into institutionalized race and ethnic categories (McAdam et al. 2001).

Cleavages become reified as insults and attacks along similar identity lines become repeated, as Roy (1994) reports. So, beginning in 1954, relatively minor village disputes over "some trouble with cows" in Pakistan became gradually transformed and understood as part of the age-old Hindu–Muslim conflict (see also Brass 1997). As violence and revenge escalate on either side of a conflict, small-scale skirmishes became redefined as collective events requiring a response (Gould 1999; Kalyvas 2003). Eventually (but not inevitably), the escalating violence developed into the Bangladesh–Pakistan civil war (McAdam et al. 2001: 128). Similarly, Gould's (1999)

---

[11]For examples of research finding little impact of ethnic heterogeneity on the onset of civil war, see Russett et al. (2000) and Fearon and Laitin (2003). For examples of research supporting the effects of ethnic and cultural distinctions on ethnic mobilization, see Olzak and Tsutsui (1998), Sambanis (2001) and Wilkes and Okamoto (2002).

analysis of collective action in Corsica suggests that, under some conditions, collective retaliation following initial disputes escalates into "generalized violence," enticing nondisputants to join subsequent episodes of collective violence. In this way, sporadic ethnic conflict becomes gradually transformed into sustained ethnic social movements, as ethnic organizations, leaders, and supporters come to frame ongoing events as ethnically motivated. In analyzing the forces that escalate group conflict, these scholars underscore the emergent properties of both identities and conflict (McAdam et al. 2001).

In contrast to this process-oriented perspective, Gellner's (1983) treatment of nationalism rests on claims that preexisting cultural differences (especially language) provide key channels and conduits of communication and links within populations that are culturally distinct. Similarly, Anderson's (1991) "imagined communities" mobilize along language lines, as written texts create a sense of peoplehood out of linguistic similarities. Some political scientists have found that *ethnic-linguistic diversity* increases the potential for mobilization along ethnic lines (Anderson 1991; Deutsch 1953). In this view, diversity inhibits smooth race and ethnic relations, creating the conditions for contentious political activity of all kinds. There is some empirical evidence supporting this claim, showing that ethnic heterogeneity has a positive and significant effect on nonviolent ethnic mobilization (Hill, Rothchild, and Cameron 1998).

Still others expect a curvilinear relationship between ethnic movements and linguistic homogeneity, with peak rates of ethnic unrest expected when levels of linguistic diversity are neither very low nor very high. This claim is supported by the analyses of Gurr (1993), Muller and Weede (1990), Posner (2003), and others, who find that group conflict intensifies when there are relatively few groups of similar size. Ethnic diversity is also likely to be increased by migration patterns, which have been associated with ethnic and racial conflict in the United States (Olzak 1992).

Although cultural perspectives may appear useful for understanding particular cases of ethnic antagonism, one drawback to this approach is that it is often difficult for researchers to determine the causal ordering of cultural distinctions and group mobilization (as in the 1990s conflict between Hutus and Tutsis in Rwanda). This is because ethnic labels and identities have emergent properties that depend on various negotiations that take place within specific interaction contexts (Barth 1969). Furthermore, any specific ethnic boundary is likely to become more salient after acts of vengeance, combat, or other conflict have occurred.[12]

Cultural views have also been used to emphasize some shortcomings of purely constructionist views. For instance, A. Smith (2000: 70) argues that the constructionist perspective overemphasizes the modern aspects of ethnicity while ignoring the symbolic aspects of identities (including cultural values and traditions) that have been carried over from premodern periods.

In studying the impact of ethnic identity some time ago, Anthony Smith (1984) outlined some of the causal sequences implied by the process of ethnic mobilization of identity. In particular, he lists several functions of identity, which serve to designate basic cultural markers that bind them to past and present histories within time and space. Furthermore, precisely because ethnic identity is at least partially voluntary, members can enter and exit an ethnic status, creating the potential for mobilizing new recruits, supporters, and fellow travelers.

Smith (1984: 119) enumerated a useful set of conditions under which ethnic identity is likely to become activated. These include (1) intervals during prolonged periods of conflict and warfare, when group identities are under siege or are threatened by others (including third parties to the conflict, as in the Cold War);[13] (2) intervals during periods of secularization or cultural change, during which a technologically superior or economically dominant culture threatens a more traditional culture;[14] and (3) intervals during periods of intense commercialization which integrate a society into a broader system of economic exchange that is dominated by more advanced technologies or more powerful adversaries (Barber 1996; Huntington 1996).

The Legacy of Colonialism and Independence Movements

A number of important macropolitical theories have emphasized the importance of colonialism in shaping the ethnic basis of social movements, including nationalist movements.[15] Because colonialist powers carved an

---

[12]For evidence, see Gould (1999), McAdam et al. (2001), Varshney (2001), and Tilly (2003).

[13]For expanded treatments, see Borstelmann (2001), Regan (2002), and Regan and Abouharb (2002).

[14]This argument has emerged as a key explanation of Islamic fundamentalism, and of religious-ethnic conflict more generally. For reviews, see Fox (2002).

[15]For examples, see A. Smith (1981), Fox (2002), Tilly (2003).

artificial grid of administrative regimes that cross-cut cultural and linguistic divisions, few administrative boundaries coincided with linguistic, religious, or cultural divisions, especially in Africa. As nationalist movements emerged from the demands for increasing suffrage of the populations within colonialist empires, some ethnic elites moved into advantaged positions, while other minorities or disadvantaged groups became subjugated. The resulting ethnic stratification system in many former colonies created a rigid system of inequalities that remains entrenched to this day in many former colonies. To the extent that these inequalities become viewed as illegitimate, they become the basis of mobilization movements aimed at redressing ancient grievances originating from a colonial past.[16] As a result, former independence leaders and modernizing elites have found themselves confronted with ethnic rebellion from a variety of competing groups.

A review of the literature on colonialism and independence movements documents how both processes (decolonialization and the expansion of civil rights) were shaped by their distinct colonial histories.[17] Because ethnic identity could be manipulated to promote loyalty, form regional militias, and generate solidarity among elites favoring independence, ethnic identity emerged as a historically important force in many former colonies. As Enloe (1973) noted, one or more ethnic groups were often singled out by the colonizers as favored elites, creating the potential for ethnic dynamics to unleash resentment and status competition for scarce government jobs within the colonial structure. Following the end of colonialism, nationalizing elites inherited the patchwork puzzles of states in various regions, which rarely overlapped perfectly with any cultural features of linguistic, religious, or conscious ethnic markers. Thus, by 1950, the stage was set for the emergence of complicated alliances and hostilities among local elites and rival colonial powers.

Nowhere is this fact more vividly experienced than in the history of independent African states, where the failures of nation building in states such as Rwanda, Sudan, Nigeria, and Somalia have sometimes involved dramatic conflicts and horrific fighting (Welsh 1996; Brown 1996; Young 2002). Colonial legacies and an absence of sustained economic growth undoubtedly interact to produce ethnic movements challenging these artificial

---

[16]See, for examples, Horowitz (1985).
[17]See Emerson (1964), Kuper and Smith (1969), Horowitz (1985), Varshney (2002).

geographical boundaries.[18] Yet, as Kuper and Smith (1969: 128) pointed out, although ethnicity predates colonialism, "Imperial states inevitably magnify these structural and cultural differences and segregations of rulers and ruled, and are typically administered through systems of multiple domination."

THE IMPACT OF DIRECT AND INDIRECT RULE

Building on Emerson's (1964) earlier work on the impact of different colonial structures, Hechter (2000) argues that nationalist movements become transformed into active social movements under specific political structural arrangements, in which colonialist or federated authorities cede formal authority to local leaders. The power of local elites then rises and falls, depending upon the power of regional identities and loyalties in more and less centralized regimes. When indirect rule breaks down and external authorities attempt to impose direct rule, nationalist movements are likely to arise. Hechter (2000: 28) specifies that nationalism will emerge under two specific conditions: (1) the rise of direct rule, and (2) collapse of a multinational empire.

Brubaker (1996) also suggests that federated (as compared to centralized) systems have fostered a plethora of "new nationalisms" in Western and Eastern Europe (see also Halperin 1998). Roeder (1991) explains the movements in Eastern Europe as fundamentally based upon the federated system of regional and ethnically defined republics in the Soviet Union. As suggested in Chapter 1, political systems of incorporation that are based upon ethnic and/or regional identities create incentives for mobilizing along ethnic lines. Because the structural bases for ethnic movements exist, powerful nationalist movements have emerged within the former Soviet republics. Thus, the federated system of Soviet territories also set in motion a number of subnationalist movements that were organized around the republics' ethnic/linguistic/political identities.

While most of these theoretical arguments suggest the conditions under which nationalism will emerge, there is an important idea that emerges when considering the consequences of changes in regime strength. This argument suggests that when a central authority is weakened (by the breakdown of empire, or by external wars, famines, or economic crises), local elites that once held power become threatened. Drawing on their power base, nationalizing

---

[18] See also Yashar (1999) for examples from Latin America.

elites can then use their ethnic base to mobilize against competing groups. Applying Hechter's formulation suggests that direct rule might encourage politics based upon status group identities (compared to class).[19]

Alternatively, when the imposition of direct rule penetrates local levels of authority, peripheries and their modernizing leaders react, often with strong social movements aimed at resisting state-building efforts based in the (ethnically different) core. This suggests that some of the presumed consequences of direct rule, including cultural homogeneity, are endogenous to the structural dimensions of direct and indirect rule. Thus it becomes very difficult to test whether homogeneous ethnic identity in a region is a cause or an effect of direct rule (see also Hechter 2004).

Ethnic Parties and Consociationalism

The extent to which political parties overlap with ethnic identity provides another dimension for analyzing state variation in ethnic incorporation regimes. In examining varying institutional arrangements, Horowitz (1985) emphasizes the fact that ethnic political parties maintain ethnic loyalties through patronage systems in which rewards are based on ethnic group membership. Such forces are particularly strong when language, religion, or some other marker can distinguish a population that is geographically concentrated in a region. Other scholars (e.g., Brown 1996) have argued that while ethnic regional concentrations are important preconditions, they do not necessarily lead to ethnic violence. Instead, these scholars tend to emphasize proximate causes or local triggering mechanisms, such as changes in political authority, collapse of colonial authorities or empires, or transition to market economies or democracies (Levine 1996: 322–35).

Theories of consociationalism once appeared to explain how ethnic divisions became obstacles to state-building in multicultural environments.[20] In this view, political systems that provided a direct correspondence between "ethnic community" and "political party" would ensure that each minority

---

[19]For expanded treatments of this argument, see Hechter (2000, 2004).

[20]With consociationalism, political parties (and other representative bodies) structured along ethnic or linguistic lines predominate (as in Canada or Belgium). Mobilization along ethnic lines will alternate between vocal protests and/or violence and activities associated with institutionalized party politics. Over time, a dynamic equilibrium may be reached in which ethnic demands become incorporated into institutional politics and party structures.

community would have adequate representation to voice its claims and disagreements (e.g., Lijphardt 1977; Horowitz 1985).

In practice, many countries that have tried to implement consociational solutions have not been successful in preventing the outbreak of ethnic violence (Varshney 2002; Wilkinson 2004). Indeed, consociational formulas that create ethnic parties have incited ethnic and racial violence more often than not. As Horowitz (2001) now observes, party identification can calcify minority status, reifying cleavages and social distance among groups. Alternatively, historical identification of ethnic groups with specific parties or ruling elites can produce subsequent ethnic resentments, fragmentation, and ethnic hostility from groups whose needs are not currently being met.[21]

Two outcomes of consociational polities are possible: cooptation—in which ethnic parties become embedded in the power structure with regularized access—or some form of ethnic conflict (or a country may vacillate between the two outcomes). My point is that either way, consociationalism is likely to maintain the salience of ethnic identity in a multinational state. Canadian politics at the national level has experienced both consequences in recent decades.

International relations perspectives on ethnic conflict address another impact of the role of ethnic party systems on the likelihood of ethnic conflict. Whether the potential for ethnic conflict is greater in countries with pluralist party systems or autocratic party systems has been hotly debated in this literature. However, the empirical findings (e.g., Brown 1996) suggest that strategies for containing ethnic conflict are more effective in more democratic regimes than in less democratic regimes. Strategies for containing violent ethnic conflict include implementation of proportional representation, direct rule, and/or granting gradualist reforms and concessions. However, Horowitz (1985, 2001), Hechter (2000), and others have documented the relative failures of proportional representation, federalism, and other structural measures designed to eradicate or diminish ethnic conflict within states. Others suggest that peaceful outcomes may depend on the future organizational strength of international human rights organizations, associations, and other non-governmental organizations that provide external infrastructures and monitoring agencies.

[21] For instance, see Olzak et al. (2003), Varshney (2002), and Horowitz (2001).

Political shifts in regimes or power arrangements at the global level can offer new opportunities for formerly disadvantaged ethnic minorities. This process is particularly intense in newly democratizing states, where ethnic movements at the local level have been encouraged by local elites. Some of these movements have become institutionalized in party politics. This is particularly true for the period preceding transition to democracy in former Soviet Union countries, where communist party leadership and mobility opportunities channeled ethnic tensions within the contests for party leadership (see Roeder 1991; Beissinger 2002). Following the breakup of communist control, a number of Eastern European countries have witnessed a resurgence of ethnic movements, as party politics has reemerged along a number of new boundaries and identities.

Competition theory arguments applied at the global level would lead us to expect that local mobilization would rise as empires dissolve and colonial power declines. For example, following the decline in communist control, gypsies in Hungary began to mobilize for civil rights in significant numbers, and Russians in Estonia and Latvia have protested for expanded citizenship rights and against the loss of language rights in those countries (Beissinger 2002). Thus, the demise of the Soviet Union has released forces of intergroup competition at the local level in much the same way as declining colonialism encouraged nationalist movements (Brubaker 1996). Whether or not such competition becomes ethnic depends upon the regional concentration of linguistic, cultural, and historical identification with ethnic boundaries and the ability of native ethnic elites to gain grassroots support.

The Role of Ethnicity in Civil Wars

The preceding discussion about the onset of ethnic conflict raises questions about the nature of the relationship between ethnic aggression and other types of war, including international war. Earlier I suggested that many scholars trace the basis of most serious and enduring forms of civil war to ethnic divisions. For instance, they ask, *under what conditions do ethnic divisions lead to non-ethnic civil wars?* Other scholars are concerned with the pace of conflict, asking, *does the presence of ethnic conflict prolong the duration of civil wars?* Furthermore, *are internal ethnic wars linked to interstate wars, and if so, how?* Several innovative lines of research have suggested that there is a strong link between ethnic cleavages and violence, in which group differences mobilize and sustain the capacity for groups to incite civil wars

(Krain 1997). For instance, Sambanis (2001) has analyzed whether or not ethnic and non-ethnic civil wars have the same causes. This line of research is tricky, because it is difficult to demarcate when civil wars have a more or less "ethnic" character (since movements might shift their bases of mobilization over time). Nevertheless, Sambanis finds that civil wars based upon ethnic and/or religious identities are more likely to erupt in countries with high levels of ethnic heterogeneity and low levels of political democracy. In contrast, in non-ethnic (or revolutionary) civil wars, economic and development indicators (especially energy consumption) have more influence on the outbreak of non-ethnic civil wars than do measures of ethnic heterogeneity and indicators of democracy. Moreover, Elbadawi and Sambanis (2000) found that, contrary to expectations, civil wars in Africa over the 1960–90 period were not the result of its ethnic or religious diversity, but rather could be attributed to fragile political institutions, high levels of poverty, and other economic indicators such as dependence on natural resources and the absence of indigenous businesses.

The empirical evidence suggests that ethnic diversity prolongs civil wars, but there are few theoretical explanations of why this should be the case. Recently, Krain (1997), Collier (2000), Fearon (2002), Collier, Hoeffler, and Söderbom (2001), and Fearon and Laitin (2003) have examined the impact of ethnic cleavages on the duration of civil wars. Collier et al. (2001) and Fearon and Laitin (1999, 2003) find that the duration of violent civil conflict increases when there is a small number of large ethnic groups, when there are conflicts over land use, and when rebels have access to external (or contraband) resources, such as primary exports (Fearon 2005). Yet, somewhat paradoxically, the capacity of either side (government or ethnic insurgents) to obtain a decisive military victory lowers the probability of a negotiated settlement among combatants, and eventually shortens the duration of the war. Not surprisingly, the evidence shows that ethnic wars and civil wars are causally and temporally related.

The political refugees from civil wars in Bosnia and other ethnic regions provide another example of how regime changes create the potential for new ethnic movements (including ethnic wars), although resettlement programs undoubtedly undercut a group's ability to mobilize in any one country. At the same time, resettlement programs (and opposition to them) often concentrate ethnic populations and create new networks that provide recruits for mobilizing ethnic violence, as examples from the West Bank in Israel, or the Kurds in Germany, suggest. Thus, transitions to democracy may mobilize ethnic movements by offering new political advantages to ethnic groups that were more easily submerged in repressive regimes.

THE ROLE OF INEQUALITY AND MOBILIZATION

Do extremes in economic inequality among regions (or countries) affect ethnic uprisings? A long-standing assumption in the literature on collective violence (beginning at least with Marx and Engels) is that inequality facilitates group violence. According to this classical view, to the extent that gaps in access to resources grow, inequality provides motivation and justification for expressing grievances in opposition to the status quo. However plausible, such theories have not met with much empirical support, and recent analyses of social movements have suggested support for the alternative view, that an increase in resources favors mobilization by formerly disadvantaged groups.[22] Perhaps because of its position in the classical literature on stratification and political sociology, the debate over the power of inequality to produce social movements continues to have an impact on the study of collective violence and civil wars, and on analyses of many forms of social movements and collective action.

By the 1970s, the literature on ethnic social movements began to grapple with the paradox that while economic and political development apparently eroded some traces of primordial ethnic identity, under some conditions it seemed to foster ethnic mobilization. One early theoretical explanation of this phenomenon suggested that ethnic movements could be traced to conditions in which an *internal colony* existed, where a regionally concentrated population experienced both cultural and economic subordination.[23] This theory reflects deprivation explanations of mobilization, but it also emphasizes the importance of an interaction effect between uneven industrialization and cultural differences among regions in core nations. In this view, cultural and economic subordination causes ethnic grievances to become the basis of enduring political contention. The sources of ethnic solidarity are thus seen as including uneven regional development that reinforces or creates inequality, dependence on external or international investment, and an occupational

[22]For an initial statement of this argument in terms of social mobilization, see Deutsch (1953).

[23]For analyses showing a relationship between regional inequality and rural uprisings, see Paige (1975) and Villarreal (2004).

structure that is highly segregated along ethnic lines. Furthermore, according to this argument, a high level of ethnic solidarity and a division of labor along ethnic lines provoke ethnic conflict in developed regions, rather than in impoverished areas (Hechter 1975).

Under some conditions, within internal colonies a *cultural division of labor* emerges, in which dominant ethnic populations monopolize administrative and supervisory occupations (and rewards), while subordinate ethnic populations are relegated to lower-status occupations (often in extractive industries). These theories offer testable arguments that suggest that ethnic solidarity and political mobilization based upon ethnic and labor-market cleavages triumph over other possible types of loyalties. While the arguments are predictive and highly convincing (see Hechter 1975, 2000; Hechter and Levi 1979), the empirical tests of this theory have yielded inconclusive results (Nielsen 1980; Olzak 1982; Olzak and Nagel 1986; Medrano 1994).

Competition perspectives have provided some alternative lines of explanation for understanding how changes in economic and political conditions within and among states can provoke ethnic mobilization. First, this perspective suggests that the shrinking of resources in states, regions, or groups intensifies competition and conflict directed against ethnic minorities. Conflict arises because groups find themselves in direct competition for smaller numbers of jobs, elite representation, political favors, and other outcomes. In this view, economic contraction provokes competition and conflict (Olzak 1992), especially among different ethnic populations at the bottom of the social structure (Olzak and Shanahan 2003).

A key variant of competition theory is offered by *split labor market theory.* This perspective holds that ethnic antagonism peaks when two or more ethnically or racially differentiated groups command different wage prices within the same labor market niche (Bonacich 1972). Three-way competition dynamics emerge because dominant-group employers maintain wage differences between two or more sets of workers split along ethnic lines. Mobilization based upon race or ethnic identity occurs as dominant groups attempt to reassert their dominance over newly competing groups, and as formerly disadvantaged ethnic groups challenge the existing power structure and majority groups resist. Evidence from Chinese contract laborers in labor camps in Colorado (Boswell 1986) and from African-American and European immigrants in a variety of urban settings in late-nineteenth-century America tends to support arguments from split labor market theories (Olzak

1992). Furthermore, this theory suggests that as the dynamics of split labor markets change over time, and as the wage gap between racially differentiated groups erodes, conflict can be expected to decline proportionately.[24]

Economic competition perspectives have implications for political competition, suggesting that a wide variety of changes in state policies will intensify competition and mobilize ethnic populations to engage in nonviolent protest movements. For instance, some Soviet and Eastern bloc observers claim that during the late 1980s, as glasnost and perestroika undercut the absolute authority of ethnic Russians within the state apparatus of many Soviet Socialist Republics, nationalist sentiment became easier to mobilize, particularly in the former republics of the Ukraine, Latvia, Estonia, and Lithuania (Ulfelder 1997, 2004). This development created the potential for new national leaders and quasi-party structures often organized around anti-Russian ethnic sentiments.

According to competition theories, changes in economic conditions can incite mobilization by formerly disadvantaged groups. In this view, declining inequality among regions (or groups) increases the likelihood that subordinated groups will mobilize, because they experience new opportunity structures or can access new resources (Olzak and Nagel 1986). Thus, increasing income and occupational mobility for black Africans in South Africa escalated rates of protest dramatically in that country and subsequently gained them new political leverage (Olzak and Olivier 1998; Olzak et al. 2003).

The fragmentation of state regimes at the end of World War I (as summarized by the word "balkanization"), the movement for colonial independence throughout the pre– and post–World War II period, and regional disputes related to the emerging Cold War during the 1950s undoubtedly affected levels of relative economic growth and inequality within countries. These reconfigurations of world politics produced a different set of dependent relations among rich and poor countries. Conventional wisdom (and prior research) has long supported claims that economic instability seems to generate

---

[24]Evidence consistent with arguments from competition theory has been reported in studies of racial conflict in contemporary South Africa (Olzak and Olivier 1998), postindustrial conflict between white and black workers in the United States (Wilson 1978; Olzak 1989), discrimination against Chinese mineworkers in Colorado (Boswell 1986), race and ethnic conflict in U.S. cities around the turn of the century (Olzak 1992; Olzak and Shanahan 2003), and cross-national analyses of the *Minorities at Risk* data set (Wilkes and Okamoto 2002).

rebellions, civil wars, and internal civil strife (e.g., Muller and Seligson 1987; Lichbach 1987; Muller and Weede 1990; Sambanis 2001).

However, as many critics have indicated, it is equally likely that economic instability results from prior conflict, or that economic declines follow the public's anticipation of civil unrest. Thus, my next question asks, *are there specific causal sequences that link declining economic conditions to ethnic mobilization, or, alternatively, are inequality and unrest coincidental, but caused by some third factor?* Answering this question with certainty is difficult, in part because the nature of most longitudinal data on states or ethnic groups does not lend itself to discovering an "initial cause." Nevertheless, it is worth pursuing some novel ways to approach these questions, because many theories of mobilization propose that economic deprivation precedes civil unrest. Only by unraveling the causal sequence of events can we begin to understand the conditions under which ethnicity becomes mobilized.

In an attempt to sort out the causal ordering of economic effects on ethnic wars, Blomberg and Hess (2002) analyze the likelihood of ethnic war, genocide, revolution, and regime change (or "state failure") using newly available data on 152 countries from 1950 to 1992. They find that while the onset of ethnic war is significantly more likely to follow recessions, the reverse causal relationship is much weaker empirically. Such evidence largely supports the notion that economic decline raises rates of internal civil war, rather than the reverse.

Sambanis (2001) and Fearon and Laitin (2003) also find that economic hardship fuels a variety of internal conflicts, including ethnic ones; this supports the grievance perspectives long suspected by international studies scholars. In particular, a US$1,000 drop in per capita income yields a 41 percent increase in the likelihood of civil war, compared to a country at the world median level of income (Fearon and Laitin 2003: 83). While such findings are not new—and they beg for more systematic study of the interrelationship between weak states, economic stability, and ethnic violence—they suggest that poverty has a powerful mobilizing effect that cannot be easily put aside (see also Elbadawi and Sambanis 2000).

Ethnicity and Modernization

Are ethnic movements truly novel, or are they simply instrumental creatures of political movements that once, earlier in history, took other forms? Without undertaking a long historical treatise on questions of colonialism, empires, and their demise, answering this question is not easy. However, as Brubaker and Laitin (1998) argue, and Kalyvas (2003) concurs, it seems plausible that religious or class-based social movements are now more likely to be couched in distinctly ethnic terms and/or demand regional self-government, whereas fifty years ago they did not. A related question concerns the historical claim that there has been a shift in locus of ethnic activity. How can we uncover the mechanisms that caused social movements to expand their scope from local concerns to encompass national goals? Brubaker (1996) suggests one answer to this question by drawing a parallel between "ethnic movements" and "nationness." In his view, nationness is an evolving institutional process that begins to crystallize as ethnic groups confront processes of state building and state expansion. Similarly, Anderson (1991) posits a causal relationship between the rise of ethnic movements that coincided with the modern period of nation building, the spread of literacy, and increasing organizational interdependence among associations, groups, and state authorities (see also Tarrow 1998; Hechter 2000).

Other scholars have questioned whether what we are witnessing is really ethnic in character and not just a social construction of past confrontations in ethnic clothing. In a provocative discussion of this issue, Kalyvas (2003) asks just how many civil wars may have been misclassified as "ethnic" or "class conflict" events because they are (by definition) reinterpreted after events have occurred and rarely as they are emerging. Yet dealing with this fact presents an extremely difficult problem for analysts who are using historical documents in trying to analyze ethnic conflict and protest. There are no simple solutions to the fact that political conflict can be continuously reconstructed and reinterpreted. However, this same problem must be confronted when conducting all types of historical analysis, not just ethnic ones. That is, just because events are interpreted and reinterpreted does not render them uninformative. We know that even an isolated incident can take on a life and identity of its own, once it is repeated in public accounts such as newspapers, rumors, history books, and academic journals. Indeed, it may be that the process by which public documents come to label similar types of collective action as "race riot" or "criminal looting" or "insurgent uprising" in different contexts and across different historical periods is worth studying in its own right.

Rather than try to discern the meanings behind the multiple messages inherent in group conflict, it may be more useful to develop a typology of events and social movements based upon the claims expressed by nationalist and ethnic movements. Nationalist movements stake territorial claims based upon a group's unique history, set of ethnic markers, language, phenotypes, or other characteristics that bind group members together, despite the absence of direct face-to-face interaction. That is, scholars claim that ethnic and nationalist movements differ from other types of social movements in that they make demands and moral claims of group identity and/or self-determination. Additionally, the claims of nationalist and ethnic movements often require some authority (usually at the national or international level) to redress an existing injustice. The injustice may be a mild one, such as the fact that the group has been ignored and unrecognized, or they may involve more serious claims of victimization through terrorism or genocide. And the claims may shift from one to the other end of the continuum over time.

The empirical regularities present in these claims in the contemporary period provide clues for understanding why the goals and aims of mobilization invoke ethnic identity claims rather than other potential identities. Some scholars find that ethnic and nationalist movements are distinct from other bases of political contests (such as regional or religious social movements) because they employ distinctly modern claims.[25] Yet the modern character of nationalist movements does not limit ethnic and nationalist movements to a specific set of modern values or contemporary themes. Indeed, many nationalist movements (e.g., Islamic nationalist movements) have invoked themes demanding a return to the past (Snow and Marshall 1984). The modern character of these movements rests on the idea that there is a shared identity of a "people" with boundaries beyond a parochial village or town (Anderson 1991).

The position taken here is that it is probably not useful to debate what was and what was not "fundamentally" an ethnic war. Instead, researchers have opted for finding evidence showing that the claims and goals of social movements have distinctly ethnic claims that shape the ethnic character of a movement. This decision has proved to be useful because both ethnic identity and contentious conflicts have emergent properties that become transformed (and perceived) as ethnic events, sometimes long after the conflict occurred. Indeed, as Kalyvas (2003) demonstrates, ethnic activity has often

---

[25] For examples, see Gellner (1983), Hechter (2000), and Wimmer (2002), but see also Snow and Marshall (1984) and A. Smith (2000).

been relabeled (by different participants, politicians, news media, or by-standers of all types) as turf wars, criminal activity, accidental mishaps, vendettas, family feuds, or even private expressions of retribution (Kaldor 1999).[26]

Who is responsible for the construction of events as ethnic? In one view, the role of alliances or brokers is increasingly the key to understanding how local events resonate with existing or newly emergent cleavages at the national level (Kalyvas 2003). Alliances create the potential for new boundaries to be formed and old ones to dissolve, as different ethnic cleavages become salient in any given political struggle. According to Kalyvas (2003), Tilly (2003), and others, only with third-party involvement will local conflicts be transformed from small-scale local skirmishes to national cleavages. Does the presence of third parties assist us in distinguishing whether movements are nationalist or ethnic in character? Or, alternatively, do ethnic movements have some intrinsic quality that allows us to define them?

Kalyvas (2003) makes a good case for the importance of third parties as key framing agents in any group conflict situation. So too, do McAdam et al. (2001) in their analysis of the critical role of social movement "brokers" who create a dynamic potential for both increasing the level of contention and for defusing it. However, it is interesting that the important "third parties" to conflict are all but forgotten in many accounts. In identifying ethnic events for analysis, the main trick is to figure out how to codify regularities in themes, claims, and expressions of ethnic social movements, without falling prey to the labeling processes that may change over time and thus be misleading.

External ("third party") forces, then, matter to internal mobilizations, and it is likely that large-scale ethnic nationalism today is more likely to be encouraged over small-scale identities as state economies and politics become more integrated. This is because the scale of social organization and political power shifts from local, parochial, and personal relations to international, associational, and impersonal multistate bureaucracies. Smaller-scale identities such as kinship, family, and neighborhoods remain relevant in local settings. But larger-scale ethnic identities have become increasingly more important as policies regarding language, education, discrimination, affirmative action, regional taxation, and redistribution are contested at the national

[26]For examples of coding strategies and techniques that have been used to operationalize these concepts in useful ways, see, among others, McAdam (1982), Olzak (1989), and Gould (1999).

(or international) level. So in the contemporary period, ethnic groups must reorganize nationally to compete effectively for state resources.

Some scholars have analyzed the Cold War period in terms of this "third party" effect, suggesting that the participants, allies and enemies, created animosities that fundamentally reflected each of the protagonists in the Cold War (Borstelmann 2001). The Cold War produced a number of cleavages and ethnic fragmentation of states, where each side was aligned with one or the other side to the war (Borstelmann 2001). In these former battle zones (especially Uzbekistan, Chechnya, Serbia) state building has been complicated by the legacy of the Cold War, and some of the old fault lines have resurged in the form of nationalist social movements. In this way, the United States and former Soviet Union became third parties to internal conflicts in which ethnic minorities solicited support from powerful allies.

Racial politics in the United States had significant international repercussions during the Cold War as well. In Borstelmann's (2001) view, existing racial inequalities and discrimination patterns in the United States were used by the Soviet Union as a key basis for making claims of moral superiority during the ideological struggles of the Cold War. As a result, fears about consequences in Cold War negotiations influenced internal politics in the United States for decades.[27]

THE ROLE OF ETHNIC ENTREPRENEURS IN MOBILIZATION

To what extent is ethnic mobilization an instrumental decision by ethnic entrepreneurs and activists who seize opportunities to advance their careers and take over power? There are several useful variants of this instrumentalist perspective. For instance, *rational choice perspectives* emphasize causal factors producing ethnic and nationalist social movements that shift the calculus of the costs and benefits attached to ethnic mobilization (Hechter 1987a, 2000). According to this view, modern ethnic movements occur with regularity because they have unique properties that allow them to overcome the free-rider problem that hampers recruitment and mobilization efforts. Because ethnic groups are able to form dense social networks more easily than other groups, solidarity is high, minimizing costs of mobilization. As a consequence, by

---

[27]For an extended discussion of the implications of the Cold War in the success achieved by the civil rights movement in the United States, see Borstelmann (2001: 266–71).

this argument, ethnic groups can efficiently apply systems for monitoring behavior, ensuring loyalty, and sanctioning members (Hechter 1987a). Building on rational choice models, Fearon and Laitin (1996) and Weingast (1998) have linked the strategic aspects of ethnic identity to violence, as elites build on existing ethnic loyalties.

Despite the advantages for monitoring and maintaining network infrastructures, the mobilization of ethnic loyalties has sometimes proved fatal to group members. As Bhavnani and Backer (2000) argue, the presence of genocidal norms (defined as a threat of sanctions to group members who decline participation in ethnic mayhem) increases the scale of ethnic violence. Moreover, under conditions of strict group monitoring (with the potential to impose sanctions or expulsion), the activation of group loyalties can provoke explosive ethnic violence. However, in this view, the scale and scope of ethnic violence can be reduced when group monitoring is weak and genocidal norms lose force. Bhavnani and Backer (2000) offer an explanation for one persistent and counterintuitive finding in the literature: Even when there is a history of intergroup cooperation, tolerance, intermarriage, and trust among different groups interacting within a region, the intensity of ethnic killing and violence may remain high. Similarly, theorists have extended prisoners' dilemma models to consider the implications of game theory for ethnic mobilization, including outbreak of ethnic war (Fearon 1998; Fearon and Laitin 2003; Varshney 2003). They find that while armed ethnic rebellions tend to last longer than non-ethnic ones (Fearon 2004), ethnic and cultural distinctions (including linguistic ones) have few systematic effects on the onset or duration of civil wars (see also Fearon and Laitin 2003).

Moreover, during periods of uncertainty (such as transitions to democracy), power vacuums encourage ethnic leaders to capitalize on the fears of ethnic minorities. Indeed, Lake and Rothchild (1998: 4) argue that "ethnic conflict is most commonly caused by collective fears of the future." This perspective emphasizes that during political crises, *the threat of ethnic victimization* becomes more credible and ethnic polarization becomes more likely, even if there are long histories of ethnic integration and peaceful coexistence (as the case of former Yugoslavia suggests). The scale and recency of prior attacks by opponents raises the credibility of these threats even further, risking the potential for proactive strikes.

Using game theory reasoning, Fearon (1998) has offered a compelling argument along these same lines. In this scenario, in a dual-ethnicity and asymmetric power situation, a minority group will prefer fighting to settling under less than optimal conditions. This is because, by definition, acquiescence is costly for the minority group, and it is preferable to resist forcefully rather than remain in a peaceful but unacceptable state of coexistence with the oppressors. Fearon (1998) explains this suboptimal outcome as resulting from the majority's inability to respond favorably to the minority's demands. By intensifying ethnic fears of persecution, and in the absence of third-party mediators, ethnic leaders are able to successfully emphasize the benefits of mobilization to their ethnic constituencies (Fearon and Laitin 1997).[28]

Applying game-theoretical models to four specific cases, Laitin (1995) compares ethnic movements in the Basque Country and Catalonia in Spain, and in post-Soviet Georgia and the Ukraine. Using models that hold a number of cultural and historical factors constant, Laitin finds that three factors predict the outbreak of violence: (1) rural social structure, which facilitates group monitoring and expedites militant commando operations, (2) tipping game mechanisms that explain the conditions under which costs to joining nationalist campaigns (and recruitment of soldiers to nationalist armies) are reduced, and (3) sustaining mechanisms, which rely on several random shocks that trigger a culture of violence that becomes culturally embedded in regional and collective memories (see also Gould 1999). While other scholars have not explored these rational choice theory arguments systematically, such arguments suggest an important theoretical strategy for linking the macro-structural determinants of political systems to individual-level arguments about the motivation to support ethnic social movements.

Other instrumental perspectives suggest that individual warlords, or ethnic entrepreneurs, gain substantial resources and loyalty during periods of political instability and widespread uncertainty (Collier and Hoeffler 2004). In this view, self-interested leaders mobilize ethnic group loyalties to gain leverage over different warring factions. Evidence from Eastern Europe provides considerable support for these perspectives, suggesting one answer to the paradox of newly mobilized ethnicities and cleavage lines. For instance, few studies found high degrees of intolerance among Croatians and Serbs prior to the outbreak of violence in the former state of Yugoslavia, suggesting

---

[28]In Fearon's (1998) view, however, escalation is due to internal factors, rather than to external involvement or international linkages.

that ethnic hatred alone cannot explain outbreaks of violence of the kind experienced in this region. Carrying this argument one step further, Fearon and Laitin (2003) have suggested that when upward mobility channels are blocked, local leaders arise to champion the case of discrimination, providing one source of ethnic leadership carrying a message that resonates locally.

Evaluation of Various Perspectives

While there is no shortage of arguments, the empirical evidence in support of a direct causal relationship between institutional frameworks, economic inequality, and ethnic mobilization has been equivocal (Sambanis 2001, 2004; Fearon and Laitin 2003; Hironaka 2005). How do institutional and political opportunity structure models fare when compared to models of economic contraction? In his empirical analysis of political conflict (measured by total deaths from nonroutine political participation events), Schock (1996) finds that political opportunity measures perform better than do measures of economic inequality or economic development. In his analysis of approximately sixty countries over the period 1973–77, Schock finds that the potential for ethnic separatism (calculated from Taylor and Jodice 1983) increases political violence overall, but that this relationship holds only in countries with relatively low levels of political institutionalization (defined by the presence of binding rules on political participation). He concludes that his results suggest that weak states are more likely to transform ethnic grievances into political conflict and that further attempts to expand their control over minorities are likely to meet with ethnic resistance (Schock 1996: 127–28).

Moaddel's (1994) analysis found support that connected ethnic divisions to other forms of conflict within states. His results found that ethnic separatism affected both regime repression and political conflict. Contrary to inequality theories of ethnic conflict, Moaddel also found little evidence that underdeveloped countries experienced more political violence, once income equality and regime repression were taken into account. However, in this study political violence (measured by political deaths, civil unrest, riots and other armed attacks, and sanctions by the state) included insurgency actions as well as state violence, making it difficult to distinguish whether political violence precedes, follows, or coincides with acts of state repression.

Another set of arguments uses a version of grievance theory to advance the view that ethnic diversity underlies group antagonism. In this view, the degree of cultural distance and diversity in a population creates tensions leading to conflict and hostility (Williams 1994; Esman 1995). However, many findings from the empirical literature cast doubt on this claim. For instance Fearon and Laitin (2003) find little relationship between ethnic linguistic diversity and civil war, while Sambanis (2001) finds a significant relationship between ethnic linguistic fractionalization and ethnic civil wars. Gurr (2003) and Olzak and Tsutsui (1998), analyzing the *Minorities at Risk* data set, find a relationship between ethnic linguistic fractionalization and the magnitude of ethnic rebellion, whereas when others use data on all types of civil war (Sambanis 2001; Fearon and Laitin 2003), they find that ethnic fractionalization has little or no effect on other types of civil war.

Furthermore, the literature on state repression and ethnic violence has shown ambiguous results. One reasonable explanation for the conflicting findings has emerged in the collective violence literature. This is the claim that the relationship between civil liberties and mobilization is curvilinear. In this view, protest would be relatively mild in settings granting either many or very few civil liberties (Muller and Seligson 1987; Gurr 1993; Moore 1998). This means that the calculus of costs and benefits attached to protest reacts to changes in the political environment. Ethnic opposition to a given regime may in turn weaken the legitimacy of a state, so that the balance of gains and losses attached to mobilizing a secessionist movement would necessarily shift over time.

Analyses of ethnic and nationalist movements run the risk of ignoring these social movement dynamics when they equate ethnicity with nationalism.[29] It seems more relevant to examine whether ethnic distinctions predict levels of instability, rather than to assume that this correlation exists a priori. Such overlapping definitions have hampered researchers' ability to test a key assumption of instrumental theories that suggest that ethnic markers (or their distribution in a population) play a key role in determining the timing, spread, or location of ethnic movements. Thus, I would argue that there are substantial research payoffs to keeping the two concepts analytically distinct.

Evaluating the empirical performance of various perspectives against each other becomes especially difficult because the key research strategies from each tradition often vary substantially with respect to their units of

---

[29] See also Brubaker (1996), Brubaker and Laitin (1998), and Varshney (2002) for expanded treatments of this point.

analysis (e.g., countries, regions, cities, or groups), selection of cases that are at risk, and measures (e.g., income inequality, geographical concentration, or linguistic fractionalization). Moreover, many perspectives are based in specific fields, such as international relations, sociology, economics, and political science, which tend to have non-overlapping research traditions and literatures. Up until recently, the literature on ethnic and nationalist movements has not engendered much dialogue across disciplinary boundaries. For example, organizational theories of ethnic mobilization focus on traces of identifiable organizations, structures, and leaders, while mainstream protest analysts tend to focus on events, and comparative historical approaches use rich detail to flesh out specific historical contingencies. Each perspective has its own set of embedded assumptions, traditions, and goals that do not lend themselves easily to direct comparison with those of other approaches.

Despite this fragmentation of approaches, an emerging tradition in political science and sociology suggests that it might be useful to begin to analyze different forms of ethnic mobilization using a singular framework (e.g., Brubaker 1996; Hechter 2000; McAdam et al. 2001). In this view, there are similar mechanisms that can illuminate key factors responsible for the emergence, persistence, and decay of these forms of social movements. Rather than develop specific theories for each subtype of movement, it seems fruitful to begin with shared causal features of these movements. With more attention to the commonalities among forms of ethnic and nationalist movements, we stand to gain more understanding about how violence escalates and diffuses, or how spontaneous protests are transformed into sustained social movements that challenge existing authority structures.

Moreover, theoretical advances in sociology, political science, and psychology have suggested that analysis of particular ethnic and nationalist movements might benefit directly from the use of arguments from social movement literature, rather than applying findings from specific regional studies or historical accounts of a single ethnic or nationalist movement. By this I mean an approach that seeks to emphasize the continuities (and discontinuities) among social movements and their forms, across a number of historical periods and regional settings, in an attempt to build cumulative theories of ethnic and nationalist change. I would argue that theories that seek to isolate specific instances of ethnic movements and nationalism do not reach beyond the specific instances, and tend to be self-limiting and descriptive rather than explanatory.

However, I acknowledge that the aim of producing general theory is a fiercely debated issue in macro-sociology. Some sociologists argue that most, if not all, macro-level processes are historically contingent and unique, unable to sustain general theoretical arguments (Skocpol and Sommers 1980). On the other hand, Lieberson (1991, 1994) and Kiser and Hechter (1991) suggest that general theoretical arguments remain fruitful goals in the study of large-scale social change and political movements. Others have staked out a middle ground, suggesting that theoretical explanations of social movements can only be done by drawing deep analogies across similar mechanisms (e.g., McAdam et al. 2001).

My view is that strategies that move away from building theoretical arguments hamper our ability to create an empirically based body of knowledge. If each type of ethnic mobilization—from civil rights movements to ethnic civil wars—is analyzed separately by country, time period, and movement goals, it becomes impossible to know when to stop creating new and unique explanations to fit each new occurrence of a nationalist event or ethnic campaign. For this scholar, comparative work that seeks to build cumulative theories that can be falsified empirically holds far more promise than do studies of movements as unique and separate events.

Research Design and Measurement Issues

Most studies investigating ethnic mobilization have focused on a single ethnic or nationalist social movement within one country. While the conventional case study approach has generated many interesting findings, few are generalizable, and most of them examine ethnic movements that were highly successful, dramatic, or historically significant (Hechter and Levi 1979; Olzak 1982). Such approaches might overlook the diffusion of similar instances of ethnic and racial mobilization and the discourse surrounding them. Virtually all ethnic subnational movements since World War II have invoked the language of national self-determination in their demands. For rather different examples that share this characteristic, consider the territorial claims made by the Irish Republican Army, the Palestine Liberation Organization, and the American Indian movement. Until recently, most accounts have not moved beyond the observation that these ethnic movements share distinctly nationalist goals based in claims of common culture and ethnic affinity.

Such research tends to have limited goals, because the findings are diffi-cult to apply to other settings. Another, perhaps more serious, methodolog-ical problem concerns sample selection bias. Sample selection bias means that a sample has been chosen on the basis of some level of the dependent variable—e.g., only countries that have experienced some ethnic turmoil.[30]

The advantage of examining over time a set of countries at risk of having ethnic and nationalist movements is that explanations of periods of protest or ethnic violence can be evaluated empirically rather than described in ret-rospect. Event-history methods track the unfolding of events and their re-sponses over time; use of these methods facilitates the study of diffusion or contagion of events. This means that questions about whether ethnic protests in one country sparked subsequent protests in other countries can be better approached using longitudinal data that contain information on countries that are at risk of having some kind of ethnic uprising, conflict, or protest. Similarly, questions about whether state repression increases or depresses the rate of protest can also be investigated empirically using these methods that follow the trajectories of movements over time.

Other researchers have used comparative research designs that include populations of regions or states that might or might not experience ethnic conflicts or nationalist movements. In this way, researchers can test theories about the emergence of various forms in different settings (Gurr 1993). Yet some of these large-scale studies have also been criticized for sample selection bias, although the magnitude of this problem has not been fully explored (see Fearon and Laitin 2003).

Clearly, there are obvious trade-offs between the amount of detail and the statistical power that can be brought to bear in each of these designs. Comparative designs have the advantage of allowing researchers to pursue questions about the diffusion of ethnic and nationalist social movements across national boundaries, while case studies can explore various historical changes in depth, holding a number of country-specific measures constant.

[30]For examples of research on sample selection bias and newspaper sources, see McCarthy, McPhail, and Smith (1996), Hug and Wisler (1998), Myers (2000), and Myers and Caniglia (2004). Causal inferences drawn from studies of highly con-tentious or dramatic events (rather than from long-term data on countries, groups, or regions) are likely to be compromised by a study design that samples on some (high or low) level of the dependent variable. Recently, researchers have shifted their focus and begun to analyze such phenomena by following a set of countries (or cities or regions) that are at risk of having an event, over some comparable time period.

Analysis of ethnic conflicts within and between nations requires research designs and methods that take into account effects of changes in political and economic structures on rates of occurrence. Gathering information on the timing of events has become a critical component of research design in studying social movements. For theoretical and methodological reasons, information about the timing of events helps researchers to adjudicate among competing theories that imply different causal sequences.

Strategies for studying these processes now emphasize the importance of gathering information on the history of events, as well as state responses to ethnic events, as one way to untangle the causal sequences. Social scientists have long been fascinated with the obstacles to state building, but only recently has ethnic mobilization been a key concern of sociologists. In my view, the most exciting trend in research on social movements and collective action has been the recasting of new theories, data, and methods that take into account the dynamic and interactive nature of movements and state (and international) responses. Only by capturing this dynamic empirically can we begin to unravel the causal connections between nationalism and ethnicity.

Event analysis (used here) provides powerful ways to analyze the kinds of dynamic processes outlined above.[31] This approach uses information on the timing and sequencing of events to estimate models for rates of collective action. Two general forms of event history analysis are relevant for studying the processes discussed here. The first involves use of count data to analyze current events of a specific type, as in studies of race riots in the United States, protest in South Africa, or ethnic conflict in a number of countries over time. These studies use a variety of longitudinal designs, including time series, panel designs, and other statistical techniques appropriate for use in analyzing count data of this type (Cameron and Trivedi 2003).

The second method commonly used in event analysis considers transitions among movements and countermovements, as in the relationship between the rate of pro-Gypsy demonstrations, and the rate of anti-Gypsy attacks and violence (and vice versa). Analysis comparing the frequency of occurrence of different types of events broadens the research design so that similar causal mechanisms can be compared across different types of

---

[31]For examples, see Olzak (1989), Gurr (1993), Koopmans (1993), Kriesi et al. (1995), Olzak and Olivier (1999), and Tilly (2003).

outcomes. Longitudinal research designs are appropriate for examining whether changes in structural conditions coincide with the occurrence (and non-occurrence) of ethnic collective actions. This becomes important when analyzing data on events that are rare, as are most separatist and secession movements (see also Hechter 1992).

Macro-level processes, which involve relationships across a number of state units, are particularly useful for capturing mobilization movements. A variety of methods for studying diffusion have proven to be useful for understanding cross-national effects in institutional economics, institutional theories of legitimation, and social movement theory and research. Such methods and techniques for analyzing diffusion have been applied successfully to the study of the breakdown of colonial regimes (Strang 1990), anti-foreigner violence in Germany (Koopmans and Olzak 2004), and civil and international wars in recent decades (Sambanis 2001; Gleditsch, Strand, Eriksson, Solleberg, and Wallensteen 2001). Another application has studied the transformation of American civil rights movement activism in other settings, such as the anti-apartheid movement in South Africa (Olivier 1990; Soule 1997; Olzak and Olivier 1998). In another application of event analysis, Mark Beissinger (2002) has suggested that many of the Soviet Union's policies of indirect rule regarding ethnicity in various republics facilitated the growth of ethnic elites and organizations that eventually led to the overthrow of the communist regime in 1989 (see also Ulfelder 2004). Such agendas have pushed the field of political sociology further in terms of being able to identify the impact of varying political structures that produce new opportunities for mobilization.

One alternative explanation for diffusion deserves mention here. Many scholars of collective action suspect that the magnitude of collective action depends on the spread of information by the media (Tilly 1978; McAdam et al. 1988; Koopmans and Olzak 2004). Skeptics of media sources of data on events (see Hug and Wisler 1998; McCarthy et al. 1996; Myers and Caniglia 2004) might assume that media reporting rates will be biased downward in dominant countries, which wish to present themselves as democratically open and relatively conflict free. If this is the case, then richer, core countries would systematically undercount ethnic events (especially violent ones), while in peripheral countries events would be overreported. Others have argued the opposite, that because of the concentration of media outlets and wire service networks, news from more developed countries will be more likely to be reported when compared to peripheral countries and regions (or regions with fewer wire services).

Instead of debating the merits of newspaper sources, it seems more fruit-ful to turn this criticism into a hypothesis that can be evaluated across both of the data sets analyzed in this book. This hypothesis builds on the notion that media coverage is likely to be more sensitive to events taking place in media-rich countries, and suggests that more developed core countries will contribute more events to the data set than will peripheral countries.

Many other problems and obstacles also arise when conducting large-scale research that compares country-level characteristics over time. Even larger questions have arisen in the literature concerning sources of system-atic bias, endogeneity, and measurement error in research on political con-flict. These issues are serious and they deserve more empirical attention. For instance, measurement error can wreak havoc with modeling techniques that test for the significance of various indicators. Flawed results mislead researchers and policymakers alike.[32] Fortunately, there are a number of measurement models now available that make use of latent trait analysis, structural equations modeling, and multiple indicator models. When the data are rich enough to provide multiple indicators for a single concept, posterior density models can be estimated, so that assumptions can be made and tested using data at the country or group level and compared (Quinn et al. 2003). However, the situation here is less applicable to this type of measurement error modeling, because we do not have a number of different indicators for each conceptual argument. In the future, however, it will be worth exploring some of these models, especially in terms of sampling bias and other concerns, across different data sets and using multiple indicators of the same concept, to see if the models produce similar or different results.

One final and important methodological issue deserves attention. Macro-level analyses and explanations nearly always invoke questions about the causal sequencing of events. It is often illuminating to explore a reverse causal argument that asks if a causal factor can also be considered a *conse-quence* of the outcome in question. So, studies of democracy and economic development have been plagued by this classic chicken-and-egg problem: do more democratic countries and regimes survive because they are richer and

---

[32]For excellent discussions of these problems, see Quinn, Hechter, and Wibbels (2003) and Clinton, Jackman, and Rivers (2004).

more economically stable, or does economic well-being contribute to the building of democratic institutions in some fundamental way?

Without sufficient information on the timing of events, untangling their causal sequencing can be hazardous, if not impossible. Furthermore, it seems facile for critics to dismiss an entire theoretical perspective by raising questions about a reverse causal argument, especially without empirical or theoretical backing. Nevertheless, given the importance of this problem, it seems reasonable to explore these arguments about endogenous effects of democracy and ethnic mobilization, to clarify our understanding of the historical development and mechanisms behind these complicated processes.

Conclusion

This chapter summarizes a number of leading approaches to ethnic movements that build on theories of nationalism, self-determination, inequality, and mobilization. Most perspectives surveyed here focus on internal features of states, including variation in economic well-being, modernization, political access, and democratic institutions. I argue that this emphasis has not led to a cohesive theoretical framework, nor can focus on the internal features of states explain the apparent rise of importance of ethnic and racial identity in the contemporary period. In the chapters that follow I advance the claim that processes of economic and political integration among the world's states have caused a rise in ethnic protest movements. In core nations, ethnic protest will be relatively more frequent, but its form is generally less violent because ethnic goals can be moderated by institutional means. In contrast, in peripheral nations ethnic protest is likely to be more sporadic, but potentially more violent when it does erupt. Whether scattered nonviolent protests develop into armed rebellions also depends on internal processes related to the political opportunities for ethnic inclusion and economic mobility.

CHAPTER THREE

Escalation and De-escalation: Trends in the Data

Is ethnic violence rising to unacceptable and detrimental proportions, as some might argue? Has there been a proliferation of ethnic protest and claims-making activity across the world's states? Or is ethnic mobilization subsiding, eclipsed by other mobilizing forces and identities? This chapter provides a first glimpse of the empirical evidence used to address these questions. I then examine some of the trends in the data that allow us to assess claims about the rising salience of ethnicity in the modern world. In the chapters that follow, I ask what types of ethnic movements seem to be increasing in intensity and which ones are declining, and I will examine some of broader policy implications of my theory and empirical analysis.

Recall that the arguments in Chapter 1 suggested that increasing the number of links with an international network of non-governmental organizations raises opportunities for mobilizing along ethnic and racial lines. Processes that connect various geographical, political, and administrative units (1) spread a human rights ideology that legitimates sovereignty and rights of self-determination, (2) carry ideas, tactics, and organizational infrastructure across national borders, and (3) allow groups and regions to compare levels of inequality across cultures and groups. Furthermore, as administrative state units are increasingly interdependent, as evidenced by increases numbers of economic, social, and political ties, then one would expect to see resistance movements against these centralizing tendencies. To the extent that discrimination and inequality are disproportionately ethnic in character, various forms of ethnic mobilization ought to result.

Examining Levels of Activity: The Minorities at Risk Data Set

In order to examine some trends in ethnic activity over the 1965–98 period, I begin by painting a broad picture of types of ethnic events that have taken place. To date, the most comprehensive data on the magnitude of ethnic protest and violence has been collected by Ted Robert Gurr (1996, 2003) in his Minorities at Risk (MAR) Project.[1] These data track 284 politically active ethnic groups throughout the world from 1945 to the present. Information collected on "minorities at risk" was originally gathered so that it could be analyzed at the ethnic-group level by using Guttman scales of severity of nonviolent ethnic protest and violent conflict. Because the ascending levels of protest and violence represent a significant escalation in goals and violence, in each case, they are analyzed separately. For theoretical reasons, an initial task will be to compare differences between violence and nonviolence, in order to answer questions about the conditions under which violence occurs.

MAR focuses specifically on ethnopolitical groups that have been designated as having "political significance" in the contemporary world because of their status and political actions. As outlined on the MAR Web site, "political significance is determined by the following two criteria: [1] The group collectively suffers, or benefits from, systematic discriminatory treatment vis-à-vis other groups in a society; [2] The group is the basis for political mobilization and collective action in defense or promotion of its self-defined interests" (http://www.cidcm.umd.edu/inscr/mar/about.asp).

While the boundary between protest and violence is not always absolute, Gurr (1993: 93) distinguishes protest from violent rebellion by delineating differences between their strategies and tactics: "The essential strategy of protest is to mobilize a show of support on behalf of reform; the essential strategy of rebellion is to mobilize enough coercive power that governments are forced to accept change." Gurr further clarifies that while protesters might use violence, it would only be in sporadic and unplanned ways. In contrast, violence takes the form of more planned campaigns, as in armed attacks, genocide, banditry, and terrorism. Gurr defines violent ethnic

---

[1] For a complete description of the scaling techniques and definitions from this project, see Gurr (1993: 93–121). The MAR data set, initiated by Gurr in 1986, has been based at the University of Maryland's Center for International Development and Conflict Management since 1988, and has been made available to researchers since 1990.

activity as ethnic activity that includes some form of coercive threat or action on behalf of an ethnic communal group (see Gurr 1993: 94–95). Another important distinction is that protest is generally directed against some (usually state) authority, while violence can be directed against some other ethnic group or groups, or it may be directed against state authorities (the MAR data set does not distinguish between these two targets of violence).

Table 3.1 presents the substantive categories that Gurr used to develop a Guttman scale of values, in which nonviolent protest values range from

TABLE 3.1

Categories of Nonviolent Ethnic Protest and Ethnic Rebellion, Minorities at Risk Data Set

Level	Nonviolent Protest	Conflict and Rebellion
0	No events recorded	No events recorded
1	Verbal opposition *Petitioning, leafleting, agitation, etc.*	Political banditry, *Sporadic terrorism*
2	Symbolic resistance *Sit-ins, blockage of traffic, sabotage, etc.*	Campaigns of terrorism
3	Small demonstrations *A few demonstrations, rallies strikes, and/or riots* *< 10,000 participants*	Local rebellions *Armed attempts to seize power in a locale*
4	Medium demonstrations *Rallies, strikes and/or riots* *< 100,000 participants*	Small-scale guerilla activity *< 1000 armed fighters* *Sporadic armed attacks (< 6 per year)* *Attacks in small part of group's area*
5	Large demonstrations *Mass demonstrations, rallies, strikes and/or riots* *> 100,000 participants*	Intermediate guerilla activity *1 or 2 traits of small-scale activity* *1 or 2 traits of large-scale activity*
6	—	Large-scale guerilla activity *> 1000 armed fighters* *Frequent armed attacks (> 6 per year)* *Attacks affect area occupied by group*
7	—	Protracted civil war *Fought by rebel military units with military base areas*

NOTE: Scale values adapted from Minorities at Risk (Gurr 1993: 95), the MARGene Documentation and Codebook (Bennett and Davenport 2005: 84–86), available online at http://www.cidcm.umd.edu/inscr/mar/data.asp.

0 to 5 and violence/conflict/rebellion values range from 0 to 7. These levels provide the key data for the dependent variables of the magnitude of ethnic nonviolence and violence.[2] The index data are further aggregated across five-year intervals (with the exception of the last interval, which covers 1995–98). For my analysis, this means that the year 1965 refers to activity levels during the 1965–69 period, 1970 refers to 1970–74, 1975 refers to 1975–79, 1980 refers to 1980–85, 1985 refers to 1985–89, 1990 refers to 1990–94, and 1995 refers to 1995–98. Thus, I analyze the MAR data at the group and country levels of analysis over the 1965–98 period.

As can be seen in Table 3.1, protest ranges from relatively mild acts of "verbal opposition," to large-scale demonstrations involving 100,000 participants or more. When scrutinized more closely, the MAR protest index refers mainly to categorical escalations in size and scale. In contrast, the categories of violence seem to indicate escalation in levels of military authority, organization, and in scope of intended violence. Thus, ethnic violence categories range from scattered acts of violence or sabotage, through the outbreak of local rebellions, to civil war.[3]

To capture some of the trends in these data, I first calculated the percentage of ethnic groups that were engaged in serious levels of nonviolent ethnic protest. I operationalized "serious," by counting those groups that engaged in more than verbal opposition and political organizing (above levels 1 and 2 in the left column of Table 3.1). Similarly, I calculated the number of groups engaged in more serious levels of violent activity, beyond that of political conflict and campaigns of terrorism (above levels 1 and 2 on the right-hand side of Table 3.1). These benchmarks were chosen for substantive reasons. For nonviolent protest there seemed to be a natural division between normal political action (such as lobbying, in category 2) and large-scale demonstrations. Thus, social movement theories tend to emphasize the distinction

---

[2] Note that earlier versions of the *Minorities at Risk* data had three distinct scales: nonviolent protest, violent protest, and rebellion. The data used here follow the 1999 revision that combines violent protest and rebellion into a single scale. Table 3.1 categories reflect the revised scales (see http://www.cidcm.umd.edu/project.asp?id=17).

[3] Gurr (1993: 89–122) used Guttman scaling techniques to produce scales ranging from 0 (no ethnic protest observed in a country over that period) to 7 (indicating protracted civil war), for successive five-year periods. Gurr originally distinguished violent protest from outright rebellion by the lack of sustained action and indications of hierarchical command structure of rebels. Both violence and rebellion indices have been collapsed and redefined in the most recent (2004) measures of the MAR data.

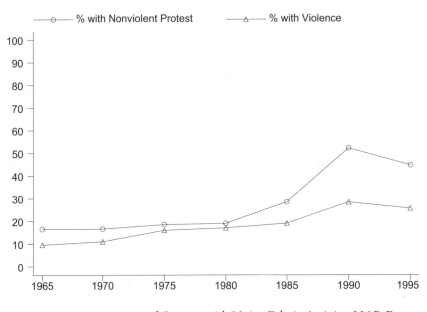

FIGURE 3.1 *Percentage of Groups with Major Ethnic Activity, MAR Data*

between conventional and institutional behavior, and spontaneous street behavior. Similarly, for violence, the escalation of activity that generates local
rebellions indicates an escalation in commitment and risk over more sporadic and less sustained violence (as indicated by levels 3 and higher in the
right column of Table 3.1).

Figure 3.1 shows trends in the percentage of groups that engage in protest
and violence above these benchmarks. A comparison of the two trend lines
us that the percentage of ethnic groups ("at risk") instigating large-scale
public protests was generally higher than the percentage of ethnic groups
instigating major forms of ethnic violence. Because protest generally in-
curs lower costs (in terms of state repression, arrests, or even death), this
result would be anticipated by most theories of collective action (e.g., see
Tilly 2003; McAdam, Tarrow, and Tilly 2001). At the beginning of 1965,
16 percent of all groups who might be expected to protest did so, and by
1990 this percentage had tripled. In 1965 the percentage of groups engaging
in violent forms of action was similar to the percentage of those engaged in
nonviolence, whereas nearly 30 percent engaged in violence in 1990.

Without further analysis, it is difficult to judge whether these levels are
high or low. However, it is interesting to notice that despite the fact that

these groups were chosen on the basis of prior activity, in 1965 the bulk of these "at risk" groups did not engage in activity that went beyond institutional lobbying, demands, and political conflict activity. As we will see in later chapters, the percentage of countries that had no reported violence is sometimes a majority, especially in the pre-1989 era. Furthermore, countries that experience violence do not always continue to do so, suggesting that state repression may intervene at some point. We will return to this point later in this chapter.

Given the differences in risks, levels of organization, and involvement of weapons, it might seem reasonable to expect different temporal patterns for nonviolence compared to violence. Instead, we see in Figure 3.1 that these forms show a strikingly similar trajectory over this period. Both violent and nonviolent ethnic activity peaks in 1990, and then both appear to be declining by 1995. These trends are consistent with the view that the end of the Cold War (perhaps temporarily) escalated ethnic mobilization (Gurr 1993). This figure also hints at the fact that protest and violence are causally connected.

Figure 3.2 shows the same time series for the percentage of countries that experienced major forms of ethnic protest and violence, using the same benchmarks used in Figure 3.1. As might be expected, the percentage of

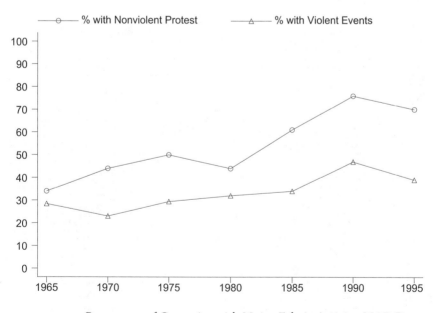

FIGURE 3.2 *Percentage of Countries with Major Ethnic Activity, MAR Data*

countries experiencing nonviolent and violent activities follows the same temporal pattern that we saw for the percentages of groups, but the pattern is more volatile when countries are examined. In fact, in Figure 3.2 the percentage of countries (with minorities "at risk") experiencing either violent or nonviolent ethnic activity remains relatively stable until after 1980, when it begins to increase. By 1990, serious forms of demonstrations and/or ethnic violence were reported in more than 70 percent of countries that had politically active minorities.[4] We see a downward trajectory of ethnic activity by 1995.

Given the MAR project's selection procedures, the relatively high percentage of countries experiencing some form of ethnic activity is not unexpected. In particular, the groups (and the countries where they reside) were chosen because they could reasonably be expected to have some form of political demands, expressions, or rebellion based upon ethnic claims. Thus, in some ways the percentage of groups and countries experiencing serious forms of ethnic activity might be lower than expected, given the sampling design that generated these data.

Event Counts of Ethnic Activity: The PANDA Data Set

To counterbalance the selection problems presented by the *Minorities at Risk* data, I analyze time series information on ethnic events gathered from a second data set, referred to as the PANDA (Protocol for the Assessment of Nonviolent Direct Action) data set.[5] The data represent a subset of Reuters news reports that were coded by the use of a system of content analysis and sentence parsing that uses information in the headline of the report to create a sequence in which categories of subject, verb, and object can be combined to create an event data set. Following standard newspaper reporting guidelines, this data set aims to answer the questions of "Who did what to whom and why?"

---

[4]Gurr (1993) and his associates judged an ethnic, religious, or communal group to be "at risk" if there was evidence of previous political activity that involved this group (as instigators or victims).

[5]These data were coded using the PANDA/KEDS software program designed and implemented, under the direction of Doug Bond, by the Program on Nonviolent Sanctions and Cultural Survival at Harvard University. As of July 1, 2005, the Program for the Assessment of Nonviolent Direct Action has closed. Doug Bond is currently president of Virtual Research Associations (www.vranet.com).

The PANDA data on ethnic events have several advantages over the *Minorities at Risk* data, beyond the sample selection bias issue.[6] First, the Reuters data cover more countries that were "born" in the 1989–90 period, after the demise of the Soviet Union. These countries have been assumed to be the locus of many, if not all, of the ethnic conflicts in the post-1990 period, but this assumption has rarely been examined empirically. Second, these data allow for a comprehensive comparison of violence perpetrated by ethnic insurgents, as contrasted with violence in reaction to ethnic movements (as the *Minorities at Risk* data set does). This allows me to focus on variation in the rate of ethnic violence by insurgents, as distinct from violent state/ethnic-group confrontations.

My use of these data followed a straightforward set of coding rules that (1) began with the initial data set of over 500,000 reported public protest events, and then (2) selected a set of events that reported ethnic or racial labels, groups, social movements, or separatist organizations, and that (3) excluded government officials or authorities as the initiators of action. Violence was coded as present if injuries to property or persons were sustained in activity generated by the instigators of activity. Violence by government authorities such as police was excluded, as was violence perpetrated by outsiders such as UN military convoys, coalition armies, or armies from neighboring countries.

At the outset, it is necessary to make a number of critical research decisions, in part because of the fact that some countries that exist at the beginning of the time series (e.g., West and East Germany, the USSR, etc.) no longer exist by the end of the observation period in 1995. For purposes of creating a broad view in this chapter, I reconfigured the data on ethnic events across a full 1984–95 period (across the Cold War divide). Arraying the data in this way requires a number of important decisions about (1) various states that did not exist as independent units prior to 1989, for example, many of the former countries under Soviet rule, Germany, etc.; (2) various states that split or became independent units during this period, such as Eritrea; and (3) states that substantially changed political form in terms of democracy and autocracy. Are these different states, or should we simply merge data and

[6]The key problem for many researchers is in making inferences about causal patterns of ethnic activity using a data set for which the sample has been chosen based upon some (prior) level of presumed ethnic mobilization or political activity. For discussion of sample selection bias issues in these data, see Fearon and Laitin (2003) and Tilly (2003).

boundaries (for example, from East and West Germany into Germany)? Answering these questions involves consideration of a number of tricky issues, and there are no single right answers.

The strategy chosen here refers to a "country" in terms of a regime with sovereign political authority and administrative control when it emerges as an independent unit. Of course, all of these countries vary substantially with respect to the viability of administrative control, strength of regime power, and so on (which will be considered in the chapters that follow). Using these rules means that, for example, East Germany and West Germany exist in the initial observation year of 1965, but both cease to exist at the end of 1989. In 1990, the country of Germany emerges as a new single state (so the unified country of Germany does not exist in the time series data prior to 1990, but East Germany and West Germany do exist in the dataset up to that point).

While these rules allow us to distinguish between new and old states (in the same territory, as in Germany) and help to avoid double counting of previous activity in formerly more inclusive states (e.g., the USSR), this decision creates problems for panel analysis, since all of the units do not all exist for all years. Because the end of the Cold War demarcates an important period in which a number of new states are "born," it makes sense to separate the analyses at that point. Also, fortunately, for those countries that move in and out of the data set in different years, new estimation techniques are now available for dealing with "unbalanced" panel observations. I have also used various methods (including bootstrapping techniques) to examine whether or not the estimates are biased, given the available units of analysis.

The PANDA event data allow us to address a key theoretical question regarding the causal sequencing of ethnic events and state repression of ethnic minorities. Unlike other data sets (including the MAR data), the PANDA set allows us to distinguish between instigator-sponsored and state-sponsored violent events. A recurring criticism of research on ethnic violence has pointed out that many existing data sets on ethnic violence conflate these two sources of violence. For instance, many studies of civil war using the Correlates of War (COW) dataset analyze the number of political deaths (as opposed to homicides, death by natural causes, etc.) in a year as a proxy for civil war. The most obvious problem with using the COW data set for this purpose is that a high number of deaths may occur due to the relative weakness of group challengers compared to a more robust state police or internal army, or deaths may increase as the result of increasing escalation and challenge to state authority (or violence may be the result of an increase in both trends). In the majority of available data sets, trends in state repression cannot be untangled from increases in group mobilization.[7]

Fortunately, in the PANDA data this is not the case. In these data there are clearly defined sets of "agent" and "target" codes that contain specific information for outcomes of violence against an ethnic/cultural/religious/nationality group instigated by state, army, or other authorities acting in an official capacity. This means that state-sponsored violence against ethnic and racial groups can be differentiated from violence and protest instigated by grass-roots groups against the state. This is a major advantage of this data set, and indeed, it affords a unique look at the relationship among all forms of violence concerning ethnicity.

The first step in the data analysis presented in this chapter will be to describe the various trends in ethnic violence, ethnic protest, and state violence involving ethnic groups over the 1984–95 period for which event data are available. Then I will compare the effect of state-sponsored violence against ethnic groups to violence instigated by ethnic groups. A third step will examine differences in factors associated with ethnic violence compared to nonviolent ethnic activity: are the causes the same or different? Finally, I will explore difficult issues involving simultaneous effects of repression on violence and vice versa, in an attempt to untangle some of the feedback loops that might affect the results.

Figure 3.3 shows that the trajectory of all forms of ethnic/cultural/religious groups and mobilization (both violent and nonviolent action) first rose and then fell during the 1984–95 period. There is an initial steep rise in the amount of ethnic activity from 1984 to 1985, followed by a ragged yet overall positive incline. After 1989, there is a steep descent in amount of ethnic activity. These cyclical patterns (and their slope) require more explanation than has been offered in the literature.[8]

---

[7]For example, Tilly (2003: 65) criticizes Gurr's *Minorities at Risk* data set because it tends to conflate measures of increasing violence with government-sponsored violence, as governments seek to contain, undermine, and deter further violence by challenging groups. According to Tilly, the problem is that the proportion of collective and violent acts contributed by each side cannot be determined using this index data.

[8]Thus, recent explorations of ethnic mobilization have documented but have not yet modeled the factors that might explain the decline in activity by 1995 (Gurr 2000; Sambanis 2001; Fearon and Laitin 2003).

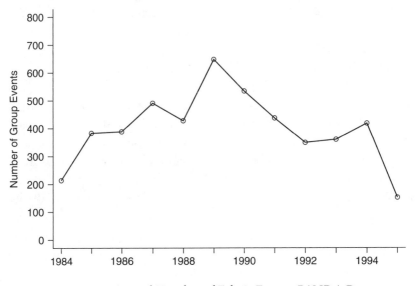

FIGURE 3.3   *Annual Number of Ethnic Events, PANDA Data*

Comparison of the trends in ethnic violence and nonviolence addresses theories that consider ethnic mobilization a singular phenomenon. For instance, Figure 3.4 shows that ethnic group violence spiked in 1985, 1987, 1989, and 1993. The trajectory of nonviolent ethnic protest over these years also peaks in 1989, suggesting that protest and violence mutually reinforced each other over these years. Moreover, both trends curve downward at the end of the 1994–95 period. As might be expected, ethnic group activity shows at least a two-to-one ratio of nonviolent to violent events for most of this period (compare the left-hand and right-hand side scales of this graph, which show this fact). In fact, during 1989–91 and again in 1994–95, the ratio of nonviolent to violent events is over three times as high. Thus ethnic violence and nonviolence show counter-cyclical trends as well as some overall similarities in terms of gradual rise and fall of activity. In the beginning of the period examined, nonviolent ethnic mobilization rose sharply between 1984 and 1985, and again in 1987, whereas after 1985, ethnic group violence remained relatively stable, averaging around 120–125 events per year, until 1995, when violence declined even further.

While these time series graphs are useful for describing the amount of ethnic group activity, they cannot address the question of what factors cause this activity to fluctuate over time. We first explore the temporal aspects of this question in Figure 3.5, which compares the trajectory of state-sponsored violence against ethnic minorities (defined as violence by state authorities, including the army, state or local police, national guard, etc.) with that of ethnic violence. This figure shows several patterns that support the idea that repression and group violence are countervailing forces. In particular, there are several years in which ethnic group violence peaked as state repression of ethnic groups declined (in 1987 and 1992–93). However, both trends curve downward at the end of the 1994–95 period. As might be expected, group challenges instigate a larger number of violent events than does state repression (as can be seen by the differing scales on the two sides of Figure 3.5), although the severity in terms of weaponry deployed by state-sponsored authority might be more lethal. The counter-cyclical trends suggest some initial support for Moore's (1995) claim that state repression and ethnic demands on state authority represent a dyadic response-reaction dynamic, in which violence by one side is countered by violence on the other. The two curves might be interpreted as reactive cycles of protest and response.

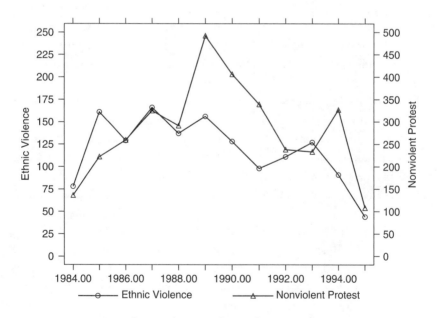

FIGURE 3.4   *Violent and Nonviolent Ethnic Events, PANDA Data*

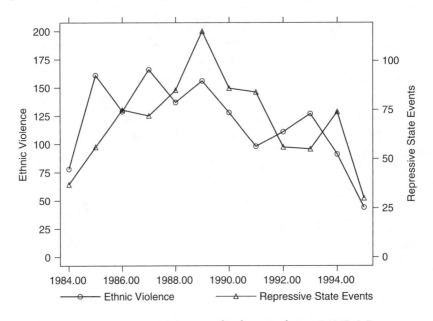

FIGURE 3.5 *State Repression and Ethnic Violence, PANDA Data*

The peaks in nonviolent protest in 1989–90 shown by Figure 3.6 may provide some evidence that ethnic protest accompanied the new democracies and new states emerging from the shadow of the Soviet Union in those years. As many others have suggested, 1989–90 was an important historical period that witnessed the end of the Cold War, the emergence of a large number of new countries, and a realignment of state coalition partners and alliances (Borstelmann 2001). Most observers have associated this period with rising conflict, as emerging states attempted to achieve legitimacy both internally and externally, a claim supported by Figure 3.6. The figure also shows that there has been a gradual decline in such tumultuous activity. Yet there is another peak in nonviolent ethnic protest in 1994, which suggests that the incidence of ethnic protest is not necessarily on the wane overall.

Does nonviolent protest react to state repression in the same way that ethnic violence does? Many important theories of collective action suggest that repression extinguishes nonviolent protest more rapidly than it does violence. This is partly because ethnic nonviolence is relatively low-cost compared to violent activity. At low levels of repression, personal injury, arrest, death, and bodily harm are less likely, so protest rates will fluctuate at relatively high levels over time in democratic and open societies. But when state repression intensifies, nonviolent protest will be sharply reduced, as its costs rise dramatically. In contrast, violence appears on the horizon when other options are either closed or nonexistent; at that point, protesters have nothing to lose. By this argument, violence by the state would be more reactive to violent challengers than vice versa. As discussed in Chapter 1, theories of collective violence by the state suggest that state authorities will be more reactive to violent challengers, since there is much more at stake when a violent overthrow seems imminent.

Figure 3.6 provides some evidence addressing these theories. In particular, nonviolent protest and repression increase and decline simultaneously and both types of activity track each other rather well. A comparison of Figures 3.5 and 3.6 suggests that violence may indeed react to the expressions of state violence after some time has passed, but that nonviolent mobilization by race and ethnic groups may respond immediately to violence by authorities. If actions and reactions are indeed simultaneous (as might be expected, given the overlapping curves to be seen in Figure 3.6), then more complicated longitudinal models that take this simultaneity into account directly will be necessary.

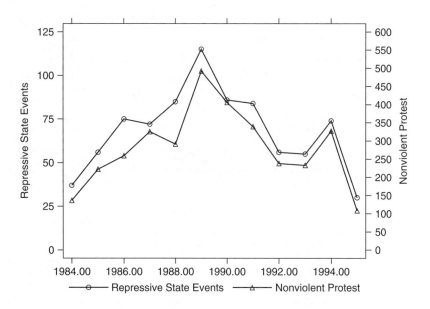

FIGURE 3.6 *State Repression and Nonviolent Ethnic Events, PANDA Data*

That these time series graphs show a gradual decline in the amount of ethnic mobilization seemingly challenges some conventional assumptions about the rising threat of ethnic violence that have been voiced by some scholars (e.g., Gurr 2000; Horowitz 1985). Yet other evidence—notably from the MAR data set examining escalating categories of violence—shows that more countries are experiencing more radical forms of violence. Moreover, there is arguably a larger threat from rising state violence against minorities, rather than the reverse, in the contemporary period. Finally, it seems reasonable to question whether or not ethnic mobilization should also be considered a sign of political health, rather than an indicator of impending threat to state sovereignty. I take up these questions in more depth in the multivariate analysis below and examine protest and violence during the Cold War and post–Cold War periods separately.

Conclusions

What lessons have we learned from this brief overview of the data on ethnic conflict and protest? We compared two different data sets that cover some of the same overlapping periods, and found substantial agreement about the general trends in ethnic activity. Nonviolent protest is more widespread than large-scale violence, and both forms of ethnic activity seem to have gradually declined since the peak period of 1989–90.

The time series graphs regarding the relationship between state-sponsored repression and ethnic violence and nonviolence seem to show that repression tracks ethnic activity, showing peaks in actions by ethnic groups and by authorities in the same years. However, there appears to be more of a reactive dynamic for violence, in which violence by insurgents is followed by repression by state authorities, perhaps attempting to constrain the violence. In contrast, repression and nonviolent protest follow a nearly identical cyclical pattern.

While these bivariate time series graphs tell us little about the causes of ethnic activity, they do address one of the more important debates in the literature warning us that ethnic activity continues to be on the rise. Both data sets, analyzed in terms of repression, ethnic violence, and ethnic nonviolent protest, suggest that ethnic activity and reactions to it were in decline by the mid- to late 1990s, even in those groups designated most "at risk" in terms of capacity, grievances, and previous insurgency.

CHAPTER FOUR

Globalization and Nonviolent Ethnic Protest, 1965–1989

To many, the civil rights movement in the United States ushered in a new era of group politics characterized by increasing ethnic fragmentation and intractable conflict. Advocates of this view point to the fact that politicians, courts, business mission statements, college admissions committees, and government bureaucrats now regularly debate the costs and benefits of policies and strategies that address the expansion of minority ethnic rights. Tactics and themes from the U.S. civil rights movement have been adopted by a variety of minority rights movements, including emphasis on language, ethnicity, religion, immigration status, and other group claims (Fredrickson 1995). Because minority rights issues also intersect with a variety of others, transnational social movement organizations increasingly add issues of minority rights to the agendas for conferences, meetings, and publications on development, inequality, monetary policy, and the environment.[1] The minority rights revolution is happening everywhere, to paraphrase Skrentny (2002).

Accordingly, public debates surrounding minority rights can have both positive and negative consequences. On one hand, because they raise awareness and public sympathies, these debates undoubtedly fuel broader acceptance of ethnic and racial identity among some segments of the population. On the other hand, as ethnic boundaries become newly invigorated, competition for scarce resources raises the likelihood that ethnic conflict and violence will result (Olzak 1992).[2] Others reject these claims, characterizing ethnic mobilization as providing signals to elites that discrimination and underrepresentation persist (Skrentny 2002).

[1] For example, research by Khagram et al. (2002) documents the successful application of ethnic rights campaigns in environmental protests against implementation of dam projects that were slated for funding by the World Bank.

[2] For a more strident view of ethnic politics, see Huntington (2004).

The process by which ethnic identification produces ethnic fragmentation has prompted further debate by academics and policymakers. Examples range broadly: Lapp civil rights in Scandinavian countries, Macedonian rejection of Albanian separatist claims, Tibetan nationalism, Pacific Islander student organizations, and a variety of other contemporary movements organized around ethnic identity. According to some scholars who are critical of ethnic and racial civil rights movements, the danger is that, over time, formerly peaceful ethnic movements may fragment and divide a society. Moreover, movements that gain momentum run the risk of transforming into guerilla movements, separatist organizations, or intractable rebellions.

Are ethnic protest movements new? Or do such movements simply masquerade as ethnic in the contemporary period? Social movement scholars provide some insights for answering this question. According to Tarrow (1998) and D. Meyer and Tarrow (1998), what is modern about contemporary social movements is that protest tactics have a uniquely "modular" quality, which means that tactics, rhetoric, and forms of protest campaigns have been readily imitated, replicated, and modified to fit local settings or issues. Protest by Palestinians against Israeli violence, Catholic civil rights marches in Northern Ireland, rallies by Turkish immigrants for better housing in Germany have often successfully adapted tactics, slogans, and routines from other movements, especially the U.S. civil rights movement.[3] However, many innovative civil rights tactics were built upon foundations of nonviolent movements espousing tactics of civil disobedience, particularly from India's anti-colonial movement (Tarrow and McAdam 2005). Petitioning and leafleting have an even longer history, as Tilly (2003) has taught us. Claims that ethnic protests are both novel and rising in number are therefore highly debatable and deserve a closer look.

To begin to address these claims, I first distinguish *nonviolent ethnic protest* from other forms of ethnic mobilization. In an ethnic protest, a group expresses a racial or ethnic grievance, most often expressing a demand directed at government officials or at the public at large. The classic examples of ethnic protest include a march for voting rights, a sit-in targeted at a discriminating firm, and a boycott of a company that has discriminated against

---

[3] Accordingly, McAdam (1995) distinguishes between "initiator" and "spin-off" movements.

some ethnic group. Forms of ethnic protest tactics are often innovative, as they try to circumvent or neutralize high levels of repression by authorities (McAdam 1983). For instance, in pre-1994 South Africa, anti-apartheid protest often accompanied gatherings such as funerals and soccer games, because few other public displays by crowds were permitted for black Africans. In many places, large-scale economic boycotts have become commonplace strategies that are easily mobilized in countries with strong organizational bases. Researchers have operationalized ethnic and racial protest as action in which a group expresses a public claim based upon some ethnic marker, such as skin pigmentation, language, historical discrimination, or regional distinctions (McAdam 1982; Olzak 1992; Cornell and Hartmann 1998). The United States civil rights movement activities are prototypical examples. These movements may be nonviolent, but they are not necessarily limited in their demands and goals.

As noted in Chapter 2, within the larger category of protest movements there are many subcategories. These categories are distinguished by the scope of their challenge to existing state authority. Consequently, activities such as lobbying, petitioning, peaceful marches, and demonstrations can be considered peaceful if participants do not engage in violence. So here nonviolence is a defining feature of protest if the instigating group is not intentionally using violence in the form of weapons, bodily harm, or other strategies of property destruction, such as firebombing, etc. This does not preclude the use of violence by authorities against protesters.

World Integration and Ethnic Protest

In Chapter 1, I observed that an ideology of human rights has diffused across the world's states at the same time that use of tactical forms of ethnic protest, violence, and rebellion has become more commonplace (Gurowitz 1999; Risse et al. 1999). A world integration perspective explains the intersection of these trends by suggesting that the diffusion of human rights ideology both activates ethnic identities and provides new opportunities for mobilizing, while it simultaneously renders existing inequalities unacceptable (see Figure 1.1).

Extending this world integration argument suggests that the centrifugal effect of human rights will begin in dominant core countries, and only gradually diffuse to the isolated periphery. One implication of this argument is that peripheral countries will have less nonviolent ethnic protest than will core and semi-peripheral countries. If the world integration approach is correct, this effect should be present even when we control for the democratic nature of political regimes.

A second integration argument relates measures of organizational involvement and ethnic protest. It suggests that economic and political ties to the world system, indicated by the number of memberships in international non-governmental organizations, ought to spread an ideology of human rights that includes ethnic and minority rights. In addition, countries with more memberships in international non-governmental organizations will experience more nonviolent ethnic protest than will countries with few connections to INGOs. Finally, my argument suggests that the recent period has seen an intensification of world integration. If this is the case, then the effects of peripheral status and international organizational memberships will be stronger in the most recent period. That is, the effects of global integration ought to intensify after the end in 1989 of the Cold War.[4]

Internal Features of States That Encourage Ethnic Protest

A number of internal features of polities or regimes also channel ethnic politics toward nonviolence. Because mobilizing protest typically extracts lower costs from participants (in comparison to expressions of violence, which risk injury or arrest), protest is easier to organize, control, and disperse, especially in democratic settings. Moreover, the public expression of dissent has attained legal support in most democratic countries as an accepted and valid strategy for vocalizing demands, expressing disagreement, and other forms of claims-making. Thus, it has become commonplace to argue that a variety of both actors and nonparticipants (including bystanders, protesters, monitors, counterprotesters, human rights observers, and police) in protest activity share a common set of understandings about legitimate protest behaviors (McCarthy and Zald 1977).

Liberal theories of democratic states also suggest that protest is more likely in democracies because the threshold of voluntary activity is lower

---

[4]Note that this does *not* necessarily imply that ethnic mobilization ought to increase monotonically over time. Rather, it suggests that the magnitude of effects of membership in international non-governmental organizations (INGOs) ought to become larger over time.

in open societies. To the extent that activities and tactics are routinized as legitimate expressions of free speech, we expect to see more protest of all types (Bollen 1989; Oneal and Russett 1997). In making this claim, my world integration argument about the diffusion of human rights parallels a liberal theory of the state (e.g., see Russett et al. 2000). Both perspectives expect that more protest will occur in countries with traditions of freedom of speech, openness of the press, and greater wealth. This implies that non-violent protest will be greater in dominant and democratic countries when compared to peripheral countries. Such perspectives linking liberal theory of the state with global theories of integration offer some testable propositions for examining factors leading to protest rather than violent outbreaks of ethnic mobilization.

First, democratic principles favor nonviolent over violent mobilization efforts of ethnic groups (Keck and Sikkink 1998). In systems where ethnic minorities have open and easy access to political institutions, and where educational and military institutions and political authority are open to minority recruitment, we expect to see more ethnic protest. Following this argument, regimes that are more democratic and grant more political freedoms to citizens are more likely to experience ethnic protest, as compared to less democratic regimes.

Second, my political incorporation argument states that the formal incorporation of ethnic groups in politics makes ethnic mobilization more likely. Through citizenship rules, ethnic political parties, and policies regarding ethnic rights, states reinforce the salience of ethnic identity for groups over other identities that might be relevant. This situation contrasts with polities that legitimate ethnic rights in terms of individual advantages or in terms of occupational-guild-like associations (as in labor unions in Sweden).[5]

These ideas require some elaboration. Recall that in Chapter 1, I applied ideas from a world polity perspective in order to understand patterns of ethnic mobilization. I suggested that countries' granting of formal rights

---

[5] Some cases of individual public policies regarding race are more hybrid, and thus more difficult to classify, than others. For example, in the United States, affirmative action policies use information on gender, race, or ethnicity to make decisions about particular individuals applying for school admission, promotions, or jobs. The legal and philosophical arguments that lie behind these policies are often motivated by reference to underrepresentation of groups. Nevertheless, most outcomes involving affirmative action policies apply to individuals.

to groups on the basis of race and/or ethnic identity increases the likelihood that more political activity (including protest) will be based on ethnic identity rather than on some other potential identities. Such an argument begins to answer questions about why ethnic mobilization appears more relevant in the contemporary period. To the extent to which ethnicity has become an increasingly legitimate platform for making demands directed at authorities, we would expect significantly higher rates of protest along ethnic lines in the recent period.

Furthermore, to the extent that a larger proportion of countries legitimate a universal human rights platform in their institutions and policies, any remaining injustices stand out as egregious violations of these (now worldwide) guarantees. Thus, we should expect more mobilization against ethnic barriers in states that regularly restrict rights of minorities. Lessons from the history of slavery in the Americas, caste exclusion rules in India and South Africa, and the implementation of restrictive citizenship illustrate how the residues from these barriers become institutionalized as enduring boundaries, hostilities, social rankings, and ethnic politics. The evidence suggests that the legacy of racial injustice has lasting effects, even if legalized discrimination has been dismantled.

Grievance perspectives would predict that policies that exclude groups from full participation will engender more resistance movements and ethnic protest. However, in highly authoritarian systems ethnic groups cannot express demands openly without risking arrest or deportation. As the presence of human rights organizations grows, however, ethnic groups can increasingly turn to non-governmental agencies to resolve claims of ethnic discrimination.[6] As human rights activists pursue treaties, rights, and proclamations outlawing injustice, remaining exclusionary rules come under the scrutiny of various international associations, United Nations committees, human rights organizations, leaders, and politicians (Coicaud et al. 2003). Thus we would expect that, over time, countries with exclusionary policies experience increasing magnitudes of ethnic protest.

A more plausible scenario is suggested by Jackie Smith (1995). According to this argument, given the rising legitimacy of human rights, demands for removing any existing ethnic barriers will be magnified (and expressed more

---

[6]For evidence, see Keck and Sikkink (1998), della Porta and Tarrow (2005), and Sikkink (2005).

freely) in democratic countries, compared to countries where exclusionary policies exist and countries that have more authoritarian and less democratic institutions. Thus, I expect that democratic countries will generate more institutionalized forms of ethnic mobilization in the form of nonviolent ethnic protest.

A fourth argument concerning internal characteristics of states rests on a large body of empirical evidence showing that mobilization opportunities also depend upon economic well-being. The literature on civil unrest, civil war, and international relations supports this claim, finding that poorer countries will not engage in nonviolent protest, while richer countries produce ethnic mobilization that is (1) nonviolent and (2) less threatening to the stability of regimes. Civil war evidently also becomes less likely with increasing income levels (Oneal and Russett 1997; Henderson and Singer 2000; Fearon and Laitin 2003). As is the case for most social movements, ethnic protest depends upon access to organizational and leadership resources, which are more difficult to obtain in countries below the world's average levels of income (but see Collier and Hoeffler 2004 for a different view).

The larger point is that movements that were once considered purely *local struggles* for expanded minority rights have become part of a *global human rights movement*. In a world where human rights are increasingly universal, widespread, and inclusive, remaining exclusions have become perceived as more egregious. According to world polity arguments, movements increasingly mobilize on behalf of excluded group members and base their demands upon universalistic principles of inclusion (Meyer and Jepperson 1991; Soysal 1994). The pressure on exclusionary countries may be internal (in the form of movements based upon the excluded identity, as in pre-1994 South Africa), or external (in the form of international sanctions, such as those against the state of South Africa prior to 1994). The prediction from this argument is that countries with policies that specifically exclude ethnic or racial groups from economic or political participation will be most likely to experience ethnic protest as a result of these practices.

Globalization and Measures of Protest

Social scientists interested in collective action have long considered studies of the life histories of movements as being key to understanding the process by which collective action unfolds and recedes. Until recently, most studies of ethnic movements have relied on case study narratives of one country. While such studies are rich in detail and history, they have not produced a unified explanation of ethnic conflict. This is because the case study approach necessarily focuses narrowly on those regions (or historical periods) characterized by ethnic turmoil—it ignores those regions experiencing little or no ethnic violence. A more balanced approach used here analyzes countries (or regions or cities) that show variation in the magnitude of ethnic mobilization.

THE MINORITIES AT RISK DATA SET

In Chapter 3 I presented categories of escalating levels of ethnic nonviolence and some descriptive statistics of violence and nonviolence for the years from 1965 through 1995. Because the Cold War period differs from the present period (and because the nature of ethnic protest is different from that of violence), I begin with a separate analysis of the magnitude of ethnic protest for the period prior to 1990. The levels of protest from the *Minorities At Risk* (MAR) data set provide the key data for the dependent variable over this period.

This chapter uses data at the group level on the magnitude of ethnic protest instigated by groups designated by Gurr to be "at risk" and thus included in the MAR data set. Groups were included in the data set if there was evidence that the group (1) had a history of systematic discrimination by the state, (2) experienced some level of political mobilization between 1945 and 1989, and (3) membership consisted of at least one hundred thousand persons.

These data have been criticized for a number of important reasons.[7] However, they remain the most comprehensive data on the topic that have been made available (Gurr and Harff 1996; Gurr and Moore 1997; Fearon and Laitin 1996). Nevertheless, using a sample of ethnic populations chosen in this way raises questions of sample selection bias—sampling that is based upon some level of the dependent variable. Does this problem compromise my analysis of these data? This issue is a complicated one that involves assessment of the populations of countries or groups that might reasonably be expected to experience ethnic mobilization. Gurr and Scarritt (1989: 375–83) explain that their sampling procedure defined this population as ethnic groups that showed some signs that they were differentially treated by

[7] For example, see Tilly (2003: 65–66).

relevant state authorities. They also required that groups "at risk" have some level of political activity at some point during the thirty-five-year period. These definitions imply that the sample may indeed be biased toward higher than average levels of ethnic mobilization than might be found in a random sample of groups. However, at this stage of research using these data, there is no simple solution to this problem. In part this is true because no other independent source of data can be used a comparison point.[8] The PANDA data set provides another comparison set, because it includes information on conflicts, protests, and rebellions that were reported by the Reuters news service.[9]

Table 4.1 lays out the percentages and frequencies of each category of nonviolent ethnic events from 1965 through 1989. Each country's intensity score is measured for three separate waves: 1965–69, 1975–79, and 1985–89. For the dependent variable, each model includes a lagged dependent variable, measured in the preceding five-year interval. However, for the first five-year panel there is no preceding decade measure available, and so I consider the first five-year period as an initial benchmark.

Gurr's definition of *nonviolent protest* includes conventional protest activity on behalf of an ethnic communal group, but excludes any activity that involves the threat or use of coercion (Gurr 1993: 94). In the *Minorities at Risk* data set, the index of nonviolent protests includes petitions, publications, leafleting, demonstrations, strikes, and rallies that range in size from small demonstrations to events involving over 100,000 participants.

There are some surprises in Table 4.1's examination of the landscape of ethnic protest during the 1965–89 period. Contrary to some expectations, the percentage in most subcategories remained fairly stable. While many

---

[8] Because of this, I am unable to use models that would estimate the amount of sample selection bias that undoubtedly affects the MAR data set. Because these data have proven extraordinarily useful to many scholars (e.g., Gurr 1993, 2000; Wilkes and Okamoto 2002; Toft 2003; Fearon and Laitin 2003; Hironaka 2005), it seems reasonable to proceed, keeping in mind that there are flaws in these data that are difficult to resolve.

[9] There is another sampling issue that arises when using the PANDA data on events: the likelihood that a news report about a specific group will be filed with Reuters may be positively influenced by prior mobilization events. In other words, previous events sensitize reporters to what might be assessed as a newsworthy event. It is prudent to assume that not every ethnic event that occurred had an equal chance of becoming part of the Reuters news record. Thus, there are possibilities of different sources of bias in both data sets.

TABLE 4.1

Number and Percentage of Countries Experiencing Different Magnitudes of Nonviolent Ethnic Protest, 1965–1989

	1965–69 (%)	1975–79 (%)	1985–89 (%)
0 No events recorded	25 (27.5%)	21 (21.0%)	6 (5.8%)
1 Verbal opposition, petitioning and leafleting	8 (8.8%)	2 (2.0%)	8 (7.7%)
2 Symbolic resistance and lobbying	25 (27.5%)	26 (26.0%)	23 (22.3%)
3 Small demonstrations	12 (13.2%)	30 (30.0%)	33 (32.1%)
4 Medium demonstrations	14 (15.4%)	16 (16.0%)	19 (18.5%)
5 Large demonstrations	5 (5.5%)	4 (4.0%)	11 (10.7%)
99 No Basis for Judgement	2 (2.2%)	1 (1.0%)	3 (2.9%)
Total Countries	91 (100%)	100 (100%)	103 (100%)

NOTE: All scale values adapted from *Minorities at Risk* (Gurr 1993: 95) and MARGene Codebook (Bennett and Davenport 2005: 82). For specific definitions of categories for nonviolent protest, see Table 3.1.

countries (in a sample of "at risk" countries) experienced little or no ethnic protest in any given five-year period, a considerable minority of them experienced major demonstrations.

This table also addresses the conventional wisdom that ethnic protest became more commonplace in the interval between the 1960s and the end of the Cold War. From 1965 to 1989, ethnic protest did indeed rise dramatically. Almost one-third of countries in the *Minorities at Risk* data set reported no protests in 1965, but by 1985–89, there were only 6 out of 103 countries that reported nonviolence. Over this fifteen-year period, the percentage of countries experiencing large-scale demonstrations, with participants numbering over 100,000, had doubled.

EXPLANATORY FACTORS

This section first examines the argument that a country's status in the world system will affect its levels of nonviolent protest. It then tests the claim that the effects of peripheral status, a country's civil liberties rating, and international associational ties produce different levels of ethnic violence and nonviolence.

The analysis includes a categorical measure of a country's status in the world system that was produced using the results from network analysis of reported trade, diplomatic, and sanctioning connections (Snyder and Kick 1979). I argue that core nations will experience more ethnic activity overall, due to the fact that those countries most integrated into a world system also tend to accept an ideology guaranteeing human rights that is based on norms of ethnic equality. In dependent nations, the organizational forces of integration into the world system exert pressures *against* nonviolent ethnic mobilization. In particular, I expect that peripheral nations that are least embedded in the world system should experience lower levels of nonviolent ethnic activity overall, while core countries will experience more nonviolent ethnic activity.

The ethnic incorporation argument (discussed in Chapter 1) suggested that states that singled out specific ethnic groups as either deserving or not deserving specific economic or political standing in a country would experience more ethnic protest as a consequence of formalizing this group identity (e.g., Soysal 1994; Schofer and Fourcade-Gourinchas 2001; Jepperson 2002). To begin to examine this argument empirically, I use data from the updated *Minorities at Risk* (2004) data set, which classifies a minority group's relative formal political status along two relevant dimensions that adhere closely to these theoretical ideas. The first dimension is that of "formal recognition," which I code as "1" if there is at least a substantial majority of group members who have formal recognition in the polity. Two examples coded "1" on this measure (listed in the MAR codebook) are Iraqi Kurds and French Canadians. This measure is coded as "0" if one of the following conditions holds: (1) there is no formal recognition, or there is de facto recognition but no distinct administrative status (the example given is that of African Americans in the United States); (2) recognition is explicitly denied; or (3) the group is formally excluded from the political process. Because this measure is coded at the group level, I used all available information to create a country-level variable, indicating "ethnic based group rights" if at least one group (excluding the dominant group) has formal ethnic group rights in the polity. A "0" indicates that ethnicity is not formally recognized in the polity for any ethnic group in that country.

A second ethnic group rights measure indicates whether or not the polity formally excludes individuals from participation based upon ethnic or racial group membership. One of two conditions holds if this measure has been coded "1": (1) the country explicitly denies rights to a given group; or (2) the country explicitly prohibits a distinct ethnic or territorial group from participating in political or economic activities (the two prominent examples are the Chinese in Malaysia and Arabs in Israel). Note that the two ethnic rights measures do not exhaust all possibilities. A third possibility is a country in which ethnicity does not enter into group considerations in the polity, or only does so informally. These countries would be coded as "0" on both measures.

The next two hypotheses concern policies of inclusion and exclusion more broadly. I measure these concepts using a Summary Index of Freedom rating (published by the Freedom House in recent years) that has been used in many studies of political instability and collective violence (Taylor and Jodice 1983). It combines an index of civil liberties and an index of political rights, each of which ranges from 1 to 7 (see Gastil 1988–98; Freedom House Web site www.freedomhouse.org/ratings/index.htm). Thus, the summary index ranges from 2, indicating a high level of rights and liberties, to 14, indicating a low level.[10]

Chapter 1 offered the argument that ethnic mobilization depends upon the extent to which countries are subject to international constraints (as indicated by world system theory). I also argued that because peripheral countries are by definition more marginal actors in the world system, memberships in international non-governmental organizations (INGOs) ought to reduce internal ethnic conflict in these settings even more dramatically. The measure of these international memberships is an annual count of INGO

[10]It may be useful here to define these concepts more concretely. For example, the political rights component of this index originally ranged from 1 (indicating the highest level of civil liberty), to a low of 7 (countries having the fewest civil liberties). An example of the coding rules used in 1978 indicating highest possible level of liberties includes "political systems in which the rule of law is unshaken; and freedom of expression is both possible and evident" (Gastil 1978: 19). In 1978, Australia, Denmark, and Canada had a score of 1 on this scale. At the lower end, a score of 7 in 1978 indicated political systems in which "the outside world never hears of internal criticism, except when through the government's condemnation of it. Citizens have no rights in relation to the state" (Gastil 1978: 19). The countries of Albania, North Korea, and Uganda had a score of 7 in 1978. It seems prudent to mind the cautionary advice of many researchers who have explored these data and found that many of these measures have limitations, especially in terms of limited variability, missing data, and other problems common to time series data sets across a large number of countries. In particular, the data might be shaped by political context and biases of news reporters, historians, government workers, and, of course, other researchers who precede us.

memberships. I use data on this indicator from three time points (1966, 1977, and 1982) that were published in the corresponding yearbooks of the Union of International Associations.

I examined several well-known measures of ethnic diversity, including the ethnic linguistic fractionalization (ELF) measure available in Taylor and Jodice 1983, which was taken from earlier analyses published as *Atlas Narodov Mira* (1964). My analysis suggested that the ethnic fractionalization index compiled by Fearon (2002) has a number of flexible and attractive qualities. Country scores range from 0 to .925, indicating the level of ethnic fractionalization in a country. This measure was created by an exhaustive analysis of data drawn from *World FactBook*, the Library of Congress Country Studies series, the *Encyclopaedia Brittanica*, and several published sources on ethnic groups in Africa and other settings (e.g., Scarritt and Mozaffar 1999 and Morrison, Mitchell, and Paden 1989) to first develop a comprehensive list of ethnic groups.

Creating this index was not without obstacles. Fearon (2002) discusses the various problems associated with defining "ethnicity"; he settles on a definition that states that an ethnic group will have a strong descent basis and self-consciousness as a group (see also Thernstrom's [1980] *Harvard Encyclopedia of American Ethnic Groups* for similar decision rules). In this book I use Fearon's measure for my analysis for several reasons: it takes the "structure" of ethnic groups seriously; it uses more recent sources than other available indicators; and it is available for a larger number of countries (N=160) than are previous measures of ethnic/linguistic fractionalization (such as the one used in *Atlas Narodov Mira*) or of ethnic heterogeneity.[11]

While various measures of inequality in a country have become available recently, relatively few measures of ethnic inequality have been developed. Such measures would be extremely useful here, not only to compare effects of overall inequality and well-being, but to capture specific indicators of potential grievances that are related directly to ethnic group membership.[12] A number of other measures were investigated, including a measure of population diversity, and one for the impact of urbanization, indicated by the

---

[11]For expanded discussions of this issue, see Henderson (1997), Vanhanen (1999), Gurr (2000), Laitin (2000), and Varshney (2002).

[12]For later years, I employ Gurr's updated *Minorities at Risk* measures of ethnic inequality, which capture relative inequality levels indexed at the ethnic group level, for the 1980s and 1990s.

percent of the population living in urban areas of 50,000 or more in 1970. Neither had a significant effect on nonviolent ethnic protest when applied in the analysis.

I also examined a variety of additional measures that have been used in previous analyses of national social protest movements. While these studies do not usually analyze ethnic mobilization separately from other forms of mobilization, it seems useful to include these variables so that the nature of ethnic protest can be compared to studies of general protest activity. My strategy will be to report only those measures that are theoretically relevant and that had systematic effects on protest.[13]

Given the centrality of concerns about measurement in the methodological literature using cross-national data, it seems important to investigate at least one theoretically relevant source of spuriousness. This is the alternative hypothesis that any systematic differences between core and peripheral countries might be due to the strong tendency of the media to publicize (or exaggerate) racial and ethnic confrontations. This hypothesis combines a main core-country effect with an additional diffusion effect. Either argument suggests that ethnic activity will be greater in the core because coverage, attention, and per capita consumption of the mass media should be greater in core countries. Put differently, the hypothesis suggests that the intensity of ethnic violence may be the same in all countries, but that the data contain upward bias in this measure of the magnitude of events in the core. To test this argument, I compared the effects of measures of per capita newspaper circulation, televisions per capita, radios per capita, and broadcast and print media control measures. Contrary to the expectation that media coverage would inflate reports of ethnic protest in a country, I found no systematic effect of any of these measures.

---

[13] For example, I initially analyzed data on ethnic protest using two measures of state repression in models of nonviolent protest. The first is a count of deaths per 1,000 persons resulting from domestic political violence, aggregated over the 1948–62 period (Taylor and Jodice 1983: 40–42). While this measure of repression has its drawbacks (in that it conflates anti-government as well as anti-insurgent deaths, and acts of government repression are likely to be systematically underrepresented for underdeveloped countries), it remains a useful gauge of internal political confrontations with authorities. Other measures indicated various repressive actions directed against minorities, available in the updated MARGene data set. However, for all three waves of ethnic protest analyzed in this chapter, I found no significant effects from these measures, so they were dropped from the analysis.

Estimation Techniques

Investigation of these arguments requires a model that estimates the effects of shifts in levels of inequality, of increasing integration into the world system, and of shifts in levels of ethnic nonviolence. This research design proposes to begin analysis at the country level, so as to exploit the excellent data provided by Gurr's (1993) scales of the magnitude of ethnic protest and violence.[14]

My hypotheses suggest that world system position and country level political and ethnic diversity characteristics will affect ethnic protest, net of the effects of prior history of ethnic mobilization. This argument requires a method of analysis that combines temporal variation, prior levels of ethnic activity, and changing levels of economic measures within countries. The choice of a method of analysis of these data was also hampered by the fact that the range of variation is extremely limited: it is aggregated into five-year totals, and it is categorical (see the list of categories defined in Table 3.1). Another problem for estimation is that the majority of cases have magnitude values of zero. This renders less than ideal the more conventional methods of estimating models that assume that events are normally distributed (e.g., ordinary least squares regressions or time series analysis). In sum, the hypotheses and form of the data require a statistical model that is appropriate for ordinal data using cross-sectional data.

To meet these requirements, I first use ordinal logit analysis, which captures the Guttman scaling method used to create the magnitude scales (see Table 3.1). For the data presented in Table 4.3, in columns 1–3 I present an ordinal logit analysis appropriate for use with data that are organized hierarchically. Using Gurr's presentation of these categorical activities as indicating a Guttman-style scale of increasing scope and violence, I analyze the group-level and country-level factors associated with broader scope and more sustained violent rebellions. Stata 2001 (release 8.0 SE) estimation techniques for ordinal logit regression allow us to examine both group-level and country-level factors in the same model, despite the fact that it is likely that the standard errors may be inflated by the use of two levels of analysis in the same model. The estimation technique allows comparison of robust standard

---

[14]See Appendices A and B for lists of the countries analyzed with these data. Because of missing data in different models, the lists of countries will differ slightly in different specifications across the following chapters.

errors to be clustered within each country, thus adjusting for autocorrelation of error terms within countries for group-level data. A comparison of models that adjusted for country-level clusters and models that did not do so showed them to be identical, so I report robust standard errors.

It turns out that for many of the relevant democratic polity, civil rights, and economic indicators, panel data are available for three waves of protest data from the MAR data set. For this reason, I present analysis using the same variables in a panel design in Table 4.3 alongside the cross-sectional analysis. The advantage of the panel design is that the generalized least squares (XTGLS) estimates for panel data allow specification of correlated error terms, which is often a problem in estimating time series data.

Results

The arguments presented above suggest that the impact of structural characteristics depends upon whether a country is in the core or the periphery of the world system. Is this a reasonable assumption? To answer this question, Table 4.2 explores whether there is a statistically significant difference between the effects in the periphery and in other countries. As suggested, there are a variety of reasons why nonviolent protest might be discouraged in the periphery, including the world system argument proposed above, higher levels of repression (which discourage nonviolent protest), and political opportunities structures in the periphery (which exclude participation by minorities).

Table 4.2 analyzes the hypothesis that peripheral countries will experience less ethnic protest than either core or semi-periphery countries, examining the data separately for each panel wave. Each of these panels examines this bivariate relationship, and comparison of the three waves tells us about the effects of world system status over time. The relationship is clear: the hypothesis that peripheral countries experience less nonviolent ethnic protest than core and semi-periphery countries is supported for the 1965–79 period, but not for the 1985–89 period. This suggests that world system status had an initial effect on nonviolence, but that this effect weakens toward the end of the Cold War period. While these period effects seen in Table 4.2 are interesting, they do not inform us about the mechanisms that underlie the patterns, nor do they tell us if these relationships have changed over the 1965–89 period.

TABLE 4.2

Relationship of Peripheral Status in the World System and Magnitude of Nonviolent Ethnic Protest, 1965–1989 (by number and percentage of countries)

	No Protest (%)	Some Level of Protest (%)	Totals (%)
		1965–69	
Non-peripheral countries	7 (15.9%)	37 (84.1%)	44 (100%)
Peripheral countries	17 (39.5%)	26 (60.5%)	43 (100%)
Total countries	24 (27.6%)	63 (72.4%)	87 (100%)
Chi-square			6.08**
		1975–79	
Non-peripheral countries	5 (11.1%)	40 (88.9%)	45 (100%)
Peripheral countries	16 (31.4%)	35 (68.6%)	51 (100%)
Total countries	21 (21.8%)	75 (78.1%)	96 (100%)
Chi-square			5.74**
		1985–89	
Non-peripheral countries	2 (4.3%)	44 (95.6%)	46 (100%)
Peripheral countries	4 (7.4%)	50 (94.0%)	54 (100%)
Total countries	6 (6.0%)	94 (94.0%)	100 (100%)
Chi-square			.41

NOTE: Chi-square tests statistics evaluated at one degree of freedom. Two-tailed tests of significance reported. * $p < .05$,   ** $p < .01$,   *** $p < .001$.

We turn next to the multivariate models of nonviolent ethnic mobilization. It seems that the patterns of effects differ considerably across three periods, which may be a function of the measures available or may reflect actual period effects in these patterns. Table 4.3 shows the results for a model indicating the effects of structural characteristics on nonviolent ethnic protest. For this analysis, I use information on nonviolent protest for three panels, 1965–69, 1975–79, and 1985–89. The table reports unstandardized ordinal logit coefficients for each of the independent variables or lagged dependent variables (robust standard errors are in parentheses below each parameter estimate). Each model was also adjusted for clustering on the country identification code.

TABLE 4.3

Comparing Cross-Sectional and Panel Estimates of Effects on the Magnitude of Nonviolent Ethnic Protest, 1965–1989 (robust standard errors in parentheses)

	Protest 1965–69	Protest 1975–79	Protest 1985–89	Panel Data 1965–89
Magnitude of prior	−.176	.856***	.660**	.170**
of ethnic nonviolence	(.222)	(.218)	(.224)	(.059)
Ln population size	.490**	.436**	.287	.306***
(lagged in last col.)	(.205)	(.214)	(.237)	(.086)
Ln GDP per capita	.029	.968*	.178	.067
(lagged in last col.)	(.560)	(.457)	(.517)	(.141)
Ethnic fractionalization	3.24**	−.718	.676	.877*
index (Fearon 2002)	(1.14)	(1.13)	(1.13)	(.430)
Demoratic regime scale	.091	.044	.165**	.036
(Polity IV) (lagged in Col. 4)	(.085)	(.059)	(.063)	(.021)
Freedom house index	.073	.218	.339**	.070
(lagged in Col. 4)	(.149)	(.129)	(.143)	(.044)
Televisions per capita	3.88	−8.89**	−3.21	1.62
	(4.07)	(.07)	(4.18)	(1.19)
Periphery status	.035	−.024	−2.07***	−.306
(0, 1)	(.604)	(.784)	(.668)	(.227)
Number of INGO memberships	.000	.001	.000	.000
(Hironaka 2000)	(.001)	(.002)	(.001)	(.000)
Group rights based	−.010	2.08**	−.077	−.290
on ethnicity (0,1)	(.745)	(.678)	(.816)	(.234)
Ethnic exclusionary	.789	1.24	−.184	.421
policies exist (0,1)	(.841)	(.743)	(.759)	(.240)
Time trend				.349**
				(.122)
Total countries	57	71	71	71
Log pseudo-likelihood	−84.9	−85.5	−90.8	NA
Pseudo R-square	.11	.24	.20	NA

NOTE: Two-tailed tests of significance reported.* $p < .05$, ** $p < .01$, *** $p < .001$.

THE INTENSITY OF NONVIOLENT ETHNIC PROTEST

I first draw attention to the fact that nonviolence shows significant effects of prior ethnic activity in columns 2–4 of Table 4.3, as expected. Prior ethnic protest only increases after the mid- to late 1970s, suggesting that mobilization attempts before the 1960s had a different underlying dynamic.[15]

[15] In previous analyses using structural equation models that captured the cumulative effect of each wave, I found that the most proximate measures were more closely correlated than were more temporally distant measures of ethnic activity (Olzak and Tsutsui 1998).

In the mid-1980s, there is evidence for an escalating effect of previous levels of activity. The first hypothesis suggested that the magnitude of ethnic nonviolence would decline with peripheral country status. There is significant support for this claim, especially after 1985, as can be seen in row eight in column 3 of Table 4.3 (and also in the pooled cross-section analysis in column 4). That is, from 1985 through 1989, the magnitude of ethnic protest is lower in peripheral countries compared to countries that are more central in global trade and diplomacy. Interestingly, net of the effect of its initial impact on the magnitude of protest, peripheral status does not affect protest magnitude during the 1970s, but it has a net negative effect during the 1980s. Thus, there is some evidence that the impact of structural characteristics does indeed change across time periods.

The second hypothesis builds on the world polity argument that a culture of human rights is diffusing across the world's states (Soysal 1994; Lake and Rothchild 1998; Hironaka 2005). For ethnic politics, this process is more intense in countries that have polities structured along ethnic lines and in countries where politics are characterized as more inclusive. In this view, protest is both legitimated and regulated by a more open and vocal political structure, with access for minorities.[16] Recall that one main hypothesis held that countries with a higher rating from the Freedom House would have higher magnitudes of nonviolent ethnic protest compared to countries having less freedom with respect to political and civil rights. This argument finds support in the middle columns of Table 4.3: that is, in the most recent period and increasingly across three panels, countries that grant civil liberties to their citizens experience more protest based upon ethnic identity. Furthermore, there was no evidence of a significant interaction effect between this Freedom House summary index and either peripheral or core status (results not shown).[17]

[16]This claim runs counter to the usual picture of ethnic mobilization that views ethnic protest as a threat to democracy. Indeed, there are good reasons to believe that the absence of protest is a much more worrisome sign. I take up this argument in detail in the concluding chapter.

[17]Following earlier analysis (Olzak and Tsutsui 1998), it seemed reasonable to explore whether there was a nonlinear effect of this Freedom House index. I first included this measure along with a second-order polynomial, and then I calculated a set of dummy variables based on index values that fell in the middle of the quintile range. None of these attempts to uncover nonlinear effects of this index measure improved the fit over the linear specification of the Freedom House index measure reported in Table 4.3.

I also suggested that as the number of international non-governmental organization (INGO) memberships rises, ethnic protest should rise, as world culture diffuses an ideology of ethnic sovereignty, civil rights, and rights to self-determination. In particular, I argued that having a large number of inter-organizational ties would inhibit ethnic violence but would promote ethnic nonviolent protest. I further argued that there would be a positive interaction between periphery status and embeddedness in world organization. This argument finds no support.

Table 4.3 contains two indicators of ethnic incorporation and exclusion, respectively, to examine a portion of the world polity argument. Recall that I used a measure of ethnic minority status from the Polity IV data set (Marshall and Jaggers 2005). This measure indicates whether or not ethnic minorities have formally classified political status in the polity. In the original data, this measure ranged across eight categories, including denied recognition, various levels of legal (or de facto) recognition, and totally restricted status (e.g., Chinese in Malaysia, Arabs in Israel). I recoded the different categories as two dummy variables. The first represents the salience of ethnic corporate status in the political system; it equals 1 if there is some form of political incorporation of minorities that is formalized in the political system, and 0 if ethnicity is not a distinctive group category in the political system. In Table 4.3 I refer to this indicator as "group rights based on ethnicity." The second measure is also a dummy variable, which equals 1 if one or more ethnic groups are formally excluded from the political or economic system. This measure is labeled "ethnic exclusionary policies," in Table 4.3.

How did the ethnic inclusion and exclusion measures fare? From 1975 through 1979, countries that designated ethnic minorities formally in the political structure had significantly higher levels of ethnic protest than countries that did not single out minorities in the polity. However, in the panel analysis (column 4), countries with exclusionary policies had moderately higher levels of protest. In particular, the ethnic incorporation argument finds support only for the years 1975–79. However, ethnic exclusion raises the level of ethnic protest in the pooled cross-section and time series analysis, conducted over the whole period.

Moreover, the results show that the effects of world integration increased in intensity over time, which also supports my argument. If my argument from Chapter 1 holds, then reactive ethnic movements would become more frequent as world integration intensifies. Two findings in Table 4.3 support this claim. The effect of peripheral status is weakly negative until the mid-1980s, and for the 1985–89 period, the effect is negative and statistically significant. The results are consistent with the view that exposure to the international world of organizational membership encourages nonviolent protest in the more recent decades.

Ethnic fractionalization has a significant and positive effect on nonviolent ethnic protest for the first wave (1965–69) and in the combined panel analysis. Why does this effect seem to disappear after the 1970s but then reappear significantly in the pooled analysis? Although it is difficult to state with certainty, one possibility is that the effect of ethnic fractionalization is captured solely during the first period. Since it is not a time-varying measure, the impact of ethnic fractionalization might be captured through its effect on the lagged dependent variable in each wave. In this view, ethnic diversity creates a favorable environment for building ethnic solidarity. In other words, the effect of ethnic fractionalization might be indirect, shaped by its prior impact on the initial magnitude of protest in that country.

An increase in repressive political activity within states often indicates that a regime is weakening or under siege (or both). At the same time, repressive strategies are sometimes effective means for states to suppress ethnic challengers (Gurr 1993). Curiously, there were no systematic effects of any measures of repression, deaths from political clashes, or military regimes, and so these variables were dropped from the model.[18] One possible explanation for the absence of effects found for repression could be the fact that these measures are related to exclusionary policies, which are better captured by a direct measure of exclusion. I take up this problem directly in Chapter 8, where I use data on events that can be distinguished by which groups were the instigators of activity.

Discussion

This chapter offers an argument that depends on finding that ethnic nonviolence has different roots in the periphery compared to the non-periphery.

---

[18] A number of other discrimination measures were explored, including measures of cultural, economic, and political discrimination, available at the group level in the *Minorities at Risk* data set. However, despite the fact that groups were included based upon some level of political activism and despite variation in discrimination measures, not one of these indicators had a significant effect on the magnitude of ethnic protest in any of these models.

Some supporting evidence has been accumulated in support for this argument. In particular, I expected and found systematic effects of a state's position in the world system on nonviolent ethnic protest. I also found that richer countries and countries with larger populations were more likely to sustain ethnic protest activity, as were states that granted more civil liberties and had more regularized democratic political institutions.

Conventional indicators of grievances and injustice received less support, as expected. The overall picture of ethnic protest prior to 1989 shows mixed support for a grievance perspective of ethnic protest. First, economic well-being is systematically associated with ethnic protest, but it appears that ethnic protest is greater in countries that systematically discriminate against and deny civil liberties to their citizens. From the standpoint of social movement theories, these findings make sense in that both grievances and resources are necessary for protest mobilization to take place.

Stepping back from the results, the portrait of ethnic protest prior to the end of the Cold War shown here reflects a much more benign view of ethnic protest as a barometer of both economic well-being and freedom which shapes mobilization capacity. However, the results show that exclusionary policies encourage ethnic protest, net of the effects of prior mobilization, population size, and other key indicators. Taken together, the most progressive states that lag behind in human rights are those states witnessing the highest levels of protest. The thrust of the results is consistent with the world integration line of argument, which I have outlined broadly in terms of economic, diplomatic, and trade integration as well as ideological diffusion of human rights mandates.

Moreover, protest is more likely to occur in modern democratic core states than in economically dependent states. We also see some evidence that cultural differentiation or ethnic fractionalization drives ethnic protest, especially in the late 1960s (but less so in more recent periods). One interpretation of this effect of ethnic fractionalization is that in highly diverse countries, ethnic mobilization initiated a cycle of protest. In this view, while ethnic differences may initiate movement activity, once these movements gain momentum, they may become independent from specific cultural features or differences of language and culture.[19]

[19] But perhaps not so disconnected from religious cleavages, as Oneal and Russett (1997) argue in their dyadic analysis of the Correlates of War data on civil war (see also Henderson and Singer 2000).

Conclusion

This chapter explored how the process of economic and political integration among the world's states has caused a rise in ethnic protest movements. In this view, ethnic protest is relatively more frequent in core countries, but is shaped by an institutional context guaranteeing civil rights and liberties. In contrast, the theoretical argument holds, in peripheral nations ethnic protest will be ineffectual and sporadic. Whether scattered ethnic protest develops into armed rebellions is likely to depend on the history of ethnic movements and on the reactions by government authorities.

Recasting traditional arguments about ethnic protest by adding factors that can be tied to the world network of organizations and trade gives us some leverage for understanding a complicated world system. To be sure, ethnic protest is a function of past confrontations and contemporary policies of segregation and exclusion. But ethnic nonviolent activity also seems to be a function of two structural aspects of the world polity. These dimensions are the incorporation of ethnic rights in state polities and the integration of human rights and civil rights within countries.

Ethnic protest appears to be at least partly shaped by processes that can be measured at the world level of analysis. Several applications using this wide-angle lens have been particularly useful in social science, including models of networks of information, labor migration, political treaties, and refugee flows, as well as of distribution of international corporations that span country borders. If these arguments hold up under scrutiny, then we will have gained more understanding of the underlying causes of nonviolent ethnic protest in the modern world.

CHAPTER FIVE

Global Integration and Ethnic Violence, 1965–1989

The previous chapter examined the effect of world- and state-level processes on ethnic movements that are nonviolent. This chapter analyzes the intensity of ethnic violence over the same period using data from the same *Minorities at Risk* data set. It tests the argument that *ethnic exclusion and the increasing integration of a world economic and political system have encouraged ethnic violence*. In addition, this chapter tests arguments from world system theory that ethnic violence is more likely in peripheral nations.

What do we know about ethnic violence? A number of scholars from various disciplines have identified a set of internal features of states that promote ethnic violence, including poverty, inequality, weak political regimes, and politics of exclusion. Powerful third parties (sometimes also called "ethnic warlords") who escalate local feuds, exploiting and building alliances, may assist in creating large-scale ethnic wars, which can then result in genocide or ethnic cleansing (Kalyvas 2003; Tilly 2003; Toft 2003). In particular, Collier and Hoeffler (2004) find that when countries specialize in exports of oil (or some other valuable natural resource), warlords expand their networks to cash in on this export commodity, making use of corruption, bribes, and arms trading (see also Fearon 2005). As a result, leaders of resource-rich regions capitalize on the benefits of ethnic warfare. Such theories have been particularly useful in identifying features of ethnic conflict in settings such as the Balkans, Rwanda, Sudan, and India, but they have been less successful in predicting communal violence in regions lacking in oil reserves and other exportable materials. Stepping back from the internal characteristics of this "greed" hypothesis (Collier and Hoeffler 2004; Collier and Sambanis 2002), we might ask what lies behind the trade network that has produced a rise of internal conflicts in recent decades.

I suggest that status in the world system and increasing integration of the world's states will additionally affect the diffusion of ethnic violence. In particular, I expect that ethnic violence escalates more rapidly in more dependent countries, and that more democratic and more dominant countries will experience significantly less ethnic violence. I expect that countries that incorporate ethnic groups into the polity will also have less violence. Finally, I suggest that the world polity perspective leads us to expect that countries with more exclusionary rules directed toward minorities will experience more ethnic rebellions than countries that grant ethnic minority rights and privileges.

Measures of Rebellion and Global Integration

For my analysis here of ethnic violence, I replicate the panel design presented in Chapter 4 for ethnic protest. The analysis includes measures relevant to the study of collective violence, including income inequality and repression, and those measures found relevant to the study of racial and ethnic nonviolent activity. Together these factors produce a longitudinal panel design that focuses on factors related to greater intensity of ethnic violence.

THE MINORITIES AT RISK DATA SET: INTENSITY OF ETHNIC REBELLIONS

I use the index of measures of ethnic rebellion (updated in 2003) collected by Ted Gurr in his Minorities at Risk Project. Table 5.1 presents the substantive categories that Gurr used to develop a Guttman scale of values (ranging from 0 to 7) that indicate the magnitude of violence of each type of ethnic mobilization. These levels provide the key data for the dependent variables of the magnitude of ethnic violence. I then report analysis of the magnitude of ethnic violence in countries from 1965 through the end of 1989.

Table 5.1 summarizes the percentages and frequencies of each category of violent ethnic event from 1965 through 1989, at the country level of analysis. As in Table 4.1, I analyze three panel waves: 1965–69, 1975–79, and 1985–89.[1] I end in 1989 for a variety of reasons, including the fact

---

[1] Of course, this is not the only specification of these measures, nor the only means of analysis that could be used with these data. Indeed, I turn to group-level analysis in Chapter 6, which exploits a grassroots-level argument about grievances and organizational features of ethnic violence. In the present chapter, I aim to explore country-level effects. For this reason, I aggregated the data to indicate the highest level of intensity that was mobilized by any ethnic group within a country's borders during the five-year period.

TABLE 5.1
Number and Percentage of Countries Experiencing Different Magnitudes
of Violent Ethnic Rebellion, 1965–1989

	1965–69 (%)	1975–79 (%)	1985–89 (%)
0 None Reported	50 (52.6%)	58 (56.8%)	38 (38.2%)
1 Political banditry	13 (13.7%)	6 (5.9%)	12 (11.7%)
2 Campaigns of terrorism	5 (5.3%)	8 (7.4%)	16 (15.7%)
3 Local rebellions	6 (6.3%)	3 (2.9%)	7 (6.9%)
4 Small-scale guerilla activity	4 (4.2%)	7 (6.9%)	4 (3.9%)
5 Intermediate guerrilla activity	2 (2.1%)	1 (1.0%)	6 (5.8%)
6 Large-scale guerilla activity	10 (10.5%)	11 (10.8%)	6 (5.9%)
7 Protracted civil war	5 (5.3%)	8 (7.8%)	12 (11.8%)
Total countries	95 (100%)	102 (100%)	102 (100%)

NOTE: All scale values adapted from *Minorities at Risk* (Gurr 1993: 95) and from the MARGene Codebook, Bennett and Davenport (2005: 84). For specific definitions of categories for violent rebellion, see Table 3.1.

that the boundaries of many countries (in the former Soviet Union as well as others) substantially changed in that year. Thus, it would be difficult to compare directly across columns beyond 1989 using these data, since the index values are not attached to the same units of analysis before and after this period for all countries (fortunately this issue is sidestepped in the event count analysis, which allows for unbalanced panel data structures).

Table 5.1 shows that both continuity and change are reflected in these frequencies. While a large percentage of countries experienced little or no ethnic mobilization in any one five-year period, a considerable minority of them experienced widespread ethnic clashes. Over this period, the percentage of countries experiencing protracted civil wars increased, but there seems to be no trend toward increasing magnitude of ethnic violence toward 1989. At the same time, the percentage of countries reporting no ethnic violence declined over this entire period (from 52.6 percent in 1965–69 to 38.2 percent in 1985–89). Given the fact that for a minority group to be included in the MAR data set it had to have experienced some prior levels of political activity or discrimination, it is surprising that only about one-half of these countries with "minorities at risk" actually experienced ethnic violence during the first two periods (1965–69 and 1975–79). But, by 1985–89, approximately 60 percent of the countries with minority groups deemed "at risk" had experienced some level of ethnic violence or rebellion.

Independent Variables

Does a country's status in the world system affect levels of ethnic violence? In Chapter 4 I reported that periphery countries systematically experienced a lower level of nonviolent ethnic protest and core countries experienced a higher magnitude of conventional nonviolent protest. In this chapter, I explore the hypothesis that there would be a greater magnitude of ethnic violence in peripheral countries. I then test the claim that the effect of international associational ties on ethnic violence depends on a country's position of dominance in the world system. In dependent nations, the organizational forces of integration into the world system exert pressures *against* ethnic violence, because these countries are more constrained internally by authoritarian regimes and the threat of international sanction (as compared to more dominant core and semi-peripheral countries). In particular, the theoretical argument leads us to expect that peripheral nations with more memberships in INGOs should experience lower levels of ethnic violence.

Much of the literature on collective violence also predicts that ethnic violence would decrease with increasing levels of democracy. I examine this hypothesis using measures from the Polity IV data set that have been used in studies of political instability and collective violence.[2]

Because peripheral countries are likely to be weaker actors in the world system, memberships in INGOs ought to constrain internal unrest in the periphery. Thus I expect an interaction effect between peripheral status and embeddedness in international organizations that will reduce internal ethnic violence.[3] Recall that my indicator of embeddedness is the annual count of INGO memberships. I have also added an ethnic fractionalization measure (from Fearon 2002), as a proxy for the cultural factors related to ethnic difference.

---

[2] Recall that I used this index in Chapter 4. It ranges from a low of zero, indicating absence of democratic institutions and rule of law, all the way to ten, indicating democratic institutions, universalistic voting rights, and party competitiveness.

[3] This argument is the mirror image of the ethnic nonviolence argument presented in Chapter 4.

The study of the effects of income inequality has generated a well-documented tradition in the empirical analysis of collective violence. It is also well known that the data are of variable quality. Nevertheless, the theoretical importance of the concept of inequality is uncontested (Muller and Seligson 1987). The importance of income inequality to political and economic stability led us to begin some preliminary analysis using a more recently compiled measure of the Gini index for eighty-seven countries (Deininger and Squire 1996). The calculation of the Gini index is based on the Lorenz curve, which plots the share of the population against the share of income received (in quintiles). A higher level on this index indicates more inequality, while a low value indicates relatively less income inequality. For two missing values (for countries that had all other data available), I added measures published in the *World Development Indicators 1997* (World Bank 1997: 55–57).

World polity arguments state that the existence of ethnic political parties should reinforce and activate ethnic identity in states because the parties formally incorporate this group identity in the political arena. In Chapter 4 I tested the argument that formal recognition of ethnic group rights in the polity would lead to more nonviolent mobilization (in the form of ethnic protest). However, predicting an effect of formal ethnic group recognition on violence is less straightforward. For instance, formalization of ethnic parties and other political institutions might undercut violence and channel grievances and claims-making toward more institutional forms. On the other hand, if these demands are not met, formal inclusionary rules based on ethnicity can conceivably encourage and sustain ethnic insurgent organizations, which might eventually turn violent. On the whole, however, I would expect that the institutionalization effect of ethnic incorporation will predominate, which suggests that states with ethnic group incorporation policies will have lesser magnitudes of ethnic violence.

However, states that restrict the rights of minorities ought to experience higher levels of ethnic violence. As a result of an increasingly integrated world society, the diffusion of human rights and the legitimacy of self-determination is likely to give rise to claims of discrimination and oppression where these rights are formally denied (Gurowitz 1999). Thus, I expect that states that deny minorities full participation in politics will experience heightened levels of ethnic violence as a consequence.

In using these data, I have remained concerned about media effects that may overinflate levels of violence in countries with greater access to television, newspapers, and other forms of communication. While this problem is nearly always present in any analysis of collective action, reports of violence are more likely to be influenced by media bias. To capture this argument, I compared the effect of measures of newspaper circulation per capita, televisions per capita, radios per capita, and broadcast and print media control measures on ethnic violence in all four models reported below. None of these measures had an independent effect on levels of ethnic protest or violence in any of the models shown below.

MODELS AND STATISTICAL TECHNIQUES

Investigation of the hypotheses requires a model that estimates the effects of shifts in levels of inequality, of increasing integration into the world system, and of shifts in levels of ethnic violence. The research design proposes to begin analysis at the country level, so as to exploit the excellent data provided by Gurr's (1993) scales of the magnitude of ethnic protest and violence (see Appendix A for a list of countries).

The hypotheses suggest that world system position and country-level income inequality will also affect ethnic violence, net of the effects of prior history of ethnic mobilization. Table 5.1 shows that many countries report no ethnic violence, thus the intensity measure for such countries is zero for those years. In Chapter 4, I discussed why conventional time series models are less than ideal when the data are either highly skewed or violate normal probability assumptions. As discussed in that chapter, hypotheses about changing conditions require a statistical model that is appropriate for categorical index data measured over multiple time points.

To meet these requirements, I chose to use ordinal logit models that take into account the implicit Guttman scaling of the intensity of ethnic rebellion (see Table 3.1 for the categories). The effects can be best understood as the result of small, incremental shifts of the independent variable up the scale (e.g., from having no rebellion to the likelihood of experiencing some form of localized political banditry.)

Results

I expected that world system position would be directly related to ethnic nonviolence and inversely related to ethnic violence. However, in Chapter 4, with the exception of 1985–89 (when nonviolent protest was significantly less likely in the periphery), I found no systematic effect of peripheral status on the intensity of nonviolence. In Chapter 1, I argued that peripheral countries might be more likely to experience ethnic violence because there is more repression, more income inequality, and fewer outlets for conventional political expression in those countries. Is this assumption justified? To answer this question, I needed first to determine if there is a statistically significant difference between the effects in the periphery and in other countries, as much of the political sociology literature would lead us to expect.

Turning to bivariate comparisons between peripheral and non-peripheral countries, notice that Table 5.2 shows no significant differences in the

TABLE 5.2

Relationship of Peripheral Status in the World System and
Magnitude of Violent Ethnic Rebellion, 1965–1989
(by number and percentage of countries)

	No Rebellion (%)	Some Level of Rebellion (%)	Totals (%)
		1965–69	
Non-peripheral countries	27 (58.7%)	19 (41.3%)	46 (100%)
Peripheral countries	21 (46.7%)	24 (53.3%)	45 (100%)
Total countries	48 (52.8%)	43 (47.2%)	91 (100%)
Chi-square			1.32
		1975–79	
Non-peripheral countries	22 (47.8%)	24 (52.2%)	46 (100%)
Peripheral countries	33 (63.5%)	19 (36.5%)	52 (100%)
Total countries	55 (56.1%)	43 (43.8%)	98 (100%)
Chi-square			2.42
		1985–89	
Non-peripheral countries	15 (32.2%)	31 (67.4%)	46 (100%)
Peripheral countries	21 (39.6%)	32 (60.4%)	53 (100%)
Total countries	36 (36.4%)	63 (63.6%)	99 (100%)
Chi-square			.52

NOTE: Chi-square test statistics evaluated at one degree of freedom. * $p < .10$ ** $p < .05$, *** $p < .001$.

magnitude of ethnic violence. I compared the effect of core, semi-peripheral, and peripheral status across three time periods. There were no other significant patterns with respect to ethnic nonviolence and violence in any of the panel waves. These results run counter to a common view that the periphery is the predominant location for ethnic violence (Gurr 1993). In the latter two panel waves in particular, non-peripheral countries experienced some form of ethnic rebellion slightly more often than did countries in the periphery. Thus, an intriguing finding from this preliminary analysis is that core and semi-peripheral countries have slightly higher levels of intensity of ethnic violence compared to peripheral countries.

Comparison of the bivariate results for ethnic nonviolence from the last chapter with the results for ethnic violence in this chapter is equally provocative. Recall that for ethnic nonviolence, the results revealed that core countries had more ethnic nonviolent protest than other types of countries, as I had hypothesized. Table 5.2 reveals that non-peripheral countries are not immune to substantial violent rebellions. However, in Table 5.3, when other factors are taken into account we see that dominant and dependent countries are not equally vulnerable to unrest. The multivariate results suggest that these world system effects interact in complicated ways with internal state characteristics.

WORLD INTEGRATION AND ETHNIC VIOLENCE

When comparing the results on ethnic violence in this chapter to the findings for ethnic protest in Chapter 4, several theoretically relevant differences emerge. In particular, world system theory arguments led us to expect that peripheral status would intensify the magnitude of violence for a variety of reasons related to the coexistence of inequality and dependent relations. Does this argument hold up? Table 5.3 suggests that it does, but only for two of the three cross-sectional intervals: 1965–69 and 1985–89. Once indicators of links to international organizations and ethnic diversity are taken into account, there appears to be a significant effect of peripheral status that increases the magnitude of violent ethnic activity. But this effect does not hold up in the panel analysis, which takes time trends into account.

As anticipated by the human rights literature (e.g. see Brown 1996; Gurowitz 1999), during the first wave (1965–69) INGO memberships subdue levels of ethnic violence. The negative and significant interaction effects between peripheral country status and international organizational

TABLE 5.3

Cross-Sectional and Panel Estimates of Effects on Magnitude of Violent Ethnic Rebellion, 1965–1989 (robust standard errors in parentheses)

	Rebellion 1965–69	Rebellion 1975–80	Rebellion 1985–89	Panel Data 1965–89
Magnitude of prior	.158	.378*	.900**	−.098
of ethnic rebellion	(.209)	(.169)	(.199)	(.149)
Income inequality	−.109*	.005	.023	−2.70
(Gini index)	(.055)	(.035)	(.037)	(1.91)
Ln population size	1.12**	.698	−.426	.469*
(lagged in last col.)	(.397)	(.428)	(.267)	(.153)
Ln GDP per capita	−.678	.132	−1.52	−.878**
(lagged in last col.)	(.732)	(.751)	(.728)	(.306)
Ethnic fractionalization	5.67**	1.13	1.25	.694
index	(2.11)	(1.41)	(1.18)	(.701)
Polity IV index of democracy	.140*	−.036	−.028	.048
(lagged in last col.)	(.066)	(.060)	(.054)	(.027)
Televisions per capita	−1.87	−6.04	5.50	.175
	(4.53)	(5.21)	(3.40)	(.387)
Peripheral status	3.75*	−.478	2.90*	.615
(0,1)	(1.53)	(1.69)	(1.46)	(.623)
Number of INGO	.003	.001	.003**	.001
memberships	(.002)	(.001)	(.001)	(.001)
Interaction between	−.011*	.001	.003	−.001
INGO memberships	(.005)	(.001)	(.002)	(.001)
and periphery status				
Group rights	−1.20	.504	−.077	.975*
based on ethnicity (0,1)	(1.37)	(1.27)	(.755)	(.410)
Ethnic exclusionary	.390	1.24	.640	1.30**
policies exist (0,1)	(.998)	(1.23)	(.951)	(.431)
Time trend				.438
				(.234)
Total countries	60	62	64	55
Log pseudo-likelihood	−66.2	−70.8	−85.8	NA
Pseudo R-square	.27	.19	.26	NA

NOTE: Two-tailed tests of significance reported. * $p < .05$, ** $p < .01$, *** $p < .001$.

memberships in the left-hand column of Table 5.3 indicate that during the late 1960s, for peripheral countries, membership in international organizations had a mitigating influence on ethnic violence, but this effect seems to have lessened after 1970.

Thus, different patterns emerge when comparing ethnic violence and nonviolence in peripheral countries. The pattern for the earliest period is consistent with the expectation that links to the world system of international organizations constrain violent ethnic activity in the more dependent, peripheral states. It is also consistent with the world culture arguments, which appear to be more relevant to nonviolent than to violent ethnic activity.[4]

ECONOMIC WELL-BEING AND THE MAGNITUDE OF ETHNIC VIOLENCE

Consider next the results concerning the impact of income inequality. Table 5.3 shows that for 1965–69, countries with *less* income inequality had a significantly higher magnitude of ethnic violence during the 1960s. This finding supports the resource mobilization proponents in the debate on the effect of income inequality on civil unrest. Moreover, this effect does not reappear in the other waves, which seems to suggest that the effect of income inequality varies across the period studied. That is, there is no ongoing effect of income inequality during the 1980s. However, the effect of gross domestic product is negative and significant in the panel analysis. The panel analysis results are consistent with a number of other recent studies showing that higher than average incomes deter ethnic violence and civil war (Sambanis 2001; Fearon and Laitin 2003). These results suggest that, while declines in income inequality may have increased the magnitude of ethnic violence initially, the impact of overall poverty rises has gained in importance when analyzed longitudinally (results from analysis of data from the 1990s will provide more evidence supporting this claim).

Comparison of models that include and exclude the Gini index is also instructive. Models that include measures of income inequality do not change the negative interaction effect of membership in international organizations for countries in the periphery (far-left column of Table 5.3). Nor are any other results significantly affected by the reduction in sample size or by the addition of the income inequality measure. Moreover, the effect of prior

[4]I also investigated models parallel to those shown in Table 5.3. I replaced "peripheral status" with "core" and "semi-periphery" measures (models not shown), and added interaction terms between these measures with the number of memberships in international organizations. Consistent with the protest analysis, I found a significant main effect of core status on the intensity of ethnic violence. This finding is surprising, given the conventional view of core countries. No interaction effects between core status and organizational memberships were found. Within the periphery, however, there are significant differences with respect to organizational links to the world system that moderate violence.

ethnic violence escalates over time, as it raises the magnitude of violence during the second two periods, in the two middle columns.

ETHNIC FRACTIONALIZATION AND REBELLION

To what extent does ethnic diversity incite rebellion? The debate over the extent to which ethnic divisions cause differences in culture, language, and identification to become contentious addresses a number of key assumptions about the nature of ethnic identification and its consequences. On one side, there is the constructionist claim that collective actions cause ethnic divisions, rather than the other way around (see Nagel 1995; Cornell and Hartmann 1998). On the other side we find scholars who claim that differences in culture stir fundamental emotions about the nature of a people, its kinship ties, and its ability to promote shared cultural understandings (Horowitz 2001; Kalyvas 2003).

Table 5.3 shows evidence supporting both claims, but the overall trend shows a weakening effect of ethnic fractionalization. In particular, the magnitude of ethnic rebellion increases with ethnic fractionalization in 1965–69, while its effect is close to zero by the end of the 1980s, and there is no evidence in the panel analysis that ethnic diversity matters. Thus, as many others have found, over time ethnic rebellion is not systematically related to ethnic fractionalization. In contrast, the effect of past rebellion increases over this period while cultural measures show dissipating effects of ethnic differences.[5]

ETHNIC INCORPORATION AND EXCLUSION

The world polity measures for ethnic incorporation and ethnic exclusion find strongest support in the 1975–80 period and in the longitudinal analysis. The last column of Table 5.3, the panel analysis, shows that states that incorporate ethnic group members formally into their polity evidently have significantly higher magnitudes of ethnic rebellions. As expected, states with exclusionary policies directed against minorities have higher risks of ethnic rebellion, as Gurr (1993) anticipated some time ago. While the cross-sectional

[5]Although it is not reflected in these tables, I investigated a number of useful measures of ethnic and cultural differences from the MAR data set, including ethnic economic disparities, linguistic distance from the leading ethnic majority group, regional differences, Islamic versus Western systems, and a number of other cultural measures of discrimination and difference. Not one of these so-called "cultural difference" measures had a significant effect on the magnitude of rebellion analyzed here, in contrast to the recent empirical literature.

analyses show much weaker results for these two measures, the panel analysis shows clear and unequivocal support for the world polity claims of ethnic incorporation and exclusion in the expected direction. In particular, the results are consistent with world polity arguments that suggest that implementation of policies of ethnic group incorporation and policies of exclusion both mobilize ethnic groups. Ethnic violence over the period is significantly higher in countries with policies that single out ethnic or racial identity for special consideration, when compared to countries whose policies do not emphasize ethnic group identity (either beneficially or punitively).

How should we compare the cross-sectional results to the pooled cross-section and time-series models? Because these models take into account different sets of lags, it is not easy to choose which of the two methods is more convincing. However, increasingly in the social sciences, longitudinal models that take time dependence and multiple panel waves into account seem to carry more weight. This is especially true for collective-action analysis, where the logic of path dependence and prior history seems relevant to understanding the unfolding of rebellions in a particular setting.

I report these findings on ethnic rebellion with several important caveats. First, note that these data are relevant for a subset of countries for which measures of GDP per capita, ethnic diversity, and income inequality are readily available over all of these periods. I suspect, but cannot verify, that countries that do not report the Gini index measures may be systematically different from ones that do. Furthermore, although these Gini index measures are comprehensive and carefully collated, they often are calculated for different decades and periods (using income and household survey data from various periods from the 1970s all the way through 1993).

Furthermore, using measures of income inequality is a less than ideal strategy for studying *ethnic* inequality for a number of other reasons. A careful reading of the literature on internal colonialism and the cultural division of labor suggests that general measures of income inequality do not adequately address the existing debates about the ethnic division of a system of rewards (e.g., Hechter 2000). It would be ideal to include indicators that tap *ethnic and racial inequality* directly. These might include measures of ethnic occupational segregation, ethnic inequality in income, differential patterns of arrest rates, discrimination, and suppression of language and cultural expressions. Unfortunately, these data do not exist for large numbers of countries at this point. Nevertheless, given the prominence of arguments that link inequality to collective violence, I could not resist the temptation to contribute to this lively debate by including the latest and most reliable income inequality measures (from the World Bank archives).

Discussion

Analysis of data on ethnic nonviolence and violence reveals different dynamics. In particular, controlling for a country's centrality in the world system, periphery countries are more likely to experience violence and less likely to experience nonviolent ethnic protest, as anticipated. In contrast to those who believe that membership in international organizations subdues ethnic violence, I found that overall this is not the case, except in the periphery. Evidently, outside the periphery, and in more recent years, linkage to the international system increases the likelihood of ethnic rebellion.[6]

These results have some implications for state and international policies regarding outbreaks of ethnic violence. The analysis found that the number of INGO memberships decreased the magnitude of ethnic violence during the 1965–69 period in peripheral countries. What is the clearest interpretation of these effects? First, this finding is consistent with the overall claim that the diffusion of a world system culture of human rights encourages ethnic mobilization and nationalism, but depresses levels of ethnic violence and outright rebellion. It may also be interpreted as evidence that the global culture of human rights diffuses from the core to the periphery, but constrains movements in countries that have limited degrees of freedom in world politics. In this view, the diffusion of an ideology supporting expansion of human rights tends to encourage more conventional and nonviolent forms of protest and discourage ethnic violence, especially in countries that are more restrained diplomatically by other, more powerful nations. Consistent with the prevailing wisdom, periphery countries do experience a greater magnitude of violent rebellion.

Extrapolating from these results, we can begin to speculate about the impact of global integration on ethnic movements before the end of the Cold War. The analysis thus far suggests that, as the least-connected countries became linked to a world system of diplomatic, economic, and cultural ties,

---

[6]In the next chapter, which focuses on the post–Cold War period, I describe how I expect these effects to be more robust, as more countries become vulnerable to changes in global economic and political network.

ethnic violence declined. As peripheral states become more densely tied to the world system of organizations, states may be overtly encouraged to institutionalize conventional routes of access for making ethnic political demands. Although I have no direct evidence on this point, the results are consistent with this line of argument.

Policy analysts might be led to interpret the results in this chapter as evidence showing a deterrence effect of membership in international organizations. International policymakers may feel vindicated by the fact that ethnic violence seems to decline with integration into a world system of organizations. But the evidence supporting this claim only held for a brief time during the mid-1960s, suggesting that such a view was overly optimistic. These results are only a first step in exploring the policy implications that can emerge from comparing ethnic violence across many countries and regions. The findings suggest that membership in international organizations moderates ethnic violence only in the periphery, where entry into the network of organizations may be fresh and novel. The results from Chapters 4 and 5 suggest that international organizations encourage ethnic social movements that were both violent and nonviolent during the period before the ending of the Cold War.

The results also hint at some interesting new research questions for policy studies of the effects of human rights organizations on immigration and migration. Jenkins and Schmeidl (1995), among others, have shown that there has been an exponential rise in the number of cross-country migrations due to internal conflicts, wars, and natural disasters. Refugee flows by definition require new solutions for settlement patterns, citizenship rules, and inter-ethnic contact and cooperation. If the findings regarding international organizations hold up in future research, then policymakers can begin to explore more integrated world-system-level solutions or diplomatic negotiations.

By operationalizing some of the observable effects of globalization, I have tried to show how ethnic mobilization, once activated, is transformed into episodes of ethnic violence and rebellions. The results suggest that diffusion of broad human rights policies that encourage incorporation of marginal groups with specific ethnic identities as deserving of expanded rights may have significant boomerang effects within and across countries. In the chapters that follow, I compare ethnic violence in a subsequent period with international war, civil war, and other aspects of internal violence. By situating ethnic violence in the broader context of political violence, I hope to under-score the global roots of internal strife.

Conclusion

This chapter has argued that the process of economic and political integration among the world's states has caused a rise in ethnic political mobilization. In this view, ethnic protest is relatively more frequent in core countries, but it is shaped by an institutional context guaranteeing civil rights and liberties. The theory also led us to expect that, in contrast, ethnic protest would be ineffectual and sporadic in peripheral nations and in nations granting few civil liberties. Whether scattered ethnic protest develops into armed rebellion is likely to depend on a region's history of ethnic movements and on the reactions by government authorities.

Recasting traditional arguments about ethnic violence at the world level of analysis affords some leverage over an increasingly interconnected and complicated world system. To be sure, ethnic violence is a function of past confrontations and slights. But it also appears to be shaped by processes that can be measured at the global level.

There are several intriguing implications of these results for the study of collective violence. First, they suggest that peripheral status in the world system does not invariably generate higher rates of ethnic activity. The find-ings further imply that, for the most dependent countries, integration into the world system tempers violence, at least during some historical periods. Although this chapter focused on a subset of collective violence, the analysis can be replicated with data on other types of violent activity. If this path is pursued, it might offer useful ideas about why ethnic boundaries have achieved such prominence in contemporary struggles for power.

CHAPTER SIX

Group Dynamics of Ethnic Protest and Conflict, 1980–1994

In earlier chapters I analyzed the effects of world-level processes on the magnitude of ethnic nonviolence and violence from 1965 to 1989. The results highlighted differences among states in the degree of embeddedness in the world system, and showed that variation among states with respect to international organizational participation seemed to vary directly with ethnic protest and violence. Moreover, state-level characteristics of income levels and prior violence predicted subsequent ethnic activity. This chapter shifts attention to the local level in order to explore the impact of ethnic group characteristics on ethnic mobilization, in addition to world-level and state-level influences. Further, this chapter updates information on ethnic activity with analysis of characteristics of minority groups and mobilization from the mid-1980s through 1994.

Examination of ethnic group characteristics allows exploration of theories of discrimination and cultural differences from the standpoint of different groups coexisting in a single polity. In particular, this chapter explores the effects of (1) cultural, language, and economic differentials of the minority group vis-à-vis dominant groups; (2) resettlement history of the group; and (3) effects of group competition over land. My goal is to understand those forms of ethnic conflict that have provided the biggest challenge to state authority and power. Indeed, in contrast to sporadic events, ethnic rebellions are enduring social movements that include goals of reconfiguring existing geographic boundaries, replacing state authorities, or overthrowing existing regimes. Do group-level characteristics matter, once state- and world-level measures are taken into account?

Extending the analysis beyond the end of the Cold War allows examination of the thesis that opportunities for mobilizing ethnic identity have expanded and proliferated, increasing the likelihood of ethnic movements. In particular, I introduced an argument in Chapter 1 that suggested that the effect of integration of the world's states on ethnic conflict has increased in magnitude, partly as a function of the disintegration of the Soviet Union. In the analysis that follows, I highlight the temporal differences that show that the intensity of ethnic rebellions has indeed increased in the way we had expected.

Has serious ethnic activity become more commonplace in recent years? If this is the case, then what accounts for it? Recently, scholars have suggested that the erosion of the Soviet Union and subsequent birth of a variety of Eastern European and Central European nations, the democratic changes in countries such as South Africa, and the realignment of countries once divided by Cold War loyalties have increased the potential for mobilization of a variety of new political conflicts (Borstelmann 2001; Wilkinson 2004). Yet only a few studies have explored this argument using data on ethnic rebellion in a number of different countries and regions of the world. As part of the agenda guiding this chapter, I seek to explore the question of whether or not the relationships among rich and poor, dominant and subordinate countries have remained stable or have changed over the last thirty years.

Effect of Peripheral Status on Group Mobilization

Recall that world system theory rests on the historical argument that the world's states have gradually come to fit into three categories: economically and politically dominant "core" nations, a less-developed "semi-periphery," and increasingly dependent "peripheral" nations. This differentiation of countries along this power and dominance dimension emerged with the diffusion of a world capitalist system, which reinforced the dependence of the peripheral nations on core nations. The consequence is that the system of inequality among nations retards a variety of indicators of development in the poorer countries, including the diffusion of minority rights. According to this view, the triumph of an integrated world economic and political system widened even the small gaps that existed between richer and poorer regions within and between countries. Global competition among nations intensifies as a result.

Given these theories, peripheral nations ought to experience more ethnic violence, conflict, and outright rebellion than do core nations (Gurr 1993).

Peripheral nations regularly experience episodes of regime change, uncertainty, and power vacuums, which are likely to lower the costs of ethnic mobilization (Fearon and Laitin 1996, 1997). Indeed, the literature on regime stability generally holds that challenges to state authority of all kinds will be more numerous in weaker or subordinate countries. Thus, we would expect more rebellions, and perhaps also more successful challenges from ethnic groups in peripheral nations compared to core countries. In contrast, core countries (especially those with strong democratic regimes) are able to absorb the shocks of changing political alignments that occur internally and externally (Kriesi et al. 1995).

But this is not the only prediction that we can make about the impact of state structures on ethnic mobilization. Issues of repression and state response seem equally relevant to mobilization of ethnic rebellion (Moore 1998). While peripheral nations may be more likely to experience regime shifts, these shifts are also more likely to be in the direction of increasingly authoritarian regimes and away from more democratic policies (J. Meyer and Hannan 1979). The combined impact of instability and authoritarian repression suggests that ethnic mobilization is likely to be more violent in the periphery, as it confronts an increasingly intransigent nation-state.

Some analyses of repressive regimes suggest that there is a curvilinear relationship between authoritarian regimes and internal collective violence (Rasler 1996). In countries exercising extreme political disenfranchisement, the only means to political power involves violent (or revolutionary) overthrow of the regime. This implies that when protest begins in periphery countries, if it is quickly suppressed rebellion can be extinguished, at least in the short run. However, when mobilization expands to encompass a larger-scale movement in peripheral countries, it ought to be more difficult to constrain. Presumably, this is because peripheral countries have more difficulties in and fewer resources for constraining large-scale ethnic movements.

Previous chapters suggested that state polities that exclude specific ethnic groups from membership ought to generate more ethnic solidarity and mobilization in response. In this chapter, I focus on factors that would increase ethnic group grievances that vary across ethnic groups. In particular, I argue that levels of ethnic discrimination and previous acts of exclusion against an ethnic minority will encourage mobilization at the group level. Protest ought to be the result when rights are more evenly distributed in a society, whereas violent actions will erupt when ethnic group rights have been violated.

The research literature on social movements suggests that there are additional structural dimensions that shape demands for ethnic rights. Democratic and autocratic states are likely to channel different types of social movements, including ethnic ones. If public policies regarding ethnic incorporation vary systematically along a core–periphery dimension as well, we might be able to tease out factors that work at the global level from those that apply to group-level differences. That is, if peripheral countries can be found to experience more ethnic violence, net of the effects of economic wealth and democratic institutions, then we will have succeeded in isolating the effects of global patterns of dependency and dominance. On the other hand, if we see a more unpredictable pattern of ethnic mobilization and world system position, then we will need to revise our notions about the effect of dependence on ethnic social movements.

What clues are offered by the research literature? At first glance, the literature might lead us to suspect that groups that are excluded and discriminated against would be more prevalent in periphery countries than in core nations (Gurr 1993; Moore 1998; Rasler 1996). Several arguments have been offered to support this claim. First, periphery nations with closed or exclusionary systems force protest movements to move underground, become exiled, or engage in outright armed rebellion. Second, in authoritarian regimes where protest is repressed with escalating levels of violence, the likelihood of armed rebellion in reaction to repression is higher than in countries where there are other (more conventional) outlets for protest and political expression (Moore 1998). Finally, there are some relevant short-term and long-term comparisons of the effects of state repression. There is evidence that repression may not be successful in suppressing movements in countries outside of the core. In particular, case studies of the Intifada, East Germany, South Africa, and Iran document a variety of revolutionary outcomes, despite conditions of extreme repression and exclusionary policies (Moore 1995; Rasler 1996; Olzak and Olivier 1998). Yet highly repressive regimes do sometimes experience breakdown, and highly democratic regimes can also invoke discriminatory patterns and exclude minorities from full participation. To understand whether discrimination and exclusion shape ethnic group reactions, we need to turn to more specific ethnic group factors.

In particular, the types of mobilization patterns expressed by groups that are more and less discriminated against are likely to vary with respect to the timing, level of discrimination, and spread of human rights ideologies within a country. Among groups that have experienced severe discrimination and exclusion, we might expect that the spread of an international culture of self-determination and civil rights would create a sharp discontinuity between expectations of full participation and the reality of a state that denies group rights. However, in state systems granting more egalitarian rights, less violent protest might become more commonplace, as groups express ethnic politics in an open political environment that is conducive to ethnic claims, grievances, and demands for representation. At the ethnic-group level, then, I would expect that more discrimination predicts violence on the part of an aggrieved group, but that violence is subdued in less democratic countries regardless of discrimination factors.

Historical and Cultural Factors

GROUP-LEVEL CHARACTERISTICS

The *Minorities at Risk* data set contains a number of relevant measures of a group's mobilization capacity. Among the most interesting are measures of geographical concentration within the country's borders. Also included in the data set are measures that might be conceptualized as grievance measures, including (1) prior history of competition over land and (2) history of government-forced resettlement.

Measures of competition and forced resettlement are likely to increase the magnitude of rebellion in recent decades, because they inflame grievances and solidify resistance. Spatial concentration of groups facilitates mobilization and encourages intergroup communication and network organization, providing a geographical center for making sovereignty claims on the basis of ethnicity (Toft 2003). If arguments about processes of sovereignty lie at the foundation of ethnic rebellions (as suggested in Chapter 1), then groups that are more geographically concentrated ought to mobilize more sustained rebellions from this territorial base.

The two grievance measures find support from a number of leading theoretical perspectives of social movements and ethnic mobilization. Competition for land can be expected to spark sustained ethnic rebellion, as groups vie for power and authority over disputed resources. Similarly, recent government policies such as apartheid in South Africa and government displacement of populations from Java to outlying islands in Indonesia have been associated with unpopular (and unsuccessful) attempts to subdue ethnic challenges to state authorities. Thus, we would expect that groups that have experienced forced resettlement programs and policies will mobilize against these repressive tactics.

STATE REPRESSION

A wide variety of studies of collective violence suggest that repression has systematic effects on the likelihood, duration, and persistence of rebellion.[1] As Gurr (1993, 2000), notes, stable democracies and countries embedded in the world system of international sanctions stand to lose international credibility and risk war if they rely on coercion as the main instrument of social control. At the same time, repression raises the specter of victimization, rendering mobilization by victimized groups more likely. As Rasler (1996) has suggested, small amounts of repression may indeed increase the level of rebellion, while large amounts of state repression (especially as measured by internal political deaths) may decrease the likelihood of rebellions. We have obtained measures of political deaths within countries relevant to this historical period. Thus, I expect that this indicator of repression will significantly decrease the magnitude of ethnic rebellion.

FORCED RESETTLEMENT AND HISTORY OF COMPETITION OVER LAND

Two other features of ethnic rebellions related to group competition and mobilization of grievances are particularly relevant to studies of ethnic rebellions. These are measures of (1) history of forced migration, as groups are forcibly removed from their traditional locations by authorities, or by a conquering ethnic group; and (2) history of competition over land resources. Based on competition theories of collective action, we expect that both of these measures will be significantly associated with higher intensity of ethnic rebellions.

MEDIA INFLUENCE

Many scholars of collective action have documented that the magnitude of collective action depends in part on the spread of information by the media (Tilly 1978; McAdam et al. 1988; Koopmans and Olzak 2004; Myers and Caniglia 2004). Extending this view, some might expect that collective action

[1] See for example, Gurr and Lichbach (1986), Lichbach (1987), Opp (1994), Francisco (1995), Gurr and Moore (1997), Olzak and Olivier (1998a, 1999), and Olzak et al. (2003).

in core countries responds to rapid and widespread media coverage. Thus, it seems reasonable that ethnic activity in core countries could be systematically over-represented in the Gurr data set, and so I include measures of access to the media in the population. I expect that countries with greater access to television will experience more intensified ethnic mobilization (independent of a country's status in the world system).

Research Design and Measures

As noted in Chapters 4 and 5, the MAR data set uses categories of ethnic mobilization that can be analyzed in three basic forms: ethnic nonviolent protest, inter-ethnic confrontations, and ethnic rebellions against state authorities. Because the category of rebellion represents a significant escalation in goals and violence over protest and scattered violence, it seems useful to provide separate analysis of this form in this chapter. Tables 6.1 and 6.2 present the substantive categories that Gurr used to develop a Guttman scale of values (ranging from 0 to 5 for nonviolent protest and from 0 to 7 for violent rebellion) that indicate the magnitude of rebellion of each type of ethnic mobilization. These levels provide the key data for the dependent variable

TABLE 6.1

Number and Percentage of Groups Experiencing Different Magnitudes of Nonviolent Ethnic Protest, 1970–1994

	1970–74 (%)	1980–84 (%)	1990–94 (%)
0 None recorded	150 (56.6%)	129 (49.1%)	50 (18.0%)
1 Verbal opposition and petitioning	14 (5.3%)	10 (3.8%)	22 (7.9%)
2 Symbolic resistance and lobbying	57 (21.5%)	74 (28.1%)	61 (21.9%)
3 Small demonstrations	28 (10.6%)	24 (9.1%)	86 (30.9%)
4 Medium demonstrations	13 (4.9%)	23 (8.8%)	40 (14.4%)
5 Large demonstrations	3 (1.1%)	3 (1.1%)	19 (6.8%)
Total groups	265 (100%)	263 (100%)	278 (100%)
Total countries	105	107	116

NOTE: All scale values adapted from *Minorities at Risk* (Gurr 1993: 95) and from the MARGene Codebook and Documentation (Bennett and Davenport 2005: 82). For specific definitions of categories for nonviolent protest, see Table 3.1.

TABLE 6.2

Number and Percentage of Groups Experiencing Different Magnitudes of Violent Ethnic Rebellion, 1970–1994

	1970–74 (%)	1980–84 (%)	1990–94 (%)
0 None recorded	204 (80.3%)	188 (72.1%)	165 (59.1%)
1 Political banditry	14 (5.5%)	16 (6.2%)	20 (7.1%)
2 Campaigns of terrorism	5 (1.9%)	9 (3.5%)	15 (5.4%)
3 Local rebellions	5 (1.9%)	5 (1.9%)	15 (5.4%)
4 Small-scale guerilla activity	11 (4.3%)	16 (5.7%)	16 (5.8%)
5 Intermediate guerilla activity	0 (0%)	0 (0%)	14 (5.0%)
6 Large-scale guerilla activity	9 (3.5%)	9 (3.5%)	15 (5.4%)
7 Protracted civil war with rebel military units	8 (3.2%)	16 (6.2%)	19 (6.8%)
Total groups	254 (100%)	258 (100%)	279 (100%)
Total countries	105	107	116

NOTE: All scale values adapted from *Minorities at Risk* (Gurr 1993: 95) and from the MARgene Codebook and Documentation (Bennett and Davenport 2005: 82). For specific definitions of categories for violent rebellion, see Table 3.1.

of the magnitude of ethnic rebellion. The analysis reports findings on the magnitude of ethnic mobilization, for the period from 1970 through 1994.

Ethnic protest is activity expressing a demand for change or articulating a specific ethnic or racial grievance, in the form of verbal, written, or symbolic expression, or in the form of large-scale demonstration. *Ethnic violence and rebellion* is ethnic activity that aims at changing the fundamental balance in power relations among various ethnic groups within a country, by changing the power balance between a given ethnic group and the state. It includes all reports of activity on behalf of an ethnic communal group. As can be seen in Table 6.1, nonviolent acts can range from petitions or small demonstrations through enormous street demonstrations (up to and including rioting) by hundreds of thousands of participants.

The evidence suggests that nonviolent ethnic protest is becoming more widespread, according to Table 6.1, with increasing proportions of countries with minorities experiencing some form of protest. In 1970–74, more than half of all groups of minorities "at risk" of experiencing some form of ethnic mobilization had no events reported. By the 1990–94 period, 82 percent of minorities instigated some kind of ethnic protest. The types of protests also changed over these decades, with symbolic acts and small-scale (less than 1000 persons) demonstrations being the modal type of activity. At the same time, the scale of protest rose over this period, with increasing numbers of events mobilizing hundreds of thousands of participants (from 1 percent of the total number of events to nearly 7 percent).

Table 6.2 shows that forms of ethnic rebellion and violence can range broadly, from scattered acts of terrorism through instances of local rebellions and civil war. More extreme forms of ethnic rebellions are distinguished from nonviolent protest and more scattered forms of ethnic violence by their (1) territorial scope, (2) armed participants, and (3) ability to sustain acts that challenge the existing relations of power and authority in a country.

Table 6.2 shows the number of countries experiencing different levels of intensity of violent rebellion over the 1970–94 period. The percentage of groups and countries experiencing extremes in violent rebellion increased during this time, and the percentage of groups recording little or no ethnic protest declined. There appears to be some empirical evidence supporting the conventional wisdom that ethnic rebellion has increased in recent years.[2]

Explanatory Variables

I include in my analysis a categorical measure of a country's status in the world system that was produced by network analysis results of reported trade, diplomatic, and sanctioning connections (Snyder and Kick 1979). In previous research, I found support for the argument offered here that core nations will experience more ethnic activity overall, due to the fact that those countries most integrated into a world system also tend to accept an ideology guaranteeing human rights that is based on norms of ethnic equality (Olzak and Tsutsui 1998). In dependent nations, organizational forces of integration into the world system exert pressures *against* ethnic violence (defined in terms

[2] Readers familiar with the MAR data set will note that my analysis for the 1970–74 interval includes 254 and 258 groups, respectively, while the full data set on rebellion includes 278 groups by 1990–94. The discrepancies are due to the fact that country boundaries and identities did not remain the same over this period and number of groups that can be followed over time and compared constitutes the numbers of cases in Table 6.2. For example, the USSR is in the 1970 and 1980 data, but not in that for 1990–94, whereas East and West Germany are present in 1970 and 1980, but replaced by a new country, unified Germany, in 1990 in my analysis.

of less sustained action, as is the case in rebellions). Based on these patterns, I expect that peripheral nations with more memberships in INGOs should experience lower levels of ethnic rebellion and violence overall.[3]

A second measure of world system integration involves arguments about links to international government organizations. Recall that this argument suggested that ethnic rebellions would be subdued in countries subject to more supranational constraints. Furthermore, if the argument that the impact of world culture is increasing in its effects, then memberships in INGOs ought to reduce internal ethnic conflict in these settings even more dramatically in the most recent periods. My measure of these international memberships is an annual count of INGO memberships in 1966, 1977, and 1982, as published in the *Yearbook of International Organizations* by the Union of International Associations.

Because my analysis is concerned with the nature of bias in recorded acts of ethnic violence, I include one theoretically relevant measure of media influence. Behind this decision lies an alternative hypothesis that suggests that any systematic difference in ethnic rebellion between core and periphery countries might be spurious. In this view, the difference in intensity of ethnic rebellion might be due to the strong tendency of the media to publicize (or exaggerate) racial and ethnic confrontations in countries with greater access to the media. Because coverage, attention, and per capita consumption of the mass media should be greater in developed countries, televisions per capita might inflate measures of ethnic rebellion. Put differently, this suggests that the true intensity of ethnic violence may be the same in all countries, but these data may reflect a bias in favor of reporting about more developed nations and an absence of reporting about less media-intensive countries. To test this argument, I include a measure of the number of television sets per capita (beginning in the 1970s).[4]

MEASURES OF CULTURAL AND ECONOMIC DISCRIMINATION

Do significant cultural, economic, and linguistic differences among interacting populations influence protest and full-scale rebellion? To answer this question, I explore the effects of four key indicators provided in the MAR III

---

[3] It would be more realistic to include estimates of changing levels of world system status, but these data are not yet available.

[4] I also examined, but found no effect of, other measures of media influence, including the numbers of radios and newspapers per capita.

and IV data sets (Gurr 1999). The first of these measures, originally coded as a categorical measure ranging from 1 to 3, indicating different types of linguistic patterns, was recoded to 1 if the ethnic group in question speaks a different language from the official and dominant language (in some cases, this language is listed as the official language but is spoken mainly by a ruling administrative group in power, as with Afrikaans during the 1980s, rather than by the language group that constitutes the largest population size). The next indicator is a composite index created by Gurr and his associates (Gurr 1999) to indicate the degree of economic difference relative to the advantaged group. This measures relative economic advantage and disadvantage, and the index ranges numerically from 0, indicating no economic difference, to 4, indicating extreme differentials in economic well-being for a group compared to the dominant ethnic or majority population. A third measure addresses cultural differentiation, which is averaged over levels of different languages, historical origin, religion, social customs, and residence (and is not highly correlated with the language differential measure). This indicator of cultural differentiation ranges from 0 to 4, with 4 indicating extreme differences in culture from the dominant or majority ethnic population in a country.

Two other measures indicate behavioral and historical traits expected to be associated with enduring cultural distinctions, grievances, and mobilization potential. The first is an indicator (measured at two time points, 1980 and 1990) indicating whether or not the focal ethnic minority group "at risk" experienced some competition with others over control of land. This measure is also coded on a scale ranging from 0, indicating no competition, to 3, indicating "condition of serious competition." (Gurr 1999: 47). A final measure indicates whether or not a state implemented a more extreme exclusionary policy of resettling the focal ethnic group. This measure (taken in 1980 and in 1990) is also coded on a 0–3 scale, with 1 indicating minor resettlement policies present and 3 indicating serious and widespread resettlement policies implemented. Both of these measures are expected to increase levels of both protest and rebellion, although the impact on rebellion is expected to be more intense.

Models and Estimation Techniques

Investigation of the hypotheses requires a model that estimates the effects of shifts in levels of inequality, increasing integration into the world system, and shifts in levels of ethnic protest and violence. My research design conducts the analysis at the country and group levels, in order to exploit the excellent data provided in Gurr's (1993) *Minorities at Risk* data set.

World system position, country-level differences in integration into international organizations, and group-level experiences with resettlement and competition are included in the models of ethnic rebellion. Each of these measures is expected to affect rebellion, net of the effects of prior history of ethnic mobilization. As in the previous chapter, analysis of these data is further constrained by the fact that the range of variation of the magnitude of rebellion is extremely limited: it is aggregated into five-year totals, and it is categorical (see the categories listed in Table 6.2). Another problem for estimation is that the majority of cases have magnitude values of zero. This means that more conventional methods of estimating models that assume that the values of the dependent variable are normally distributed (e.g., ordinary least squares regressions or time series analysis) are inappropriate and often misleading. In sum, the theory, hypotheses, and form of the data require a statistical model that is appropriate for categorical index data measured over multiple time points.

To compare results from this period with the analysis conducted over earlier periods, I use the same variant of the multinomial logit model, ordered logit analysis. This model is particularly well suited to data with ordered categorical dependent variables. In particular, it allows us to make predictions about the likelihood of a specific outcome (for example, in Table 6.2, comparing the likelihood of a country having no rebellion with the chances of that same country having large-scale rebellious activity). There are several advantages to using ordered logit rather than the simpler logit analysis, which collapses the dependent variable categories into 0, 1 categories. As Tilly (2003) has pointed out, such aggregation methods conflate vastly different manifestations of ethnic activity, such as civil wars and sporadic local violence. By using this method, the integrity of Gurr's original intentions (regarding the scaling distance among categories) is kept intact.

In particular, I use the ordinal logit (ologit) procedures available in STATA 8 (StataCorp 2001). This technique produces maximum likelihood estimators of the effects and robust standard errors. Wherever relevant, I report predicted likelihoods for various countries, to emphasize the importance of distinguishing among different ethnic forms of activity.

Results

My arguments suggested that the impact of structural characteristics depends upon whether a country is in the core, semi-periphery, or periphery of the world system. Is this a reasonable assumption? In particular I suggested that core countries would experience more nonviolence, while peripheral countries ought to experience more violent forms of ethnic rebellion and intergroup conflict. Was this the case? To answer this question, we first must determine if there is a statistically significant difference between the levels of rebellion in the periphery compared to other countries.

Table 6.3 compares results for the ordered logit model indicating the effects of country and group-level characteristics on ethnic protest and violence. The columns report unstandardized coefficients for each of the independent variables or lagged dependent variables. As expected, we find that previous levels of ethnic mobilization have strong, positive, and statistically significant effects on levels of protest and violence. This result reaffirms the decision to include prior levels of ethnic activity in the models, and underscores the importance of estimating the effects of previous mobilization when trying to untangle complicated causal relationships.

EFFECTS OF THE WORLD SYSTEM ON THE MAGNITUDE OF ETHNIC REBELLION

Consider first the pattern of effects in periphery and semi-periphery countries. My first argument suggested that the magnitude of ethnic violence would be greater for groups in countries that are in the periphery, and that ethnic protest would be greater in the core. I found no support for these claims during this period. That is, the magnitude of ethnic rebellion is not significantly greater in periphery countries, and the magnitude of nonviolent protest is not significantly lower in the periphery, when compared to both semi-periphery and core countries.

I hypothesized that as the number of INGO memberships rose, ethnic protest would rise in response to the diffusion of world culture and the spread of human rights ideology from the core to the periphery. In examining the effect of the number of organizational links to INGOs, we can see that INGOs had no impact on nonviolent protest, and only affected ethnic violence in the latter (1990–94) period. In the 1980s, the number of memberships in international organizations had no effect on the intensity of ethnic rebellion.

TABLE 6.3

Effects of Ethnic and Racial Group Characteristics on Levels of Ethnic Protest and Rebellion, 1980–1994 (robust standard errors in parentheses)

	NONVIOLENT PROTEST		VIOLENT REBELLION	
	1980–84	*1990–94*	*1980–84*	*1990–94*
Previous magnitude of	1.06***	.378***	.339***	.516***
ethnic activity	(.294)	(.118)	(.102)	(.149)
Group's proportion	2.39	3.27**	.980	2.32**
of the population	1.72	(1.04)	(1.30)	(.903)
Log population size	.527**	.108	−.025	−.171
	(.181)	(.199)	(.223)	(.143)
Log GDP per Capita	.769*	−.166	−.594	−1.31**
	(.367)	(.259)	(.499)	(.419)
Televisions per capita	−4.05	2.94	.604	.454
	(3.02)	(1.74)	(2.27)	(1.88)
Periphery status	.373	.040	.142	.551
(0, 1)	(.644)	(.419)	(.452)	(.493)
Number of INGO	−.001	.000	.002	.002***
memberships (Hironaka 2000)	(.001)	(.000)	(.001)	(.000)
Group Characteristics				
Speaks distinct (non-official)	.781	.485	.606	.571
language (0,1)	(.567)	(.382)	(.392)	(.335)
Economic differentials	−.044	.036	.004	.175
index	(.109)	(.076)	(.099)	(.091)
Cultural differentials	.662**	.302**	.211	.247
index	(.213)	(.145)	(.201)	(.180)
Competition for land	−.141	−.034	.327**	.618***
during 1980s	(.216)	(.145)	(.160)	(.197)
Resettlement of minority	−.314	.215	.720**	.108
population during 1980s	(.293)	(.217)	(.228)	(.345)
Number of groups	151	166	168	180

NOTE: All group characteristics provided by the *Minorities at Risk Project*, by the Project Director Ted Gurr and his associates. For details, see the MARGene Codebook, Bennett and Davenport (2005). For specific definitions of categories for ethnic protest and violent rebellion, see Table 3.1. Two-tailed tests of significance reported. * $p < .10$, ** $p < .05$, *** $p < .001$.

By the early 1990s, the situation had changed radically. Indeed, for the 1990–94 period, the effect of the number of INGO memberships is strong, positive, and significant, suggesting that international links are associated with higher levels of ethnic rebellion in this period.

How should we interpret these findings? These effects suggest that international organizational memberships raised the magnitude of ethnic rebellion only over the 1990–94 period. Taken together, the results suggest that the impact of world-level organizations gradually spread the ideology of civil rights, resulting in higher levels of ethnic rebellion for those countries most affected by these ties. It also suggests that by the 1990s, the impact of a highly interconnected system of organizations across international borders increased the intensity of ethnic rebellion in countries most embedded in this network. Does this make sense? Evidently, since the end of the Cold War and the disintegration of the Soviet Union, exposure to the international world of organizational membership encouraged ethnic rebellions. This finding supports earlier research that found that the diffusion of world culture (as indicated by membership in a large number of international organizations), would increase the magnitude of ethnic protest and rebellion (Olzak and Tsutsui 1998; Tsutsui 2004).

ECONOMIC WELL-BEING AND THE MAGNITUDE OF ETHNIC REBELLION

Turning to the effects of poverty and inequality, we see the expected inverse relationship between economic health (as measured by GDP per capita) and ethnic rebellion. This finding supports predictions drawn from the research literature on inequality, social movements, and collective action. As anticipated, protest levels are higher in wealthier countries, at least in the 1980–84 period. However, by 1990–94, this effect disappears. For ethnic rebellions, it is declining wealth that raises the likelihood of more intense activity that will challenge state authority.

In addition to models in Table 6.3, I also included measures of income inequality (using the estimated Gini index for a large set of countries presented in Deininger and Squire 1996), but it did not have any effect, and its inclusion did not change any other effects reported by the model. Contrary to what many relative deprivation and grievance theories might expect (e.g., Gurr 1993), when we hold constant previous levels of rebellion, states with higher levels of income inequality do not experience a higher magnitude of rebellion. Instead, they experience a systematically lower level of ethnic rebellion, and this is relatively constant over the thirty-five-year period.[5]

---

[5]Note that the income inequality data are available for only a subset of countries in the MAR data set on ethnic rebellion. As mentioned before, I suspect, but cannot verify, that countries that do not report the Gini index measures may be systematically different from ones that do.

Fearon and Laitin (1996) report that increases in GDP per capita lower the magnitude of ethnic rebellion significantly. To investigate this relationship, I included various specifications that included GDP per capita at varying times in each of the models shown. It appears that after 1984, the relationship with GDP tempers the intensity of ethnic rebellion significantly. It is perhaps important that this negative relationship of gross domestic product and ethnic rebellion remains negative across the whole period, in models that include indicators of world system dependency (peripheral status) and other development measures, including per capita count of television sets in a country. Thus, the distribution of wealth and the overall economic well-being within countries appear relevant to levels of ethnic rebellion during this period.

CULTURAL AND ECONOMIC DISPARITIES

An alternative hypothesis that might explain the fact that we did not find the expected relationship between income inequality and rebellion is that ethnic mobilization—both protest and violence—might be better analyzed in terms of *group-level grievances*. Fortunately, we can explore this hypothesis using the rich data provided in the *Minorities at Risk* data set. In particular, a wide variety of studies have claimed that historical experiences with discrimination and oppression shape the magnitude of reaction and rebellion. Is there evidence for this claim?

In order to examine various cultural difference and grievance indicators, I examined cultural distinctions that exist between minorities and majorities in countries, as coded from the perspective of "minorities at risk." These measures include gauges of economic, cultural, and political disparities between a minority group and the dominant ethnic group. I compared effects of broad summary index measures as well as specific group grievance measures. Not one of these grievance measures was significant in any direction. Net of the effects of linguistic heterogeneity in the country as a whole, not one cultural measure of disparity or economic hardship had an effect. This suggests that once country-level measures of inequality and past mobilization are taken into account, economic and cultural differences do not distinguish among groups experiencing higher and lower levels of rebellion.[6]

[6]Using the MARGene data set (2003), I explored several time-varying measures of economic disadvantage available at the group level. None of these indicators (including changing levels of these measures) had a systematic relationship with group levels of ethnic rebellion.

Interestingly, a dummy variable indicating that the group spoke a distinctive language had no systematic effect on the level of violence or protest. Gurr's (1999) measure of linguistic distinction (from the official language) had no systematic effect on ethnic mobilization. This finding also has parallels in others' research on more violent forms of ethnic conflict. For example, Horowitz (2001) finds that "deadly ethnic riots" appear unrelated to measures of cultural differences, and Fearon and Laitin (1999) found no effects on ethnic rebellion by measures of linguistic distance from ethnic groups in positions of administrative state power. On the other hand, it seems reasonable to suspect that because prior levels of ethnic rebellion are so strongly associated with subsequent levels thereof, these cumulative effects of prior rebellions may capture the effect of linguistic distinction. Once unleashed, these rebellions take on a cultural reality of their own, unrelated to continuing linguistic differences.

Does an absence of effects for linguistic distinction contradict the finding reported earlier for the ethnic fractionalization measure? Not necessarily. The earlier measure (provided by Fearon 2002) is measured at the country level of analysis, and indicates a general level of diversity. The MAR data set measures cultural or linguistic isolation of a specific group (from the majority population). While linguistic variables have been found to affect a wide variety of ethnic movements, it seems clear that minorities that "speak a different language" in their host country do not systematically produce higher levels of ethnic rebellions.[7]

Based upon prior research, a number of other measures of territorial concentration, group solidarity, and "indivisible territory" claims were investigated. For example, Toft (2003: 43) presents results that suggest that spatially concentrated majority groups and groups residing in a presumed homeland will generate more ethnic violence than more dispersed groups, groups that are concentrated minorities, or urban minorities. To capture the categorical nature of the data, I used ordinal logit techniques rather than ordinary least squares regression, and I added a number of additional measures to Toft's analysis. In supplementary results, I found no systematic relationship with measures of spatial concentration or length of territorial residence.

[7]One possible explanation of this finding is that linguistic separation does not automatically trigger outright rebellion, but rather is more likely to be related to more conventional and nonviolent forms of protest, such as civil rights protest and demands.

I redoubled my efforts using a number of other indicators and specifications of territorial and group concentration available in the MAR data, and I varied these measures over time whenever possible.[8] Not one of these spatial or group solidarity measures had an impact on levels of rebellion, with the single exception of the indicator of forced resettlement as a function of state policy, as discussed below.

FORCED RESETTLEMENT AND COMPETITION OVER LAND

Two other hypotheses related to cultural distinctions were included to test the notion that rebellion (in particular) would be sensitive to a group's experiences with direct competition over land resources and with policies of resettlement. Each of these experiences would be expected to exacerbate the set of grievances and create a polarized sense of identity and victimization within states. Thus, I expected that both measures—competition and resettlement—would increase the magnitude of both protest and rebellion by groups that were affected by these processes.

Resettlement affects the magnitudes of protest and violence in opposite ways. Table 6.3 suggests that while competition for land decreased the magnitude of protest activity (insignificantly in the 1990–94 period), competition with the state or with other groups for agricultural or grazing resources significantly raised the magnitude of ethnic rebellion in both periods. Evidently, competition over land decreases the ability of groups to mobilize nonviolent demonstrations, and encourages instead more violent forms of action. Such findings are consistent with competition theories that have suggested that competition over scarce resources fosters more violent forms of aggravated ethnic confrontations.

The results for resettlement policies are more mixed, receiving support in the expected direction for nonviolent protest only in the 1990–94 period and for ethnic rebellion only in the 1980–84 period. Thus, there is some evidence from this analysis that resettlement policies underlie grievances and facilitate mobilization by ethnic groups who are already "at risk" of mobilization in some form. The results also suggest that policies of resettlement

---

[8]For examples, see the CONCENX8, CONCENX9, GROUPCON, and CATNESS measures (Gurr 1999). For an attempt to improve on these measures, see Fearon and Laitin (2002), where, recalculating these measures, the authors report positive effects of regional concentration on the magnitude of rebellion in 1960 (using the MAR data set).

that aim at reducing ethnic conflict by removing ethnic groups may have the unanticipated effect of increasing both protest and rebellion.

Comparing World Polity and Group Level Effects

This chapter offers a theoretical argument whose utility fundamentally depends on finding that there would be positive and significant effects of world system integration on ethnic mobilization in countries most closely linked to the world system. I also expected to find, as others have, that peripheral countries were most vulnerable to serious ethnic rebellion. In particular, I expected to observe systematic effects of world system links, as indicated by the number of memberships in INGOs, on ethnic mobilization. The analysis found support for one of these two main theoretical arguments, but only in the most recent period examined (1990–94). In addition, the post-1990 period mobilized more protest and sustained more violent rebellion than did previous periods. This suggests not only that the end of the Cold War has produced more ethnic tensions, but that the new international network has created pressures that heighten those tensions.

Contrary to theories suggesting that ethnic violence and protest are based upon the existence (or degree) of cultural distinctions, this chapter found that group characteristics—including economic and linguistic distinctions, geographic concentration, and group solidarity—had little effect on violent mobilization. Yet a group's experience with forced resettlement mattered to both protest and violence, and competition for land increased rates of ethnic violence substantially. Does this mean that cultural explanations are not useful for understanding ethnic movements? Not exactly. The evidence in this chapter instead suggests that under some conditions, ethnic groups' mobilization capacities have been encouraged by repressive state policy. Such evidence suggests promise for analysis using cultural distinctions and group mobilization as a function of prior mobilization and state repression, and not vice versa.

Policy Considerations

The results presented raise some troubling questions for international policies regarding the most sustained types of ethnic violence. The results in this chapter show that the number of INGO memberships had a significantly positive effect on ethnic rebellion in the 1990s. These findings are consistent with the overall claim that the diffusion of a world system culture of human rights encourages ethnic mobilization and nationalism, but that this effect may be more recent than we had anticipated.

Taking this argument one step further, in Chapter 1 I posited that ethnic violence would be increasingly encouraged as the least-connected countries became linked to a world system of diplomatic, economic, and cultural ties. As peripheral states become more extensively connected to international organizations, ethnic groups may be indirectly encouraged to make political demands for national liberation and/or group sovereignty, and ethnic equality. Although I provide no direct evidence on this point, the results presented above seem to be consistent with the general argument that one consequence of global integration has been to encourage organizational isomorphism on the part of ethnic social movements and global social movement organizations. That is, we might expect that countries that are linked together in a common network of associations will begin to resemble one another in a variety of ways, including ethnic mobilization patterns. Indeed, I found no significant differences in these patterns among core, peripheral, and semi-peripheral countries.

Can we infer from these results that the system of international organizations encourages ethnic rebellion? As noted in the previous chapter, such claims require more empirical scrutiny over longer periods of time before any conclusions can be drawn about the instrumental or moderating effect of world system linkages. Taken together, Chapters 4, 5, and 6 suggest that there is an interesting trajectory over time regarding ethnic nonviolence and violent ethnic rebellion. This pattern would indicate that there is a sequential effect of becoming linked to a world system of international organizations. In other words, the effects of entry into the world system may depend on the development of the human rights ideology in different historical periods. Early on, the effect may have been to stimulate ethnic mobilization, especially in core countries. In Chapter 7, we shall examine whether the more recent period finds international organizations moderating ethnic violence and rebellion.

Conclusion

In this chapter we saw mixed effects of links to international non-governmental organizations. Linkages with the world system were found to encourage ethnic rebellion when we compared the effects on the magnitude of rebellions in three time periods. What do these results tell us about the historical evolution of patterns of ethnic violence?

The temporal patterns seen in this chapter provide some insights into this question. Instead of seeing an overall trend toward moderating ethnic violence in the periphery (as we did in Chapter 4), we see opposing effects of the international system in each period. Does this indicate that the effect of the world system depends upon its own historical development as a viable network? That is, there may have been an initial effect of a global international culture and ideology that raised levels of protest and conflict of all types. Over time, however, these linkages may temper violence and moderate the most serious forms of rebellions. As a country or group's connections to the system of INGO memberships become increasingly numerous and thus institutionalized, its power to suppress internal ethnic conflicts may rise proportionally.

At the same time, I suspect that these temporal or sequential patterns may also be shaped by specific national and group histories of conflict, and other features of changes in the constellation of states that move into and out of the set of dominant core nations. Clearly it will be important in the next decades to analyze how shifts in world system position (from semiperiphery to core, for example) may come to affect the internal politics of ethnic rebellion.

This chapter argued that the process of economic and political integration among the world's states has led to a gradual rise in more sustained forms of ethnic mobilization. In this view, ethnic rebellion is relatively more challenging to state power in recent years than it was during the Cold War period. However, the results also suggest that rebellion rose alongside the development of increasingly dense intergovernmental ties. Whether scattered ethnic protest develops into armed rebellion is likely to depend on the history of each ethnic movement and on the reactions by government authorities. In the chapter that follows, we turn to some of the political contexts of repression, democracy, and international war that shape these processes.

CHAPTER SEVEN

Globalization in a New Era: Ethnic Violence since 1989

My global integration argument holds that as nation-states have become increasingly linked together in networks of military, economic, and diplomatic associations, national political boundaries weaken and political regimes become vulnerable to internal challenges. If this is correct, then international forces of integration would have more immediate effects on countries after the end of the Cold War, compared to previous periods (Borstelmann 2001). This is particularly true for the case of ethnic conflict, which many observers claim rose sharply as a result of the breakup of the Soviet Union. I examine these arguments and compare findings from the *Minorities at Risk* data set with data on events compiled from Reuters' news accounts in the PANDA data set.

This argument does not state that international processes linking local communities are new. Instead it argues that the effects of globalization have intensified. As political associations (such as the European Union, NATO, the UN) expand their scope of activities once controlled only by state politics, new possibilities arise for creating audiences and targets for social movements. Ethnic movements span borders, activists (and terrorists) travel across international borders (both legally and illegally), and ideologies supporting human rights follows these paths (Brass 1991; Horowitz 1985; Keck and Sikkink 1998; O'Brien et al. 2000). As military, economic, trade, and other international associations grow in number, the actions of individual nation-states become less salient (relative to regions, city-states, or other powerful actors within states). As states become more enmeshed in a world system of diplomats, economics, and financial and military obligations, state actions become more constrained, and reactive ethnic movements have arisen to wrest power and authority away from host states.[1]

By the end of 1989, the configuration of the world's states had changed dramatically as the Soviet Union was transformed into a number of new nation-states, the Republic of South Africa was being transformed into a majority-rule democracy, and a number of other countries were establishing new regimes and party alliances. Some of these changes signaled important shifts in ethnic configuration within and among states, as local elites encountered new opportunities, through international non-governmental organizations, to make political alliances independent of national authorities that could stimulate economic development. Such shifts also created rifts among elites, as new power brokers and warlords arose to fill the power vacuum left by departing administrations.

These changes also seem to have been joined increasingly by rising tides of ethnic violence in the Balkans, Eastern Europe, India, and other places, where political changes accompanied the challenges to fragile new states as well as to older, established ones. From Northern Ireland to Bosnia, ethnic conflict appeared to threaten social order in old and new states. Scholars such as Gurr (1993: vii) have concluded that "conflicts between communal groups and states have come to be recognized as the major challenge to most parts of the world." Although this observation has been widely repeated, there have been few systematic analyses of patterns of ethnic violence that have emerged since the watershed events of 1989. This chapter provides a new look at this period. I analyze data from two key sources: the PANDA/KEDS data using Reuters newswire reports from the 1990–95 period (described in Chapter 6) and the *Minorities at Risk* data set for 1995–98 (recall that the 1990–95 MAR data is analyzed in previous chapters).

This chapter has two goals, both methodological and theoretical. The first task will be to summarize the relationship of ethnic rebellion and violence, economic inequality, and embeddedness in the world system during the tumultuous 1990–98 period. I will contrast findings from the two data sets, which complement each other in a number of ways but differ in other

[1]This argument does not imply that nation-states are disappearing or are experiencing a decline in authority. Nation-states are the main partners in interaction with international associations and organizations, and nation-state authorities continue to arbitrate citizenship disputes, control resources, and initiate large-scale armed conflicts.

important ways. A second goal is to analyze violent events using the PANDA data set and compare these findings with the patterns on ethnic rebellion and violence using the MAR data set (summarized in earlier chapters). Do event report data show similar or dissimilar patterns? How do the world system characteristics fare when the rate of ethnic mobilization is examined with event report data rather than with the categorical data?

Cultural and Economic Factors

For some time, scholars have debated whether economic and cultural features within and between states form the underlying sources of group conflict leading to terrorism, war, and ethnic violence. Yet only recently have empirical findings specified why these group identities might incite violence. For instance, Sambanis (2001) finds that civil wars based upon ethnic and/or religious identities are more likely to erupt in countries with high levels of ethnic heterogeneity and low levels of political democracy. In contrast, economic and development indicators (especially energy consumption) have more influence on civil war than do measures of ethnic heterogeneity and indicators of democracy. Moreover, Elbadawi and Sambanis (2000) found that, contrary to expectations, civil wars in Africa over the 1960–90 period were not due to the continent's ethnic or religious diversity, but rather to high levels of poverty, fragile political institutions, and various economic indicators of dependence on natural resources and the absence of indigenous businesses.

ETHNIC DIVERSITY AND ETHNIC VIOLENCE

Because of its capacity to partition societies, language acts as a potentially divisive factor in multilingual settings. Since the early 1960s, ethnic-linguistic fractionalization (ELF) measures have been used as proxies for solidarity that predict potential conflicts within states. Scholars have argued that state building, economic modernization, and cohesion will be seriously impeded to the extent to which groups are highly diverse, compared to conditions of relative homogeneity of the population (Deutsch 1953; Eisenstadt and Rokkan 1975; A. Smith 1991).

While ethnic diversity appears to play a role in the rhetoric and claims of most ethnic separatist movements (e.g., see Horowitz 2001), the empirical evidence showing a relationship between high levels of diversity and ethnic mobilization has been equivocal. Indeed, few studies of unrest of any kind find that diversity by itself incites ethnic violence, and some scholars have suggested that the rising salience of ethnic identity results from ethnic violence, not vice versa.

Fearon's (2002) new measure of ethnic fractionalization improves over earlier ones (notably ELF) because it is theoretically informed and painstakingly gathered using a variety of sources (see also Vanhanen 1999, 2001; Laitin 2000; Reilly 2000). Dissatisfied with existing ethnic fractionalization indices (e.g., see Roeder 2001) Fearon identified 823 ethnic and "ethnoreligious" groups in 160 countries, and calculated a new diversity index, one that is relatively independent of the much-used (but perhaps flawed) index created from data published in the 1964 *Atlas Narodov Mira*. Not only is this earlier source outdated (and does not include new states), but the earlier indices drawn from the *Atlas* do not take into account structural distance between linguistic groups. Fearon's highly detailed and careful analysis produced two new indices: the ethnic index and a cultural/linguistic fractionalization index, which allowed me to compare the role of ethnic, linguistic, and cultural distinctions within countries. However, because they are highly correlated, I choose to report only those results that used Fearon's (2002) ethnic fractionalization (EF) index.

In using these measures, I depart from traditional arguments about the disruptive and disintegrating role of ethnic diversity, and argue that we should not expect to see systematic effects of ethnic heterogeneity. My argument holds that, once economic and dependency forces at the world-system level are taken into account, ethnic fractionalization should have little systematic effect on ethnic violence. Indeed, I would argue that the variation in ethnic violence once attributed to ethnic diversity was masked by the covariation of world-system-level factors and factors related to internal development within various economies. I test this argument directly with Fearon's (2002) index, which was created using more recent information on ethnic group distinctions than were earlier indices.

ECONOMIC INSTABILITY AND ETHNIC VIOLENCE

Conventional wisdom (and prior research) has long supported claims that economic instability seems to generate a wide variety of rebellions, civil wars, and internal civil strife (e.g., Muller and Weede 1990; Muller and Seligson 1987; Lichbach 1995). However, as many critics have indicated, it is just as likely that economic instability results from prior conflict as that economic decline follows the public's anticipation of civil unrest. In an attempt to sort out the causal ordering of economic effects on ethnic wars, Blomberg and Hess (2002) analyze the likelihood of ethnic war, genocide, revolution, and regime change (or "state failure") using newly available data on 152 countries from 1950 through 1992. They find that while the onset of ethnic war is significantly more likely following recessions, the reverse causal relationship is much weaker empirically. Such evidence largely supports the notion that economic decline raises rates of internal civil war, rather than vice versa.

Ethnic diversity also prolongs the duration of civil wars. Recently, Fearon (2004, 2005), K. Gleditsch (2003), Fearon and Laitin (2002), Collier (2000), and Collier et al. (2001) have all examined the impact of ethnic cleavages on the duration of civil wars. Collier et al. (2001) and Fearon (2004) find that the duration of violent civil conflict increases when there are a small number of large ethnic groups, when there are conflicts over land use, and when rebels have access to external (often contraband) resources. Yet, somewhat paradoxically, the capacity of either side (government or ethnic insurgents) to achieve a decisive military victory lowers the probability of a negotiated settlement among combatants, and eventually reduces the duration of the war. Not surprisingly, the evidence shows that ethnic wars and civil wars are causally and temporally related.

The Minorities at Risk Data: Ethnic Rebellion since 1995

Conventional assumptions suggest that the incidence of ethnic turmoil may be rising uncontrollably in the contemporary world, creating the conditions for intractable conflict that would threaten world peace and economic stability among nations. At first glance, there are many dramatic examples over the last fifteen years that seem to support these claims. Indeed, the last decades have been punctuated by nearly continuous accounts of mayhem and ethnic violence from a variety of countries and continents, including Bosnia, Northern Ireland, Chechnya, Somalia, Sri Lanka, and so on. Yet few have tested this assumption systematically across a number of countries and groups using clear-cut guidelines for coding events and magnitude of violence.

This chapter first questions the assumption that ethnic violence rose during the 1990s. Table 7.1 reports several relevant statistics to provide some answers to this question. Over the 1995–98 period, the percentage of "at risk" minority groups engaged in political activities involving little or no

TABLE 7.1
Number and Percentage of Groups Experiencing Different Magnitudes
of Violent Ethnic Rebellion, 1990–1998

	1990–94*(%)	1995–98(%)
0 No Events Recorded	165 (59.1%)	180 (64.3%)
1 Political banditry	20 (7.2%)	20 (7.1%)
2 Campaigns of terrorism	15 (5.4%)	8 (2.9%)
3 Local rebellions	15 (5.4%)	17 (6.1%)
4 Small-scale guerilla activity	16 (5.7%)	13 (4.6%)
5 Intermediate guerilla activity	14 (5.0%)	15 (5.4%)
6 Large-scale guerilla activity	15 (5.4%)	10 (3.6%)
7 Protracted civil war	19 (6.8%)	17 (6.1%)
Total groups	279 (100%)	280 (100%)
Total countries	116	116

NOTE: All scale values adapted from *Minorities at Risk* (Gurr 1993: 95) and from the
MARGene Codebook and Documentation (Bennett Jr. and Davenport 2005: 82). For specific
definitions of categories for violent rebellion, see Table 3.1.
Descriptive data by categories of ethnic violence and rebellions from 1990–94 are replicated from
Table 6.2 for purposes of comparison.

violence is more than two-thirds of this highly selective sample (Gurr 1993).
Given that this sample of groups was chosen on the basis of previous ethnic
political activity, the fact that the majority of groups had no reported ethnic
rebellions is significant. Ethnic rebellion appears to be relatively rare, despite the conventional view that ethnic movements are ubiquitous. Moreover,
the incidence of the most serious type of ethnic rebellion declined over this
period. Table 7.1 shows that groups engaged in protracted civil wars dropped
slightly (from 19 in 1990–94 to 17 in 1995–98) and large-scale guerrilla activity declined even more across the two periods. Moreover, the percentage
of "groups at risk" with zero recorded events of ethnic rebellion actually
increased over this same period. Both trends suggest that the end of the Cold
War had a moderating effect on serious and sustained ethnic violence.

Comparing Table 7.1 with Table 6.2 (which also analyzed violent ethnic
rebellion at the group level) affords a broader view of the temporal trends in
ethnic violence (note also that the last column of Table 6.2 and the first column of table 7.1 are identical. They are added here to facilitate comparison
with data from the late 1990s). While the number of groups with no recorded
violence declined over the thirty years examined (from 81 to 64 percent
of all groups in the potential risk set), the percentage of groups engaged in

the most serious and continuous levels of ethnic violence doubled (from 3 to 6 percent of all groups, from the 1970s to the end of the 1990s). Moreover, from the 1980s through the end of the 1990s, the number of groups engaged in protracted civil wars has remained more or less constant, suggesting that the most serious forms of ethnic rebellion did not dissipate over this period.

Other scholars have suggested that while the proportion of groups engaged in ongoing ethnic movements may not have increased in the contemporary period, the scope of ethnic activity may have shifted. Has the scope of activity expanded beyond local areas over the observed period? Chapter 6 showed that in 1970 only 11 percent of ethnic groups engaged in rebellions that ranged beyond local boundaries, but by the 1995–98 period analyzed in Table 7.1, more than one-fifth of all groups are found to have mobilized beyond small local rebellions (level 3 in Table 7.1). Examining the percentage of groups organizing extralocal guerilla activity (by aggregating the percentage of groups in levels 5–7), over the 1990–98 period, Table 7.1 shows a gradual increase in diffusion of ethnic rebellion beyond local territories. However, in Table 6.2, we see that in 1970–74, only 6.7 percent of groups were active in extra-local guerrilla activities, while by 1995–98, 15 percent of groups mobilized guerrilla forces beyond local boundaries (in both cases the percentages are summed over the most serious categories 5–7). Thus the longitudinal evidence suggests that the percentage of groups engaged in extralocal armed rebellion by communal groups more than doubled over these years (1970–98).

Consider next the hypotheses about the effects of organizational integration, inequality, and competition among groups as key processes driving the expansion of scope of these social movements. Table 7.2 presents an ordinal logit analysis appropriate for use with data that are organized hierarchically (see also the discussion of analyses in Chapters 3 and 4). Using Gurr's presentation of these activity categories as indicating a Guttman-style scale of increasing scope and violence, I analyze the group-level and country-level factors associated with broader-scope and more sustained violent rebellions.[2]

With respect to the world system hypotheses, note that for two out of three models (controlling for peripheral and semi-peripheral status in the

---

[2] Recall that Stata (8 SE) estimation techniques for ordinal regression allow us to examine both group-level and country-level factors in the same model, despite the fact that it is likely that the standard errors may be inflated by using two levels of analysis in the same model. The estimation technique allows comparison of robust standard errors to be clustered within countries, thus adjusting for autocorrelation of error terms within countries.

TABLE 7.2

Effects of World System Status on Magnitude of Violent Ethnic Rebellion, 1995–1998 (robust standard errors in parentheses)

	(1)	(2)	(3)
Previous magnitude of	.667***	.657***	.656***
ethnic rebellion	(.122)	(.122)	(.112)
Ln population size	.103	.137**	.087
in 1995	(.156)	(.155)	(.179)
Ethnic fractionalization index	−.239	−.158	−.193
(Fearon 2002)	(.824)	(.816)	(.956)
Ln GDP per capita	−.0002**	−.0002**	−.0002**
	(.000)	(.000)	(.000)
Income inequality	−.010	−.012	.004
Gini index	(.026)	(.025)	(.026)
Group-Level Characteristics			
Competition for land	.614**	.659***	.595**
during 1980s (MAR)	(.196)	(.205)	(.216)
Islamic minority group	.824	.840	.710
in non-Islamic country (0,1) (MAR)	(.434)	(.439)	(.451)
Transnational support	1.25**	1.29**	1.19**
from kindred ethnic grp	(.414)	(.428	.411)
(0,1)(MAR)			
Number of INGO memberships	.001*	.001**	.001
	(.000)	(.000)	(.001)
World System Status Measures			
Peripheral status	.816**		
	(.360)		
Semi-periphery status		−.829**	
		(.356)	
Core status			.102
			(.768)
Log likelihood	−171.6	−171.6	−173.5
Pseudo R-square	.28	.28	.27
Log likelihood test statistic	7.2*	7.3*	3.7
for the addition of			
world system status			

NOTE: Two-tailed tests of significance reported. * $p < .05$,   ** $p < .01$,   *** $p < .001$.

world system), the addition of two key measures significantly improved the model over a less constrained model. That is, information on membership in INGOs and on world system status significantly improves our understanding of the mechanisms that increased the level of ethnic rebellions, as can be seen at the bottom of Table 7.2. Moreover, the hypotheses regarding the impact of non-governmental organizations find support in models controlling for periphery and semi-periphery status. This suggests that countries with more memberships in INGOs experienced significantly higher levels of ethnic rebellion during the most recent period, holding constant world system position. As expected by many scholars, peripheral status raises levels of ethnic rebellion, net of the effects of income levels and income inequality. This finding is especially interesting given the criticism that world system measures would be diminished if appropriate economic controls were added to the model. It is equally interesting in light of the fact that in earlier periods core nations experienced more violence than did peripheral regions.

The results in Table 7.2 also show strong support for a competition hypothesis in all three columns (and the coefficients are all significant). These results provide evidence that competition over territory expands a group's mobilization capacity, creating a movement's potential beyond levels of scattered and sporadic violence. These results regarding territorial competition have implications for group mobilization over time. This is because indicators of competition are taken from between ten and fifteen years prior to measures of ethnic rebellion, and competition measures are net of the effect of previous rebellion levels. These results suggest that when a group has experienced competition over land, this history significantly raises the possibility that larger-scale rebellion will result, when compared to groups that have had little or no competitive conflict over territory. Furthermore, as sovereignty arguments introduced earlier suggest, the link between land, competition, and ethnically defined rebellion may have intensified during the 1990s compared to earlier periods.

In contrast to the analysis in Chapter 5 (for the period before the end of the Cold War) we see no significant effects for ethnic diversity in Table 7.2. In particular, contrary to many predictions offered in the literature on ethnic diversity and conflict, Fearon's (2002) ethnic fractionalization measure is *not* associated with higher levels of rebellion. In column 2, this indicator of ethnic fractionalization shows a negative (insignificant) effect on levels of ethnic rebellion.[3] Should readers be surprised that ethnic fractionalization does not raise the magnitude of ethnic rebellion? Perhaps not. If ethnic fractionalization is a proxy for levels of cultural segregation of ethnic communities,

[3] I substituted two other measures of linguistic diversity in these models—the *Atlas Narodov Mira* (1964) index, and Vanhanen's (1999) ethnic heterogeneity index. However, neither of these indexes had any systematic effect on the rebellion rate. Chapter 6 also showed that linguistic isolation (measured at the group level) had no significant effect on either ethnic protest or rebellion.

then high levels of ethnic fractionalization would impede highly coordinated rebellion, not encourage it. Moreover, there is considerable evidence supporting the view that ethnic rebellions have political rather than cultural roots. Very few studies have found any significant evidence linking linguistic diversity (or distance from the majority language) to actual incidence of rebellion.

The findings for various economic indicators are generally aligned with expectations, but perhaps not as powerfully as had been anticipated. Specifically, while GDP per capita has a consistently negative and significant effect, as many others have found, controlling for peripheral, semi-peripheral, or core status does not diminish the power of economic income levels. This is revealing because some may have expected that any effect of world system position would disappear once GDP per capita was included in the model. The World Bank indicator of income inequality, the Gini Index, did not increase the likelihood of more sustained rebellion, as some of the literature on income determinants of civil unrest might have led us to expect. Evidently, ethnic rebellions are encouraged by more general forms of economic hardship in ways similar to civil wars and other unrest within countries (Fearon and Laitin 1999).

Table 7.2 shows a strong positive effect of support from kindred groups on the magnitude of rebellion, as anticipated. While this generally fits contemporary views about the source and nature of current political instability within some regions, the relationship between ethnic rebellion and religious movements is a complicated one that requires much more exploration in the empirical literature (using more nuanced measures and variables than are currently available).[4]

Net of the effects of income inequality, prior mobilization, and world system linkages, the presence of an Islamic minority tended to influence the capacity to mobilize an ethnic rebellion in the contemporary period (outside of core countries, which seems reasonable). While this result was not central to the theory, it is intriguing because it suggests that both religious and ethnic identities interact in powerful ways that can destabilize or stabilize countries. I take this issue up in using measures of religious fractionalization in the next chapter.

[4]To be sure, designation of groups as "minorities at risk" was designed to capture some *potential level* of solidarity among communal groups of all types. Yet it seems important to note that I found that few cultural measures of language, religion, or ethnic identity mattered when they were included in other analyses (not shown).

The key hypotheses surrounding world system measures find support from my analysis: in all cases, higher levels of embeddedness in INGOs raise the magnitude of ethnic rebellions, as hypothesized. So too does peripheral status in the world system, net of the effects of income level and income inequality (which are not correlated highly with peripheral status, as might be expected). Gurr's (1993) anticipation that peripheral countries experience more and higher levels of rebellion finds support here.

Column 2 of Table 7.2 shows that countries designated as being in the semi-periphery have significantly lower levels of ethnic rebellion when compared to core countries and peripheral countries, despite the fact that many scholars would argue that the opposite should happen. How can this apparent contradiction be explained? With the ending of the Cold War, former Soviet Union countries (almost all designated as being in the semi-periphery) became established as separate nations, thus decreasing the likelihood that ethnic rebellion against the Soviet Union by these nationalities would continue. According to this argument, many would have expected that ethnic minorities within the newly independent countries would become majority rulers, suggesting that an ethnic nationalist movement would lose momentum and motivation for continued mobilization. So, given that this period of 1995–98 experienced the birth of a variety of nations within this semi-periphery category (and because world system measures are unfortunately static ones), the negative effect of this status on rebellion becomes more understandable in this context.

Finally, note that core nations are neither more nor less likely than periphery or semi-periphery nations to incite more serious ethnic rebellions, once other economic and political measures are taken into account. While this may be surprising to some, it makes sense to think about the nature of core status apart from the usual measures of wealth and democracy that are often (incorrectly) associated with core status. Clearly, in column 3 of Table 7.2, measures of links to INGOs and economic hardship are more relevant to ethnic rebellion than are the countervailing influences of dominant status within the core.

Event Count Analysis: PANDA Data, 1989–1995

In Table 7.3 I present an analysis of variation in counts of violent events by state. These events include both ethnic group confrontations and ethnic challenges to state authority, and the events analyzed reported use of weapons,

TABLE 7.3

Effects of World System Status on Annual Counts of Ethnic Violence
1989–1995 (robust standard errors in parentheses)

	(1)	(2)	(3)
Lagged count	.123***	.121***	.120***
of ethnic violence	(.019)	(.018)	(.019)
Ln lagged population	−.075***	−.074***	−.075***
size in 1000s (World Bank)	(.014)	(.014)	(.017)
Ln lagged GDP per capita	−.001**	−.001**	−.002***
in 10s (World Bank)	(.000)	(.000)	(.000)
Income inequality	.021	.027*	.024*
(Gini index)	(.012)	(.012)	(.012)
Ethnic fractionalization index	.111	−.114	−.465
(Fearon 2002)	(.440)	(.449)	(.445)
Islamic minority group in	.501**	.560**	.403
non-Islamic country (0,1) (MAR)	(.250)	(.245)	(.252)
Competition over land	.412***	.385***	.355***
during 1980s (MAR)	(.087)	(.087)	(.087)
Resettlement of minority population	.168	.168	.134
during 1980s (MAR)	(.095)	(.094)	(.095)
Televisions per capita	2.60	3.35**	3.29**
	(1.43)	(1.45)	(1.40)
Time trend	.029	.025	.035
	(.030)	(.030)	(.030)
Lagged number of INGO memberships	.001***	.001***	.001***
in 100s	(.000)	(.000)	(.000)
World System Status Measures			
Periphery status	−.277		
	(.274)		
Semi-periphery status		−.204	
		(.235)	
Core status			.954**
			(.350)
Wald chi-square	154.1	154.1	160.1
Number of countries	90	90	90

NOTE: Two-tailed tests of significance reported. * $p < .05$, ** $p < .01$, *** $p < .001$.

artillery, or firebombs, and mob attacks or armed resistance. In addition, my coding scheme required that, in order to be included in the data set, the Reuters reports were required to show distinct evidence that ethnic or racial loyalties primarily motivated the events.

I first constructed a cross-sectional time series data set for 630 cases (7 years × 90 states) to analyze variation across states and over time in a classic panel design. I expected that the disturbance processes (i.e., error terms that are correlated within states across time) would be correlated across state-level observations, due to gradually changing but unobserved characteristics within states. Moreover, I assumed that autocorrelation processes would be strongest in adjacent years and less correlated in distant periods. To examine these assumptions, I experimented with several specifications of the correlation matrix of these unobserved correlations, and found, consistent with other panel models of collective action, that a first-order autocorrelation specification provided a relatively good fit with the data, when compared with other possible specifications (including random effects models and models of unconstrained correlated errors).

In this analysis, I use an estimation procedure that is appropriate for this type of event count analysis, the method of generalized estimation equations (using the XTGEE routine in Stata 8 SE). Because there was evidence of overdispersion, a negative binomial distribution for the dependent variable was modeled (King 1989; Barron 1990, 1992; Barron and Hannan 1991; Long and Freese 2001).

Table 7.3 uses several publicly available measures over time to construct this panel model of violence for 1989–95. In particular, the World Bank Indicators website (www.worldbank.org/data/wdi2005/index.html) offers the excellent and updated measures of population size, GDP per capita, and income inequality (Gini index) used here. Two key measures from the *Minorities at Risk* data set, originally measured at the group level (competition over land, presence of Islamic minority) were aggregated to the country level, indicating whether or not the country experienced any competition among groups during the 1980s, or whether there was an Islamic minority group present in the population of a non-Islamic country. Table 7.3 also includes measures of the two key world system indicators: the number of memberships in INGOs and world system status.

Because information on the dependent variable (counts of violent events involving ethnic groups) was collected from Reuters news service accounts, I suspect that media location and concentration may influence the data in systematic ways that bias the accounts. For example, it seems reasonable that countries with more media outlets, more diffusion of television and/or radio, etc., will generate more "news" and thus report more events as a result. To control for this media bias effect, I also included a measure of the number of television sets per capita in a country for 1990.

We see many similarities to the ethnic rebellion analyses that preceded this one: increased GDP per capita consistently and significantly decreases violence, while competition over land during the 1980s significantly increases violence in all three columns of Table 7.3. There is also some good evidence in support of the claim that income inequality elevates ethnic violence, measured in terms of annual counts of events that were ethnic and violent. Given the predictions by some scholars, the absence of an effect of the time trend in Table 7.3 is interesting. This finding brings into question the conventional view that ethnic violence is a continuing or rising threat to world peace.

Some scholars attribute rising ethnic violence in recent decades to the rising number of conflicts involving Islamic minority populations, as victims, perpetrators, or both. Certainly events in Bosnia, the Middle East, and India would suggest that Islamic religious minorities are associated with higher levels of group conflict (e.g., see Barber 1996; Petersen 2002; Varshney 2002; Toft 2003). Yet few comparative analyses across countries at risk of violence actually exist. Do countries with identifiable religious minorities have more ethnic violence? I explored this question several ways, by including estimates of the size of Christian, non-Christian, and religious-fundamentalist minority populations in a country where the ruling authorities are not Christian, non-Christian, or fundamentalist (Reynal-Querol 2002). Only one of these measures showed significant relationship with ethnic violence. In Table 7.3, the presence of Islamic minorities in a non-Islamic country (e.g, not ruled by Islamic law and leadership) has an impact on violence in all but the last column. While violence and ethnic rebellion are two different dimensions of ethnic mobilization, they are generally positively related to the presence of an Islamic minority in a country. Thus, much of the violence during the 1990s involved Islamic minorities as victims as well as participants in ethnic violence (see Toft 2003). The findings in Table 7.3 suggest that ethnic violence as a distinct label may include more general communal and religious violence (the coding rules included events involving all types of communal markers, including ones that combine religious and ethnic identities).

Turning to the key hypotheses regarding world system measures, we see both similarities and dissimilarities with ethnic rebellion results. First, we see that integration into the network of non-governmental associations significantly raises the number of violent events in a country, net of the effects of income and income inequality, ethnic fractionalization, and population size. This suggests that integration in the world system not only has the by-product of inciting ethnic rebellions that are larger in size and scope, but it also is systematically associated with violence. This finding runs counter to many expectations held by the international relations literature, which has suggested that substantive links among nations act as a constraint on violence within nations, raising the costs of mobilization and especially violent mobilization. At least as measured here among the ninety countries for which these indicators were available over this period, this relationship between international organizational membership and restraint of violence does not seem promising.

The bottom section of Table 7.3 presents somewhat different results regarding world system status and violent events than were presented in the previous table. Specifically, Table 7.2 shows that peripheral countries are significantly more likely to have experienced ethnic rebellion over the 1995–98 period, while this effect appears (weakly) negative in the preceding (1989–95) period. Moreover, although both Tables 7.2 and 7.3 show a positive effect of core position on ethnic violence, this effect is only significant in the event count analysis. While the direction of the effects is similar for semi-periphery and core countries in both tables, the coefficients have opposite signs for the effect of peripheral position. Evidently the effect of peripheral status during 1995–98 was to raise the magnitude of ethnic violence, while there was no significant effect of dependency in the previous time period.

These patterns can be reconciled in at least two ways: (1) these two periods represent a shift in locus of ethnic violence/rebellions, with respect to world system status, and/or (2) ethnic rebellion and counts of ethnic violence measure quite different dimensions of the problem. I take up this debate in the discussion that follows.

Discussion

This chapter draws a broad picture of ethnic mobilization that includes analysis of national and group-level forces that produce sustained ethnic movements ranging from small-scale, sporadic violence to large-scale civil wars based upon ethnic/religious/communal identities. The second analysis focuses only on ethnic violence, and suggests that while ethnic violence occurred with some regularity during the period examined, only a small percentage of groups instigated major rebellions. Moreover, the results for both sets of analyses agree that national economic hardship and histories of territorial struggles raise the rate of ethnic confrontations, but that core nations are at higher risk of violence than are less dominant nations in the world system. Given the different time periods under consideration and the different data structures (cross-sectional versus panel analysis), it is striking that measures of GDP per capita, membership in INGOs, and competition over land had the same effects on ethnic mobilization.

Some differences in the analyses of ethnic rebellion and violence are less easily explained. To be sure, the countries in the data set are not equivalent— data on several countries became available only for the 1995–98 period, and so these countries are not analyzed in the event count analysis. Furthermore, the index constructed from the *Minorities at Risk* data (ranging in scores from 0 to 7) does not neatly map onto exact event counts (country-level counts range from 0 to 96 over 1989–95). For instance, the correlation of the sum of event counts over the 1989–95 period with ethnic rebellion is .07 for 1990–95 and .12 for 1995–98. These correlations suggest that the rebellion index varied independently of the frequency of events generated by these movements. Finally, given the different data structures, should we have expected similar results? From this perspective, there is very little reason to expect identical results. For example, the design is cross-sectional, which aggregates the magnitude of events over time, whereas in the event count analysis we have a longitudinal panel design, which aggregates annual numbers of events.

Is there any way to reconcile the differences in results concerning peripheral and core countries with respect to rebellion and violence? Given the fact that the analyses cover different dimensions and different time periods, it is difficult to assess these differences with certainty. Furthermore, it is not clear that we should expect the patterns to dovetail, because Gurr's ethnic rebellion scale concerns scope rather than levels of violence. Other differences in the findings may be systematically related to differences between cross-sectional and longitudinal analyses, suggesting that the level of aggregation matters (five-year periods compared to annual counts).

Conclusion

What lessons have we learned about ethnic mobilization at the end of the 1990s? One straightforward finding is that integration of the world's states (measured by number of memberships in international organizations) continued to have a decisive impact on more unruly and more violent aspects of ethnic mobilization. This finding deserves attention because it begins to suggest some ways that nationalism, nationalist ideology, and ethnic social movements are causally linked together in the modern world. That is, a key question in the literature on race and ethnic conflict asks why this form of political activity appears to have risen in recent decades. One possibility is that international organizations diffuse information about mobilization forms and content; thus the increasing connections among states have intensified the pace of diffusion of ethnic social movements.

The diffusion imagery attached to the density of international relations helps us understand why nationalist, regional, and ethnic movements invariably make claims that they are "a people." At the minimum, such claims invoke demands for basic civil rights attached to some communal or regional identity, and protests that these claims are not now being met. To the extent to which these social movements demand territorial and/or administrative control, they run the risk of conflict with existing state apparatus.

The findings regarding world system status and ethnic violence also help us in understanding why the countries most active in the international network of economic and power relations are not immune from ethnic challenges. The explanation offered in this book suggests that an ideology of group rights and sovereignty, claims-making activity, leaders, information, and tactics is spread organizationally throughout the world, but the impact of this human rights ideology differs across regions.

The results also suggest several lines of inquiry that address various policy concerns about the nature and remediation of ethnic conflict. The data on ethnic rebellion from the most recent period suggest that as countries become more connected to each other by rapid communication, organizations, diplomatic ties, and regional associations, the pace of ethnic mobilization may not be sustained in the long run in wealthier countries.

Finally, we asked at the outset if the ending of the Cold War substantially changed the nature and character of ethnic rebellions. When comparing the results in this chapter to previous analyses of ethnic rebellion, we find more continuity than discontinuity, despite the fact that state regimes and boundaries have changed in major ways since 1988.

CHAPTER EIGHT

Democracy, Ethnic Violence, and International War

This chapter broadens the scope of this book by considering whether ethnic social movements also encourage outbreaks of civil war and/or international war.[1] The underlying motivation for this analysis comes from research in international relations that suggests that democratic regimes lower the likelihood of involvement in civil war or international war. One common view holds that countries granting more civil rights and other freedoms to minorities will undercut the mobilization potential driving conflicts within and among countries (Gurr 1993). A natural next step in this literature is to ask under what conditions ethnic divisions and turmoil lead to civil and international war.

To motivate my argument, I draw on several leading ideas from the study of social movements to consider how change occurs in political structures of states. This literature draws attention to variation in the levels of openness in a system and variation in participation of ethnic minorities as full citizens in the polity. The key finding from this line of research suggests that democratic regimes and political systems with routinized access to civil rights will experience fewer violent conflicts that rarely erupt into full-scale wars or other conflicts. Moreover, democracy systematically lowers the rate of most types of intergroup and interstate conflict, including ethnic conflict (Sambanis 2001). Countries transformed into democratic polities show substantially reduced inclination toward civil war (Mitchell, Gates, and Hegre 1999). In order to assess claims that ethnicity underlies much of the existing turbulence in the modern world, I compare internal and external sources of group conflicts and their interconnections.

[1] For a review of the conceptual and operational problems involved in defining and measuring civil war, see Sambanis 2004.

Theories that focus attention on causal mechanisms that exert pressures at the global level of analysis link these internal and external forces together in a single narrative. In particular, as globalization has created a number of similarities among local regions, the diffusion of world-level social movements across borders has broadened the scope of local concerns. The research literature suggests that the mobilization of local or communal identities (in the form of cultural nationalism, political nationalism, diaspora movements, and other forms of ethnic mobilization) has become widespread as a consequence (Prazniak and Dirlik 2001).

The intersection of ethnic and nationalist movements with internal civil wars and international wars provides a natural starting point to begin this discussion. Although the similarities and definitions overlap, there are some important distinctions as well. Because ethnic movements often challenge existing regimes based on claims of ethnic sovereignty, discrimination, and non-representation, these claims often bring movements and states into conflict when states deny the validity of these demands. To the extent that powerful, autocratic states successfully resist such challenges, ethnic movements may never surface, despite high levels of mobilization and grievances. Alternatively, weak states may encourage bold challenges, if ethnic leaders perceive weakness and inability of the state authorities to resist challenges. Ethnic identity provides a natural (and low-cost) cleavage ready-made for mobilization, especially when groups can conceivably invoke claims regarding past slights, retaliation, or discrimination (Petersen 2002; Horowitz 2001). To many scholars, it appears that ethnicity underlies many (if not most) of the world's civil wars.

Recent empirical evidence has prompted a reconsideration of this view. For example, Fearon and Laitin (2003) find that ethnic and political grievances are unrelated to outbreaks of civil war: neither language differences nor ethnic divisions appear to raise rates of civil war. Moreover, it is not just "plural" societies (or multinational states) that find themselves plagued by unrest (Toft 2003). Nor does direct evidence of discrimination against ethnic minorities exacerbate the likelihood of civil war (Fearon and Laitin 2003). Grievances do not predict civil war, either ethnic or non-ethnic (Sambanis 2001). While Collier and Hoeffler (2004) find that reliance on primary exports (especially oil) increases the risk of civil war, Fearon (2004, 2005) finds that this effect disappears when state strength is taken into account. Thus, many of the conventional notions about the dangers of ethnicity and war seem unfounded.

Moreover, findings suggest that democracy does not inevitably prevent or even subdue ethnic turmoil (Gurr 1993, 2000; Sambanis 2001, 2004; Regan 2002; Fearon and Laitin 2003). This has led to a new debate over the conventional assumptions that democracy channels and institutionalizes group conflict, undercutting efforts to challenge state authorities in a violent manner. Hence, some have argued that the reverse causal process is equally plausible.[2] Thus, skeptics ask if the relative absence of ethnic violence creates more durable and stable democracies (and not the other way around). If this were the case, then a problem of endogeneity will plague any empirical investigations of these arguments. The fact that endogenous processes are implicated in the analysis of longitudinal event histories of conflict within states having differing institutional structures means that the assumption that democracy is an exogenous characteristic of states should be scrutinized more carefully. The goal of this chapter is to use new information on political regimes, ethnic violence, and civil war to begin to address some of these substantive and methodological issues.

Political Opportunities and Ethnic Violence

Recent advances in political opportunity structure (POS) theory provide the insight that regime types shape mobilization movements that express demands or claims within the political system. As Chapter 3 suggested, exclusionary and inclusionary systems are likely to have vastly different implications for ethnic groups, as they perceive, organize, protest, and otherwise attempt to affect political outcomes. In particular, highly exclusionary systems are also more likely to deploy repressive tactics against ethnic social movements. Because of this, exclusionary countries might be expected to have relatively higher thresholds for mobilization, whereas more democratic and competitive systems have more open opportunity structures that lead to more protest and mobilization.

DEMOCRACY AND CONFLICT

A wide variety of recent studies find that more democratic regimes diminish chances of civil wars, including ethnic ones (Mitchell, Gates, and Hegre 1999; Reynal-Querol 2002; but see also Fearon and Laitin 2003 and Sambanis 2001, 2004). A common argument supporting this finding suggests that

[2]A similar endogeneity argument has been posed for democracy and economic development (see Muller and Weede 1990, among others).

democratic regimes dampen the potentially divisive effect of ethnic diversity and fractionalization, especially when political systems rank high on measures of inclusiveness, such as regularized institutions that are readily available to minority groups, organizational links to the polity, and the presence of a large variety of voting and civil rights. Such findings are consistent with political opportunity structure theories suggesting that political structures that are more open and fluid to demands of various interest groups (including ethnic identity groups) are less fragile and less likely to generate fierce opposition. Kriesi et al. (1995), for example, have argued that pluralistic regimes that are also decentralized can absorb demands from a variety of sources, without resorting to state-sponsored violence, repression, and other means of social control. Such "sponge-like" regimes absorb grievances and channel them, and as a result are likely to experience more (nonviolent) protest but fewer violent challenges to state authority.

Parallel findings reported by Sambanis (2001) and Fearon and Laitin (2003) show that civil wars are a response to general political and economic factors rather than to narrow ethnic issues (such as ethnic diversity, linguistic fractionalization, and other possible sources of group cleavage). Moreover, Reynal-Querol (2002) suggests that religious fractionalization diminishes chances of ethnic war, because where religious cleavages cross-cut ethnic ones, they create the potential for coalitions and political alignments based on extra-ethnic loyalties and identities.

Autocratic Regimes and Conflict

If democratic regimes lower the likelihood of ethnic wars and violence, then do autocratic regimes granting few civil and political rights raise rates of violence? Answering this question is not straightforward, in part because of the complicated role of repression in nondemocratic regimes. State repression is most effective when it is not used, remaining a strong, potent, but unused instrument of state power (and/or terror). In some ways, continuous use of repressive measures signals the weakening of state power. This is because repressive states risk losing international and national legitimacy at the same time that they are bearing the high costs of maintaining elevated levels of police surveillance, troops, intelligence networks, etc. Alternatively, in autocratic states, mobilization may not occur because it ensures a deadly response by authorities. Somewhat paradoxically, while the use of state repression may indicate state failure, the absence of ethnic conflict may not indicate the absence of ethnic tensions.

The implications of change in political opportunities for violent movements are less clear. Previous research suggests that government regimes alternately deploy both repression and reform, and that this vacillation has shown different kinds of effects depending on variation in political structures, economic climates, and mobilization infrastructure of challenging groups (Olzak et al. 2003). For instance, Gamson (1975) contends that government concessions lead to "new advantages" or to "cooptation," and expects both situations to dampen the motivation to protest, especially decreasing activity by radical protest movements (see also Gamson and Meyer 1996). However, Rasler (1996) and Marsh (2001) provide an alternative view that regards government concessions as a sign of increasing political opportunities for protest movements, which would raise the rate of protest. Rasler's (1996) research on Iran supports this argument, suggesting that reforms increased dissent because they sustained the involvement of old participants while convincing bystanders of the rising utility of protest.[3]

Lichbach (1987) provides additional insight into this process by suggesting that the effect of repression depends upon levels of state accommodation to protest movements, arguing that it is the inconsistency of state actions that matters. Moore (1998, 2000) extends these ideas and advances the idea that states vacillate between concession and repression as rational strategies of social control. His findings suggest that accommodation and repression become substitutes for one another, as the state authorities shift from one strategy to the other in response to dissident protest behavior (Moore 2000).

Previous research on government repression also has found that the effects of repression depend upon the political context, the resources and relative strength of protest movements, regime stability and strength, and public support of movement activities. Initially, social movement theorists hypothesized that the effects of repression were likely to be curvilinear (e.g., Tilly 1978, among others). This argument holds that the rate of protest would decline at both very high and very low levels of repression and that shifts away from either extreme would increase protest. On the other hand, by distinguishing between the effects of different levels and types of repression

---

[3] See also Olzak et al. (2003) for analysis showing a positive effect of reforms on the rate of anti-apartheid protest in South Africa.

on diverse forms of racial collective action in South Africa, Olivier (1989, 1990) finds that the effect of repression depended on the type of force used by the South African state against protesters. Specifically, Olivier finds that nonviolent protest increased significantly at very high numbers of detentions, but decreased when South African police had used physical violence at prior protests (Olivier 1989; but see Olzak and Olivier 1999). Alternatively, Gupta, Singh, and Sprague (1993) contend that the effects of repression vary by regime type, economic conditions, and ideological orientation of the state. Their results suggest that government repression provokes a higher level of protest demonstrations in democratic countries, but that extreme levels of repression decrease dissident activities in nondemocratic states, because protest becomes too costly (Davenport 1995; Gupta et al. 1993).

Differential policies and treatments regarding official minority populations add complicating dimensions to the study of the impact of repression and reform. Perceptions of fairness and justness of government acts are key determinants of compliance with (or resistance to) government policies (Levi 1997), and such perceptions are often shaped by specific group identities, and reified by institutional labels such as the official terms "Coloured" in South Africa and "nonwhite" in the United States census. Recent theories of ethnic collective action have suggested that when civil rights are applied on the basis of ethnic/racial identities, mobilization is most likely to happen along these boundaries (Koopmans and Statham 1999; Koopmans and Olzak 2004; Olzak and Olivier 1999; Cornell and Hartmann 1998; Marx 1998).

Altogether this discussion suggests the hypotheses that (1) *political regimes that fall at the extremes of the democratic and autocracy scales will deter ethnic violence and internal violence*, and (2) *political regimes that place more restrictions on civil rights will have higher rates of ethnic violence and internal civil war, all else being equal.*

Civil Wars and Ethnic Conflict

Study of the nexus of civil wars, revolutionary coups, uprisings, and ethnic conflict has been difficult for a number of reasons, including, most predominantly, the endogeneity of causes. A variety of feedback loops often present serious obstacles for researchers wanting to make causal inferences, in addition to having flawed indicators, or relying on cross-sectional data that masks temporal relationships. Furthermore, until recently, few large-scale data sets have been both reliable and easily available. Fortunately for scholars and policy analysts alike, the research environment on social and political indicators has blossomed, in terms of newly available data and methods. Research on the ethnic bases of civil wars has suggested that while civil wars seem to be associated with ethnic divisions, few measures of ethnic fragmentation and/or linguistic heterogeneity seem to be associated with a higher risk of non-ethnic civil wars (Sambanis 2001). Such results are puzzling and require more careful analysis comparing these forms of conflict. Thus, it seems important to analyze ethnic strife separately from other non-ethnic forms of rebellion, as has been done here.

In particular, Sambanis (2001: 272) defines non-ethnic civil wars as "wars aimed at securing power for a new elite or the acquisition of control of economic resources [and] territories." The differences between causes of non-ethnic and ethnic civil wars reported in Sambanis's (2001) analysis of over 160 countries are intriguing. Non-ethnic civil wars are more likely to be associated with poorer economic performance, and unassociated with ethnic linguistic fractionalization, democracy, and the peak period of Cold War tensions. On the other hand, Sambanis finds that the rate of ethnic war rises with net changes in the direction of more democratic regimes and with increasing ethnic heterogeneity (but see Fearon and Laitin 2003).

Studies examining theories of civil war range broadly and include measures associated with modernization and the displacement of traditional regimes, loyalties, and groups. These indicators, sometimes referred to as "social mobilization indicators," include high literacy rates, high educational levels, and the expansion of women's rights (Deutsch 1953). Such forces actively coordinate and facilitate ethnic mobilization among groups in which trust has been established, raising both the rates of cooperation and the risk of high levels of ethnic violence (Fearon and Laitin 1996). Finally, some of the economic literature points to reliance on specific exports, including the presence of oil as a key trade export. In some theories, high export benefits and high income inequality in a country encourage widespread corruption and graft among officials. These conditions tend to increase benefits attached to "greed" (which encourages civil war), and decrease benefits attached to political horse trading and negotiation (which would decrease the likelihood of civil war) (Collier et al. 2001). As Collier et al. and Collier and Hoeffler (2004) explain, once insurgency is under way, the temptation for warlords to loot natural resources becomes irresistible. These economic theories have thus been able to explain the apparently paradoxical finding that while civil war is associated with more poverty, richer nations (and nations that specialize in oil exports) may also experience relentless wars (Fearon and Laitin 2003; Fearon 2005).

Other researchers have argued that linguistic fragmentation plays an important role in determining ethnic civil war (but not revolutionary war) (Sambanis 2001). The explanations for these findings tend to emphasize the fact that fragmentation along ethnic lines increases the demands for ethnic resources at the same time that fragmentation increases the costs of coordination and control for the state. Either way, in this view, the state's costs rise with ethnic heterogeneity. Others have instead suggested that religious fragmentation is more divisive than ethnic diversity because (1) religious identity generally precludes multiple affiliations and participation (but a single ethnic identity can be constructed from populations speaking multiple languages or within a population including people with diverse national origins), and thus (2) religious identity is more exclusive than inclusive, marking large differences in world views and cultural explanations of external events (Reynal-Querol 2002). Elbadawi and Sambanis (2002) specify cross-cutting cleavages using an interaction term calculated as the product of religious and linguistic fragmentation indices. They argue that this interaction effect should dampen the rate of internal civil wars. Although they do not find support for this claim, the cross-cutting religious and ethnic cleavage argument remains an intriguing one because it seeks to identify the source of mobilization in structural boundaries and identity politics.

Democratic polities have usually been linked to lower rates of civil war, especially in analyses that control for wealth, primary export concentration, and a number of other key variables associated with core country dominance and centrality. However, Elbadawi and Sambanis (2002) do not find a strong effect of democratic political regimes, when controlling for complications due to endogenous processes. Democratic institutions are likely dependent on economic growth and institutional routines, which provide buffers against internal strife (Collier et al. 2001; Fearon and Laitin 2003). Democratic regimes also have a number of safety valves, including (usually by definition) a number of routes of access for expressing political demands and choices more freely than in nondemocratic regimes. In their two-stage least squares analysis that attempts to control for the simultaneity of some of these processes, it is interesting that Elbadawi and Sambanis (2002) do not find strong effects of prior democratic regimes. It seems apparent that the once-accepted association of democratic polities with lower rates of civil war may require further analysis.

Finally, Fearon (2004), Regan (2002), and others ask what causes civil war to persist over longer rather than shorter time periods. Using proportional hazard analysis, Regan (2002) analyzes more than 150 conflicts that occurred between 1945 and 1999 and finds that third-party interventions prolong civil wars.[4] Contrary to the predictions of many international politics theories, third-party interventions complicate negotiations, fund and supply armies, and lend legitimacy to conflicts that might be contained within states. Some scholars find that the effect of third-party interventions on the duration of civil wars intensified during the Cold War (Hironaka 2005). However, Regan (2002) finds that the duration of civil war is reduced if third parties intervene in favor of opposition or regime authorities, but duration increases when the intervening third parties are "neutral" (not affiliated with either side in a civil war conflict).

The diffusion literature carries this point one step further by suggesting that geographic regions provide loci for intensifying conflicts, as the number of groups and ties among combatants escalates. Such arguments suggest that there are strong spillover effects from neighboring countries (Regan and Abouharb 2002). It seems reasonable that such spillover effects provide access and opportunity to kindred groups within neighboring countries, as combatants, arms, and ammunition are exchanged most easily across adjoining borders. Thus, I include measures of civil violence in bordering countries in my models of ethnic and civil wars.

Following this literature, I expect that *internal war will share many of the same economic and political causal factors with ethnic violence*, even though *ethnic fractionalization will not raise rates of ethnic violence and internal war*. In particular, I expect that smaller and poorer countries, countries more embedded in the world system, and countries granting fewer civil rights will have more ethnic violence and a higher level of internal civil war. I also expect that international and interstate war will increase along with the incidence of civil violence in neighboring countries.

---

[4]See also Box-Steffensmeir, Reiter, and Zorn (2003), Varshney (2003), Fearon (2004), and Hironaka (2005).

Political Regimes: Polity IV Data

Ted Gurr and his associates some time ago compiled a major cross-national data set (Gurr, 1990) that aimed at producing a comprehensive data set that chronicled a number of key dimensions of political authority structures— weak or strong, authoritarian or democratic, competitive or pre-ordained, monopolistic or inclusive, and so on. Since the first publication of these Polity measures (see Gurr 1990), there have been considerable improvements in the data, and new researchers (Marshall and Jaggers 2005) have made a fourth version of this data easily accessible to scholars interested in capturing key dimensions of democratic state theory.

Efforts to compile this encyclopedic data set were motivated by a number of factors, both methodological and theoretical. First, as many scholars doing cross-national research consistently find, existing measures of state structures or regime durability are not only vastly incompatible from study to study, but they lack internal consistency and validity over time. Thus, democracy in one period cannot easily be compared to the meaning, activities, and institutionalization of democracy in the same country ten or fifteen years later. Second, the Polity compilers tackled a key definitional problem that has plagued comparative research from its inception. This is the problem of the multidimensionality of core concepts in political science and political sociology: What exactly is "democracy," and how do the different aspects of democracy relate to one another? The researchers assembling this data confront the multidimensional nature of central theoretical concepts of authoritarian (or autocratic) regimes, democratic regimes, and legitimacy directly by first unpacking these ideas into their composite areas of authority: judicial, executive, and legislative. Marshall and Jaggers (2005) conceptualize democracy in terms of high levels of competitiveness in political participation (in contrast to one-party domination), high levels of diversity in recruitment, retention, and openness in positions of elite authority, and high levels of institutionalized limits on executive authority. These dimensions are useful because they allow different branches of government activity to be coded separately, which allows us more flexibility in operationalizing concepts of democracy. Democracy, in other words, is a variable.

I use the Polity IV data in two different analyses here. First, I examine to what extent political structures shape the magnitude of ethnic violence in recent decades. The second analysis uses measures of democracy and autocracy to examine their impact on civil wars (internal challenges to state regimes), interstate wars (between two or more states), and international wars (internal wars that involve third-party states). While there are many theories that suggest that "weak" or "ineffective" states are unable to contain and control their populations, which necessarily leads to fragmentation and conflict (see, e.g., Hironaka 2005), it is equally likely that prior mobilization weakens otherwise stable states. It is important therefore to analyze these questions using a longitudinal framework that can begin to untangle these mutually reinforcing processes.

There are several well-known shortcomings to using the Polity IV measures for democratic and autocratic regimes—problems related to the fact that a large number of countries have undergone substantial changes and periods of "interruption" in regime authority. In the original Polity data (Gurr 1990), these interruptions are coded (-66) if a country's political regime has been interrupted (often due to foreign occupation), (-77) for periods of complete collapse of central political authority (usually due to military intervention), or (-88) for a transition period, in which new institutions are being planned and organized, constitutional conventions called together, etc. The problem arises because these codes become "missing data" points when an analysis attempts to use them. After considering several possible alternatives (including, coding these interruption intervals to zero, or creating a second "interruption" dummy variable—see Fearon and Laitin 2003), I decided to follow a mixed strategy suggested by Elbadawi and Sambanis (2002). In their analysis, a comparison of various solutions to dealing with "interruptions" led them to implement a method of averaging index levels for regime types using information from the five-year period preceding each interruption. Following this logic, the transition periods become average extensions of past regimes and their legacies, rather than building in substantial shifts that would occur if these periods were set to zero (which would mean recording a large shift from levels of -6 or -7 to 0, for example, in East Germany over this period, as it evolved from East Germany into part of the new entity of unified Germany).

My own analysis showed substantial differences in the patterns of effects found for levels of autocracy and democracy when using five-year averages compared to using a method that omits all transition intervals. However, the main effects of income levels and integration into the world system did not differ when using "0" or five-year averages. As might be expected, both newly emergent countries and former Soviet-bloc countries generated a major source of transitions. Careful consideration of the types of regimes, elites, and other continuities in these countries suggests a combined strategy that (1) uses the Elbadawi and Sambanis (2002) method of coding these "transition" periods as a continuation of past and present regime types, and (2) constructs a dummy variable indicating that a country's political regime had experienced major "disruptions" or a "breakdown of authority." Further support for this strategy is that it is a preferred interpretation stated in the Polity IV codebook.

A second research decision involved the question of whether to combine the "polity" scores (as Elbadawi and Sambanis 2002 have done) or to treat the scales of "democracy" and "autocracy" as independent scales. While there is no correct answer (because the solution depends on the research goals and questions), in this analysis I have specific hypotheses about the relationship of autocratic and democratic regimes that suggest that ethnic movements are shaped by specific substantive characteristics of each of these two scales. Thus, I would not expect the effects to be simply mirror images of one another. Moreover, it seems problematic to combine an autocracy–democracy scale into a single dimension, a priori, without examining this assumption empirically over a long period of time. To draw comparisons with earlier work, I begin the analysis with two measures that have been used in other analyses with success.

I offer two sets of analyses. The first seeks to answer the question of whether or not types of political regimes that are more and less inclusive with respect to political and civil rights affect the incidence of ethnic violence. The second task explores the relationship between ethnic violence and outbreaks of different types of (non-ethnic) internal, interstate, and international wars. While some scholars have suggested that ethnic violence lies behind most if not all civil wars and other serious challenges to state authority (e.g., Sambanis 2001, 2004), others disagree (e.g., Fearon 2004). Fearon (2004, 2005) and Fearon and Laitin (2003) suggest that civil wars are fundamentally unrelated to ethnic mobilization; their research finds that local ethnic entrepreneurs and warlords, representing economically driven movements, spur ethnic movements. According to this view, rural warlords exploit grievances among poor populations having relatively low access to military posts and mobility. Geographically, such movements are likely to flourish among groups based in rough and mountainous terrain where it is easy to mount challenges to and difficult to defend state control.

Until recently, it has not been possible to examine the connections among different types of international and internal wars, ethnic movements, and regime stability. With access to more appropriate longitudinal and international data, and new methods for exploring different levels of war involvement, these questions can be answered more precisely.

Armed Conflict Data Set, 1946–1999

A wide variety of cross-national data sets containing information on armed conflicts and war have been analyzed by many scholars, including the most widely cited, the Correlates of War (COW) data set (Singer and Small 1994; www.correlatesofwar.org), and the more recent State Failure data set (see Goldstone et al. 2000; www.cidcm.umd.edu/inscr/stfail), which builds on the same set of criteria for a variety of different types of state failure outcomes (these range from state failure related to overthrow of a government, to peaceable evolution to democracy, as well as other forms of regime change). As many have noted, the COW data have a number of virtues, including straightforward definitions and operationalizations of key outcome measures and reliability across studies, which facilitates comparison of the findings. However, there are several shortcomings of these two key data sets (which are themselves related). These limitations include the facts that (1) an event requires a minimum of 1000 battle deaths in order to be classified as a war, and (2) to be included in the data sets, conflicts had to show evidence of at least 1000 participants (defined as armed insurgents, demonstrators, and/or troops). As this last definition implies, the coding rules for the COW project and the State Failure project conflate government-sponsored violence and challenger-instigated violence (and this difference may not be easily sorted out in the existing data sets). Finally, definitions of "ethnic wars" tend to rely only on anti-state activity, rather than inter-ethnic conflict. The data sets that result from using this method can yield relatively low numbers of event counts, hampering the application of many useful statistical techniques and estimation methods that require larger event counts.

To begin addressing some of these issues (most notably the problems associated with the Correlates of War restrictive threshold of counting only wars with 1000 or more battle deaths), Nils Petter Gleditsch, Håvard Strand,

Mikael Eriksson, Margareta Solleberg, and Peter Wallensteen (2001) created the Uppsala data set on armed conflict, which uses a 25-casualty threshold for defining war.[5] These scholars point out that, in contrast to the COW data, this lower threshold implies that conflicts such as the Catholic–Protestant violence in Northern Ireland (in which combined deaths were more than 1000 over a decade, but rarely exceeded 1000 at any one event) could be included in the analysis, whereas a higher threshold might exclude these obviously relevant events (e.g., see Sambanis 2004.) The advantage of using these data is that conflicts can be analyzed and compared with the ethnic violence count data obtained from the PANDA event data set (using information published by Reuters, 1988–95).

N. Gleditsch et al. (2001: 5) define an armed conflict as "a contested incompatibility that concerns government or territory or both where the use of armed force between two parties results in at least 25 battle-related deaths." Of the two parties, at least one is the government of the state. Further, a state is defined as a sovereign entity whose boundaries and authority are internationally recognized and not disputed by another sovereign entity. An ordinal scale of magnitude of conflict yields three quantified categories: minor (at least 25 battle deaths, but fewer than 1000 for the entire course of the conflict), intermediate level (at least 25 battle deaths per year, and an accumulated total of 1000 deaths for the entire course of the conflict), and large (at least 1000 battle deaths per year). The flexibility of these data is further enhanced by the researchers' commitment to update the data annually (published in an issue of the *Journal of Peace Research*). Moreover, research on armed conflict and collective violence is often plagued by the fact that violence by instigators and state authorities often cannot be distinguished. In the Uppsala data set, the addition of a specific location code allows researchers to distinguish involvement in conflict from the location of conflict, with respect to a specific country. Thus, these data represent a significant advance over the COW data set.

More specific kinds of war-related conflict are coded into three different types: internal conflict, defined as conflict between a government of a state and internal opposition groups; interstate conflict, or conflict between two or

[5] See the *Armed Conflict Dataset Codebook* (Strand, Carlsen, Gleditsch, Hegre, Ormgaug, and Wilhelmsen 2003, 2005). These data are available online at www.prio.no/page/CSCW_research_detail/Programme_detail_CSCW/9649/45925.html (accessed November 21, 2004).

more states; and international conflict, in which a government meets internal opposition and confronts external state intervention by a third-party state or states.

An important piece of information to note here is that the Uppsala data set's definition of internal conflict would logically include ethnic violence, if the ethnic violence was directed against the state and met the criterion of 25 battle deaths. This means that some ethnic and non-ethnic wars are included in the index of internal war. Thus, the Uppsala data provide a nice comparison with the PANDA data set, which is restricted to ethnic contention (among different ethnic groups or with state authorities).[6]

Analysis of Ethnic Violence

Turning to the analysis of ethnic violence and political regimes from 1989–95, the results in Table 8.1 are remarkably consistent with those reported in Chapter 7. Each of the four models in Table 8.1 adds political characteristics of regimes in separate models containing measures of democracy, autocratic regimes, civil rights restrictions, the spread of violence from bordering states, and periods indicating the interruption of authority.

The results are strikingly similar to those shown in Chapter 7, which analyzed the effects of economic and political factors on the magnitude of ethnic violence using the MAR data. Table 8.1 shows how smaller countries and poorer countries experience higher rates of ethnic violence, while ethnic fractionalization has no effect on the number of violent ethnic events. As seen in Chapter 7, resettlement of minority populations and history of competition over land among minority groups raises the rate of ethnic violence across all specifications, net of the effects of regime types. Examination of the impact of religious fractionalization on all four models shown in Table 8.1 reveals no systematic effect on ethnic violence. It is revealing that one measure of political opportunity (level of autocracy) is negatively and

---

[6]For comparison purposes, I derived an estimate of "non-ethnic internal wars" by subtracting the number of ethnic wars (from the PANDA data set) from the relevant category of all "internal wars" in the Uppsala data set. This yielded a rough indication of the level of internal conflict not based on ethnic identity. I then compared the results using the new ethnic and non-ethnic internal war categories, by re-running the results shown in Tables 8.2 and 8.3. With one important exception, there were no differences in the results. This exception is that prior ethnic violence had *no* effect on non-ethnic violence in the following year.

TABLE 8.I

Effects of Political Structure on Annual Counts of Ethnic Violence,
1989–1995 (robust standard errors in parentheses)

	(1)	(2)	(3)	(4)
Constant	2.21	2.55	2.08	1.52
	(1.70)	(1.65)	(1.93)	(2.02)
Lagged count	.126***	.128***	.127***	.126***
of ethnic violence	(.023)	(.023)	(.024)	(.025)
Ln lagged population size	−.073***	−.073***	−.074***	−.077***
in 1000s	(.018)	(.018)	(.019)	(.018)
Ln lagged GDP per capita	−.328	−.315	−.297	−.232
	(.174)	(.174)	(.193)	(.208)
Ethnic fractionalization	−.142	−.131	−.078	−.409
index (Fearon 2002)	(.468)	(.451)	(.480)	(.506)
Religious fractionalization	−.001	−.001	−.004	−.003
(Reynal-Querol 2002)	(.007)	(.006)	(.007)	(.007)
Resettlement of minority	.262**	.253**	.277*	.281**
population during 1980s (MAR)	(.105)	(.103)	(.113)	(.100)
Competition for land during	.351**	.332***	.371**	.372**
1980s (MAR)	(.116)	(.111)	(.129)	(.120)
Time trend	.010	.006	.016	.021
	(.027)	(.028)	(.027)	(.028)
Lagged number of INGO	.001***	.001***	.001***	.001***
memberships (Hironaka 2000)	(.000)	(.000)	(.000)	(.000)
Periphery status	−.592	−.594	−.546	−.423
	(.395)	(.373)	(.406)	(.402)
Political Structure				
Democratic regime (Polity IV)	.056			
(scale 0–10)	(.031)			
Autocratic regime (Polity IV)		−.080*		
(scale 0–10)		(.036)		
Lagged restrictions on civil rights			.001	
(none = 0 to many = 7)			(.072)	
(Freedom House 2002)				
Number of border states with major				.094
violence (State Failure, phase III)				(.120)
Interruption of authority	.944*	.948*	.867*	.648
(0,1) (Polity IV)	(.371)	(.382)	(.353)	(.437)
Total countries	121	121	119	118

NOTE: Two-tailed tests of significance reported. * $p < .05$, ** $p < .01$, *** $p < .001$.

significantly related to ethnic violence. Thus, a key hypothesis about the effects of political liberties and the politics of exclusion finds no support in Table 8.1.

Earlier chapters found that evidence supports the world polity approach, suggesting that, as an ideology of human rights diffused broadly across countries (from the core to the periphery), states that grant formal recognition to specific racial or ethnic populations (in terms of territorial rights, administrative control, special language rights, etc.) run the risk of encouraging ethnic politics based upon these boundaries. Similarly, I argued that policies that specifically excluded populations from citizenship participation would create the potential for mobilization against these rules. The reasoning for the latter argument is based upon the idea that regimes that do not uphold egalitarian rights with formal inclusionary laws and policies will come to be seen as illegitimate and unacceptable. Thus, countries that formally incorporate ethnic groups into the polity and countries that exclude ethnic populations will be more likely to encourage ethnic mobilization than will countries that incorporate citizenship on some other basis (see Table 1.1 in Chapter 1).

Following the analysis presented in Chapter 4, I calculated two dummy variables to indicate (1) formal recognition of group rights, and (2) political exclusion of specific minority groups in the state. As I had in Chapter 4, I used the *Minorities at Risk* data set measures of formal recognition and exclusion, which defined a number of different categories of exclusion and special status rights granted to specific minorities. I analyzed the effect of two measures (formal recognition and formal exclusion) over the 1988–95 period: the existence of special recognition of rights, and whether or not any minority group was excluded from participation in a country. Unlike the analysis from the period prior to the end of the Cold War, this one found no effect of these measures for the post–Cold War period, net of the effects of democracy and autocratic regimes seen in Table 8.1.

However, during this period, ethnic violence appears to follow periods of state transition. Three of the rows in the bottom section of Table 8.1 examine the impact of different regime types, coded from Polity IV measures, along with an indicator that equals one for "period interruptions" and zero otherwise, as outlined above. Rather than code periods of regime interruption as qualitatively different, I (1) divide the information on five-year averages in democracy and autocracy and (2) add a separate measure indicating regime breakdown or transition. Thus, the impact of autocratic (or democratic) regimes and their breakdown can be examined simultaneously (see Elbadawi and Sambanis 2002 for a similar strategy).

The results are intriguing in part because they do not fit easily with conventional expectations from the literature about the power of democratic regimes. First, and most importantly, democratic regimes did not systematically prevent ethnic violence during 1989–95. During this period, not only did a large number of new states become viable political entities, these states tended to have relatively higher scores on the autocracy scale. In the view of some scholars, ethnic tensions should therefore have erupted at the end of Soviet control, perhaps threatening the chances for peaceful transition to democracy in those newly emerging countries. In columns 1–3, Table 8.1 shows evidence supporting the expectation that interruption of authority sparks ethnic violence.

The literature on autocratic regimes suggests that nondemocratic regimes suppress all forms of civil society, including rights to express ethnic grievances, to protest, and to organize for making demands on the part of subordinated groups. Such a view suggests that ethnic violence would be suppressed in more autocratic regimes. Column 2 of Table 8.1 supports the view that autocratic regimes have significantly lower rates of ethnic violence, and those regimes that became more autocratic over this period had significantly diminished rates.

Countries granting few civil rights did not experience more ethnic violence. This finding runs counter to a number of popular social movement theories. For instance, consider the view proposed in Chapter 1, that ethnic social movements are fundamentally organized around a set of claims based in group discrimination and denial of rights of sovereignty, citizenship, and/or other political rights. Grievance models of mobilization would argue that although ethnic movements are more likely to be repressed in autocratic regimes, when grievances reach some untenable level, ethnic violence will erupt. Column 3 in the lower portion of Table 8.1 shows that countries that restrict civil rights for at least some of their citizens are not significantly more likely to experience higher rates of ethnic violence, controlling for a number of economic and ethnic diversity characteristics. In other words, the absence of political liberties does not produce more violent ethnic social movements.

In the bottom part of Table 8.1, column 4 shows that the number of neighboring states with civil violence (including both ethnic and non-ethnic forms) had no systematic effect on the rate of ethnic violence over this period. This indicator specifically measures the geographical vulnerability that comes from being surrounded by violence (from the State Failure data set). However, previous eruptions of ethnic violence did increase subsequent ones, as measured by annual counts of ethnic violence in Table 8.1. In each column, annual memberships in INGOs systematically raised rates of ethnic violence, as did previous resettlement policies and competition for land. The pattern of results suggests that ethnic violence is most sensitive to internal characteristics and histories of discrimination and poverty, but that it is also shaped by international links in the form of INGO memberships.

Evidently, periods of regime transition and breakdown also fuel ethnic conflicts, an effect seen even when controlling for the democratic or autocratic nature of the political regime (in columns 1 and 2). That is, net of the effect of low levels of civil rights, countries that experience substantial transitions in regime types have higher rates of ethnic conflict. Examination of the reverse causation process was revealing here: using two-stage least squares analysis, we find no relationship of ethnic conflict with these breakdowns, once other factors (especially economic ones) are taken into account. The political process of breakdown appears more relevant to ethnic conflict than do political grievances.

Relationship Between Ethnic Violence and War

Scholars have claimed that ethnic violence motivates and prolongs the majority of contemporary outbreaks of internal and international wars (e.g., Gurr 1993, 2000; but see Gurr and Moore 1986; Fearon and Laitin 1996). Yet evidence given in support of this claim has been ambiguous, partly because internal war and ethnic violence overlap in complicated and time-dependent ways, so that early conflicts that are not easily contained often become the subsequent bases of full-blown civil wars, making the links seem more directional than they might actually be if analyzed over time. Thus, it is important to (1) measure the impact of previous ethnic violence on internal civil wars, in an effort to untangle the causal relationships, and (2) analyze these processes over time, as they unfold and change character.

Table 8.2 addresses this relationship in three columns that distinguish ethnic and non-ethnic wars (internal war), wars between two states (interstate war), and civil wars that also engage external sovereign states in a given

TABLE 8.2

Democratic Regimes, Ethnic Violence, and War, 1989–1995, Ordinal Logit Models (robust standard errors in parentheses)

	Internal War	Interstate War	International War
Lagged count	.281***	−.071	.230***
of ethnic violence	(.082)	(.062)	(.058)
Ln lagged population size	.007	.082*	−.063**
in 1000s (World Bank)	(.017)	(.039)	(.020)
Ln lagged GDP per capita	−1.31***	.201	−.586
(World Bank)	(.364)	(.331)	(.749)
Ethnic fractionalization	1.56	1.01	4.11**
index (Fearon 2002)	(.863)	(.591)	(1.63)
Religious fractionalization	−.033**	−.024*	−.008
index (Reynal-Querol 2002)	(.010)	(.011)	(.010)
Resettlement of minority	.367*	−.010	−.126
population during 1980s (MAR)	(.166)	(.155)	(.348)
Competition for land	.179	.065	.168
during 1980s (MAR)	(.164)	(.161)	(.399)
Time trend	−.142**	−.319***	−.447
	(.049)	(.058)	(.314)
Lagged number of INGO	.000	.001**	−.002
memberships (Hironaka 2000)	(.000)	(.000)	(.002)
Periphery status	−.760	.336	−2.54*
	(.671)	(.510)	(1.18)
Political Opportunity Structure			
Democratic regime scale (Polity IV)	−.044	−.038	−.093
(scale 0–10)	(.057)	(.050)	(.135)
Number of border states with major	−.041	.392**	.301
violence (State Failure, phase III)	(.155)	(.126)	(.252)
Wald chi-square	73.25	85.23	117.9
Number of observations	900	900	900

NOTE: In all models, the parameter for the lagged dependent variable is set to 1.0. Two-tailed tests of significance reported. * $p < .05$, ** $p < .01$, *** $p < .001$.

country location (international war). The key finding from this table supports the hypothesis that lagged counts of ethnic violence have a systematic effect on the magnitude of war (see also Sambanis 2001). Evidently the relationship between ethnic violence and the outbreak of serious internal and external war is not spurious, nor is it muted by including a number of economic and cultural factors, which also shape the nature and seriousness of both types of conflict.

The results for internal war in the first column show a striking similarity in the pattern of effects found for ethnic conflicts (compare the first column in Table 8.2 to column 1 in Table 8.1). The findings reflect those from earlier chapters, suggesting strong parallels between ethnic mobilization and internal civil war. First, the pattern of results suggests that a strong similarity exists among the causal mechanisms producing ethnic violence, ethnic protest, and internal war. For instance, low per capita income and resettlement of minorities encourage both internal wars and ethnic violence, net of the effect of prior ethnic violence. Second, there is a positive relationship between previous levels of ethnic violence (measured by event counts in Table 8.1) and the magnitude of internal war (in Table 8.2). This finding suggests that ethnic violence provokes substantially higher levels of civil war (see also Hironaka 2005).

Previous chapters have also offered several arguments about the relationship between a country's integration into the world system (measured by increasingly high memberships in INGOs) and ethnic violence. I found positive and significant effects for the number of memberships in INGOS on ethnic violence (for various years) in Tables 7.3, 6.3, and 5.3. And in virtually every specification in Table 8.1, countries that have more international organizational ties also experience more ethnic violence. However, this same measure of embeddedness does not appear to raise rates of other types of war, and the measure is only significant for the models of interstate war in the middle column of Table 8.2. This, too, suggests that a similar dynamic may be at work between internal ethnic violence and interstate wars (see also Sambanis 2001; Elbadawi and Sambanis 2002). To understand this similarity, we have to take into account the effect of violence occurring in bordering countries. That is, the middle column of Table 8.2 tells us that interstate wars are more severe in states deeply embedded in the network of international social movement organizations and in states where violence occurs on their borders. Both of these contingent patterns highlight the fact that a variety of international ties have had immediate effects on the stability within countries in recent decades.

The political opportunity structure (POS) measures first test the classic argument from the international relations literature that democratic polities are less likely to experience major wars. Although this argument seems reasonable, and is often used as a justification for entering wars, there is little evidence from this historical period that supports this claim. While the relationship is generally negative, it is not significant, once economic factors are taken into account.

Although there is no evidence showing a consistent relationship between democracy and ethnic violence, autocratic regimes act as a powerful deterrent to ethnic violence. Autocratic regimes suppress, deter, or submerge ethnic violence significantly more than do less autocratic regimes, according to the analysis shown in Table 8.1. Neither democratic nor autocratic regimes influenced internal, interstate, and international war (only the model including democratic regime scales are shown). The patterns in Tables 8.1 and 8.2 run counter to many theories of international politics.

Problems of Endogeneity

As discussed and analyzed in the previous chapter, there are several reasons to treat with caution the absence of results for an effect of democracy on ethnic violence. A key problem in analyzing the role of democratic institutions on the outbreak of ethnic violence and war is the obvious one of endogeneity (e.g., see Elbadawi and Sambanis 2002; Sambanis 2004). That is, democracy may indeed prevent civil wars, but the reverse causation is equally valid, as war certainly inhibits the smooth functioning of democratic institutions.

Such reasoning calls for more analysis. Using several well-known techniques for analyzing the impact of simultaneous causation (and multiple feedback loops) I conducted a number of tests to find out if endogeneity affected my results. First, I used instrumental variables analysis, specifying an equation regressing geographical region, lagged democratic polity, and political and civil rights on a democratic political regime scale. Then, in the second stage, I used the instrumented variable, and found no relationship with ethnic violence. I also conducted residual analysis, creating a "democratic polity" residual that was then entered into the same models as reported in Table 8.2. This measure also had no significant effect, indicating that there is weak evidence supporting an endogeneity argument. Finally, I examined the plots of the residuals over time, to see if any patterns could be detected that might influence these relationships, and was relieved to see relatively random distributions. As Elbadawi and Sambanis (2002) point out, this investigation does not mean that endogeneity can be rejected, given the fact that others have found evidence for such a link. Yet, using the same method as these authors, I found that the fitted values of the lag of the level of democracy in the polity also showed no relationship with war prevalence.

While the evidence suggests that, over the period examined, democratic regimes do not systematically diminish the prevalence of war, there is evidence for spillover effects of violence in neighboring countries on interstate war. Stepping back from the details, this pattern makes sense, given the definition of interstate war as conflict between two countries (as opposed to conflict that is internally driven). Thus, forms of conflict between state actors are deeply influenced by the rates of conflict that surround those same actors.

When I examined the effects of periods of interruption on all three forms of war conflicts, I found that internal interruptions had no independent effect on non-ethnic civil war, interstate war, or international war. It seems more likely that the causation goes the other way—that international wars often produce internal state disintegration. However, there is still room for skepticism, as the analysis may not be capturing the timing of such dynamics correctly, since the analysis covers a relatively brief (but highly volatile) seven-year period.[7] It is interesting, however, to take note of the absence of effects of regime interruptions on international and civil war with their more systematic positive effect on ethnic violence, as can be seen in Table 8.1. One plausible interpretation of these results suggests support for the "greed" hypothesis that weak and unstable regimes present opportunities for ethnic warlords to incite violence (Hironaka 2005; Collier and Hoeffler 2004).

War and Restrictions on Civil Rights

The results of the preceding analysis show that the pace of ethnic violence is lower in more autocratic countries, bringing into question the assertion that grievances fueled by demands for more civil rights form the basis of ethnic social movements. Are civil wars also motivated by an absence of civil rights, or do autocratic regimes influence the likelihood of civil wars independently of civil liberties? While these measures are likely to be associated, it seems important to begin to tease out the relative weight of these factors on various forms of internal and international conflict.

---

[7] For these reasons, it seems reasonable to explore these issues using the event count data (rather than the armed conflict data), because the ethnic events data can be arrayed over a longer time period. In Chapter 9, I analyze a number of additional specifications of endogeneity and other sources of estimation problems.

Denial of civil liberties appears to fuel internal civil wars, even though this same measure was not associated with ethnic violence. Turning to the evidence in Table 8.3 (in contrast to Table 8.1), we find that countries that grant relatively few civil rights to their citizenry experience more severe internal wars. However, interstate and international conflicts are not influenced by an absence of civil rights in countries that participate in such conflicts. Why would this be the case?

TABLE 8.3

Civil Rights, Ethnic Violence, and War, 1984–1995, Ordinal Logit Models (robust standard errors in parentheses)

	Internal War	Interstate War	International War
Lagged count	.277***	−.083	.221***
of ethnic violence	(.078)	(.063)	(.053)
Ln lagged population size	.009	.106**	−.061**
in 1000s	(.017)	(.040)	(.020)
Ln lagged GDP per capita	−1.28***	.252	−.525
	(.366)	(.338)	(.726)
Ethnic fractionalization	1.60	1.02	3.94**
index (Fearon 2002)	(.885)	(.612)	(1.53)
Religious fractionalization	−.035***	−.025**	−.008
index (Reynal-Querol 2002)	(.006)	(.010)	(.010)
Resettlement of minority	.337*	−.030	−.160
population during 1980s (MAR)	(.165)	(.155)	(.290)
Competition for land	.189	.082	.178
during the 1980s (MAR)	(.164)	(.161)	(.351)
Time trend	−.143***	−.323***	−.418
	(.049)	(.058)	(.325)
Lagged number of INGO	.000	.001***	−.001
memberships (Hironaka 2000)	(.000)	(.000)	(.002)
Periphery status	−.729	.349	−2.33**
	(.433)	(.504)	(.803)
Political Structure			
Lagged restrictions on	.237**	.072	.421
civil rights (none = 0 to many = 7)	(.118)	(.116)	(.425)
(Freedom House 2002)			
Number of border states with major	−.078	.389**	.249
violence (State Failure, phase III)	(.150)	(.134)	(.217)
Wald chi-square	80.3	93.1	78.8
Number of observations	888	888	888

NOTE: In all models, the parameter for the lagged dependent variable is set to 1.0. Two-tailed tests of significance reported. * $p < .05$, ** $p < .01$, *** $p < .001$.

Social movement political perspectives shed some light on this question. Over time, social movement activity requires both motivation and political access. While countries that restrict civil rights undoubtedly hinder the capacity of groups to mobilize within the country, the absence of civil rights increases grievances related to the suppression of liberties. If the momentum for increasing civil liberties has grown more intense in recent decades, then the pressure within states lacking civil rights ought to be rising. What is interesting about these findings is that they suggest that the absence of civil liberties within a state encourages internal mobilization, but not necessarily armed interference by external actors.

Another unexpected finding concerns the effects of ethnic fractionalization. Countries that are more ethnically diverse have higher levels of severe international wars, but not of internal wars. Once again, a global integration perspective is helpful in explaining results that show relatively weak links between ethnic diversity and internal war. Seen in a broader context, ethnic diversity within a country increases the number of possible ethnic and linguistic ties to kindred groups outside the country. In this view, ethnic fractionalization not only indicates internal divisions that impede nation-building, but it also increases the potential to make external links—to diasporas, refugee flows, migrant communities, and ethnic kin once residing in the same area. Thus, what others have judged a divisive force has the potential for creating new network ties with kindred communities across administrative state boundaries. Such links potentially encourage international wars, as groups with strong kinship ties and political sympathies mobilize resources, munitions, and troops to attack rivals in nearby countries.

It is interesting, however, that violence in nearby states affects only interstate violence and not international violence. Recall that international violence is defined as the classic "third-party" intervention, while interstate violence is conflict between two or more combatant states. As suggested above, this pattern may be related to the character of international war, which is defined as internal war that also mobilizes at least one other external state actor. The positive and significant effect of being surrounded by neighboring states experiencing unrest suggests that diffusion of violence directly affects the likelihood of war between sovereign states (interstate war). In contrast, internal wars with third party interlopers are not influenced by conflicts in neighboring countries. In retrospect this finding makes sense, especially if escalation in the number of territorial disputes over boundaries also increases the likelihood of full-scale war between countries. Clearly this investigation of geographical diffusion deserves more attention and better measures of diffusion, both spatially and temporally, in order to further clarify the processes underlying these results.

Conclusion: The Political Dimension of Ethnic Conflict

This chapter analyzed the interrelationships among ethnic violence and war, using a social movements and political process framework to illuminate a set of dynamics that generate group conflicts in the contemporary era. To capture the political process arguments, the discussion turned to several key indicators of political structure and regime change that have been used fruitfully to explain some of the temporal processes generating group conflict. Of particular interest here was addressing the claim that democratic regimes experience more stability and less group conflict. The empirical evidence did not support this argument.

Instead, I found that more autocratic regimes deter ethnic violence, but that countries granting fewer civil rights are also more likely to experience higher levels of internal civil war. Democratic regimes had slightly higher levels of ethnic violence but slightly lower levels of internal civil war (but neither finding was statistically significant). Similarly, countries that restrict civil rights experience more internal civil wars on their soil, when compared to countries that grant more extensive civil rights. Thus, although democracy does not appear to deter ethnic violence, the absence of civil liberties apparently does increase the likelihood of internal war in the most recent period. This finding suggests that democratic regimes are less likely to have violent uprisings because they allow more civil liberties, which serve to absorb grievances within institutional channels.

As recent research (Reynal-Querol 2002) suggests, cultural factors also matter. Religious fractionalization had no effect on rates of ethnic violence, but apparently religious diversity deters internal and interstate conflicts. This finding draws a parallel with earlier nation-building research (e.g., Eisenstadt and Rokkan 1975), which suggested that cross-cutting cleavages provide a hedge against more detrimental overlapping cleavages and identities that can undercut nation-building. As Reynal-Querol points out, it would be fruitful to investigate the overlap between religious and ethnic cleavages simultaneously, to see if this proposition regarding nation-building holds more generally in terms of regime stability.

The distinctions between democratic, authoritarian, and transitional political regimes might be justly criticized as being relatively crude indicators of political variation within countries. It is true that such blanket categories tend to gloss over details about the nature and types of administrative structures, voting rules, relative access of civil groups to the political system, centralization of authority, and a number of other factors. Nevertheless, after considerable analysis, I found that a wide variety of measures of political openness, party competition, ethnic and regional tenure of official positions, and other factors had no discernible effect on the rate of ethnic violence or international and internal war (see the Polity IV data set for an exhaustive list of measures available). Rather, the broader categories of civil rights and autocracy matter much more to outbreak of ethnic violence and war.

Many international factors apparently fuel conflicts as well. In particular, I found that membership in INGOs substantially increases the rate of ethnic conflict (but this same measure had little effect on internal war). Moreover, INGO membership had a significant effect on the rate of interstate war, suggesting that some types of connections among countries facilitate more global forms of interstate conflict. Although the literature indicates that dependent countries are more vulnerable to open warfare and conflict, the empirical analysis shows the opposite to be true: in most cases, peripheral countries had significantly lower rates of international and internal conflict (see also Sambanis 2004).

The relationship of ethnic violence with conflicts of other types suggests support for many of the conventional fears that ethnic and nationalist social movements drive up rates of internal and international conflicts. However, this relationship seems unaffected by linguistic or cultural markers of ethnicity alone, suggesting that ethnic collective action is propelled by more than ethnic or cultural differences. Rather, ethnic violence has powerful spillover effects that produce more severe degrees of other types of conflict, especially internal civil war and international wars. Internal wars and ethnic violence are more likely to erupt when there is economic hardship, but evidently democracy does not deter either form of internal strife. Ethnic violence is instead a function of prior discrimination and state oppression, and it appears to fuel at least some forms of civil war under these conditions.

CHAPTER NINE

Models Incorporating Endogeneity

Research on repression and ethnic violence emphasizes an interactive and dynamic relationship between state action and group response. For example, in the study of civil war, the classic "tit-for-tat" model of reactive violence and revenge suggests some of the difficulties in trying to ascertain which side first initiated an escalating dynamic of violence. Choosing which side to start with—the state or the challenger—has often been a matter simply of a given discipline's preference. Yet this choice has far-reaching consequences for any analysis and research design.

The literature in political science tends to focus on causal factors related to regime characteristics (such as political structure, authoritarian rule, lack of democracy, military expenditures), that encourage repression (e.g., Moore 1998, 2000; Hegre et al. 2003; Sambanis 2001, 2004). On the other hand, literature on repression in the social movement field tends to focus on characteristics of the challengers, as in case studies of social movements, their resources and infrastructures, and calculation of political opportunity structures, or "conflict carrying capacity of states"(e.g., Jenkins and Bond 2001). The costs attached to focusing on just one side of the interaction are considerable, especially if the overall escalation and decline of activity is a function of the interaction dynamic itself (Bhavnani and Backer 2000).

Recently, the dynamics of state–challenger interactions have become a subject of research on civil war and ethnic conflict. In particular, researchers have tried to untangle the causal sequencing of events by using information on the exact timing of insurgency and state repression. This research (including theoretically driven simulation models) suggests that there is often a significant and immediate response from either side of a conflict (Fearon and Laitin 1996; Cederman 2004). Others have suggested that the asymmetric nature of state resources implies a curvilinear relationship, in that group response rises and then falls as repression escalates to some extreme level (Olzak and Olivier 1999). Taking into account levels of democratic institutions complicates the relationship between state repression and insurgency even further, suggesting that the relationship between repression and insurgent rebellion depends upon a number of factors that in turn depend upon each other in complicated ways. Following this line of argument, Hegre et al. (2003) find that civil war is relatively uncommon in both highly democratic and highly authoritarian regime types.

Taken together, this research suggests that potentially serious problems of endogeneity should be considered when drawing inferences from models of ethnic mobilization. Put differently, if we assume that various measures of time-dependent factors of state response to insurgents are a function of prior ethnic group mobilization, then we face a problem of infinite regress: how far back can we observe this process, and when do we stop? Taking these issues seriously means that many if not most regression techniques (that assume exogeneity) are inappropriate, because the error terms across independent variables will be correlated (see Baltagi 1995; Baltagi and Chang 2000). In technical terms, it is fairly well known that under conditions of endogeneity, standard errors will be biased, which can lead to misleading results. Thus, it is worthwhile to try to find some solutions to this problem.

These issues have long plagued cross-national research on group conflict, civil war, and unrest. In particular, there are substantive reasons to believe that economic stability, political democracy, state violence, and group insurgency are all intertwined and involve simultaneous causation. For example, some scholars have suggested that economic well-being declines with substantial violence, which not only disrupts the normal flow of trade and economic activity, but siphons off resources when state authorities divert resources to fighting combatants. Wars both internal and external are likely to be costly, which necessarily affects economic well-being.

Similarly, it seems reasonable to suspect that state authorities and insurgent movements have nearly simultaneous causal effects on each other's rates of violence. States are likely to react in kind to violent challenges, and groups that are repressed are often motivated by revenge and tit-for-tat responses. Indeed, even a brief perusal of newspapers reporting on the Israeli–Arab conflict suggests that the amount of time between action and reaction for state and oppositional groups appears to be increasingly shorter.

The possibility that structural factors and outcomes are mutually re-inforcing presents distinct problems for researchers attempting to untangle causal effects. This chapter tackles the issue in a number of ways that apply standard econometric assumptions along with models that use newly avail-able panel estimation techniques to sort out some of the complications raised by considering issues of endogeneity and simultaneity. While none of these methodological solutions by itself is sufficient, by confronting this problem head-on I hope to alleviate at least some of the problems normally associ-ated with models that ignore these factors. Indeed, if models that take into account endogeneity are sufficiently different from those that do not, we will have learned something important about the benefits of exploring two-way causation processes.

Endogeneity of Ethnic Violence and State Repression

To create two-way causal models of state repression and ethnic mobilization, I begin with the notion that actions and reactions by state and challenger groups follow an important stimulus–response pattern that is embedded both in time and place. While this idea seems plausible, it creates a number of problems for assessing the effects of various state- and world-system factors on rates of ethnic violence and protest. In particular, assumptions about general linear models begin with the claim that error terms are uncorrelated with panel covariates over time. If this initial assumption is violated, then other types of models will be required.

There are several standard techniques in econometrics that estimate the magnitude of the effects of endogeneity. Here I analyze a model of state vio-lence that uses panel generalized least squares estimates adjusted for unbal-anced panels and heteroskedasticity, and estimates a first-order autocorrela-tion effect over time. The next step uses these results to estimate a predicted residual term, which removes variation in state violence due to structural variables included in the first stage of this process. Here this included a time trend and two variables indicating strength of the military sector of the state: estimated military expenditures as a proportion of the central govern-ment's expenditures, and percent of the labor force employed by the military sector (both are obtained from time series data available from the World Bank's *World Development Indicators* series). This first set of equations were

TABLE 9.1
Ethnic Violence and Violent State Response, 1984–1995, GLS Panel Model Estimates (standard errors in parentheses)

	(1)	(2)	(3)
Lagged residualized count	.713***	.753***	.779***
of state violence	(.054)	(.056)	(.056)
Ln lagged population size	.002**	.003***	.003***
in millions	(.001)	(.001)	(.000)
Ln lagged GDP per capita	.072	.093**	−.027
	(.038)	(.038)	(.043)
Ethnic fractionalization	.993***	.758***	.601**
index (Fearon 2002)	(.213)	(.227)	(.209)
Religious fractionalization	−.008***	−.009***	−.009***
index (Reynal-Querol 2002)	(.001)	(.001)	(.002)
Resettlement of minority population	.342***	.327***	.250***
during 1980s (MAR)	(.077)	(.079)	(.075)
Televisions per capita	.008	.855	.182
1990	(.441)	(.543)	(.501)
Time trend	−.026**	−.020**	−.009
	(.009)	(.008)	(.008)
Lagged number of INGO memberships	.000	−.000	−.000
(Hironaka 2000)	(.000)	(.001)	(.001)
Periphery status	−.101		
	(.079)		
Semi-periphery status		−.401**	
		(.137)	
Core status			1.15**
			(.413)
Lagged democratic regime index	.017**	.014**	.007
(scale −10 to 10, Sambanis 2002)	(.005)	(.005)	(.004)
Constant	50.72**	38.21**	18.40
	(17.03)	(17.31)	(16.50)
Wald chi-square	282.3	252.0	267.4
Number of observations	955	955	955

NOTE: Lagged count of state violence residualized (unbalanced panel estimates with autocorrelated errors with Baltagi panel estimator—see text). Two-tailed tests of significance reported. * $p < .05$, ** $p < .01$, *** $p < .001$.

highly significant and had a chi-square value of 156.1, with three degrees of freedom.

Table 9.1 indicates that endogeneity may be a problem in studying the effect of state violence on ethnic violence: the residualized count of events of state violence had a significant and positive effect on the rate of ethnic violence, and this effect was net of the effects of GDP per capita, ethnic and religious fractionalization, history of resettlement, and world system indicators. Moreover, the influences of all other variables in the model are unaffected by the presence of this estimated residual term. The pattern of effects remains intact when this variable is not included; however, the inclusion of this residual term significantly improves over the model that does not include it.

The next stage in the analysis explores two-stage least squares methods of estimating the simultaneous effects of measures of violence initiated by state and challenger groups. The technical requirements of two-stage least squares generally include the presence of instrumental variables that are associated with the endogenous measure but uncorrelated with the dependent variable. Such measures have often proven difficult, if not impossible, to obtain in cross-national data. This is also the case here, where it could be argued that measures of military expenditures are endogenous to the process. For example, it is plausible that countries with higher military expenditures create dissent against an increasingly repressive state. However, few theories exist about how military expenditures (apart from acts of repression, or police expenditures) might directly affect ethnic conflict.

Using measures of military expenditures and proportion of the labor force as instruments in the first stage, I employed two-stage least squares panel estimating techniques to obtain three sets of results that estimate the feedback loops between state and ethnic violence. Table 9.2 presents these results.

TWO-STAGE LEAST SQUARES ESTIMATION: STATE REPRESSION
AND ETHNIC VIOLENCE

What can we learn from these two-stage least squares models? First, note that the effect of state violence remains strong in columns 1, 2, and 3, controlling for peripheral, semi-peripheral, and core status in the world system. Second, find that, for the 1984–95 period, ethnic fractionalization has a significant and positive effect on the rate of ethnic violence, while religious fractionalization significantly decreases this rate (but there is no significant interaction between these two fractionalization measures). Contrary to what we found in earlier chapters, which examined a much earlier period (1965–85) and an overlapping recent period (1989–95), ethnic diversity seems to encourage mobilization that is both ethnic and violent in nature. However, religious fractionalization produces a countervailing tendency, which undercuts

TABLE 9.2

Effects of State Violence on Ethnic Violence, 1984–1995, Two-Stage Least Squares Panel Estimates (standard errors in parentheses)

	(1)	(2)	(3)
Lagged count of state violence	2.05***	2.00***	1.74***
	(.287)	(.270)	(.259)
Ln lagged population size in millions	.003**	.003**	.003**
	(.001)	(.001)	(.000)
Ln lagged GDP per capita	−.109	−.068	−.131
	(.161)	(.151)	(.141)
Ethnic fractionalization index (Fearon 2002)	2.67***	2.50***	2.34***
	(.654)	(.624)	(.592)
Religious fractionalization index (Reynal-Querol 2002)	−.021**	−.025***	−.022***
	(.001)	(.007)	(.006)
Resettlement of minority population during 1980s (MAR)	.360**	.355**	.358**
	(.148)	(.140)	(.132)
Televisions per capita 1990	1.32	1.68	.176
	(1.70)	(1.56)	(1.46)
Time trend	.004	−.003	.098
	(.210)	(.198)	(.188)
Lagged number of INGO memberships (Hironaka 2000)	.001	.000	.001
	(.001)	(.001)	(.001)
Periphery status	.276		
	(.436)		
Semi-periphery status		−.885*	
		(.316)	
Core status			1.83***
			(.470)
Lagged democratic regime index (scale −10 to 10) (Sambanis 2002)	.030	.028	.035
	(.033)	(.035)	(.029)
Constant	7.44	7.35**	−193.56
	(419.32)	(394.65)	(373.9)
Chi-square	128.4	148.2	168.9
Number of observations	974	974	974
Between group R-square	.72	.75	.77

NOTE: Instrumented variable: Lagged count of state violence. First-stage instruments: Lagged proportion of labor force in military, military expenditures as percent of central government expenditures (World Bank Time-Series Indicators). F-tests of significance for first-stage regressions (regressions on group means) significant below .001 level of significance (xtivreg in STATA, StataCorp 2001). Two-tailed tests of significance reported. * $p < .05$, ** $p < .01$, *** $p < .001$.

the salience of ethnic or racial identities in a country. As Collier and Sambanis (2002) and Reynal-Querol (2002) report, religious fractionalization provides a deterrent to civil war. These results suggest some additional similarities in patterns for ethnic conflict and civil war.

We find another consistency with the findings reported in earlier chapters for resettlement patterns. Evidently, state-sponsored resettlement of ethnic minorities encourages mobilization efforts that become violent, and this holds for earlier periods as well as through the mid-1990s. Thus, at least one of Gurr's "grievance" measures appears to have potent effects on ethnic violence within countries, and these grievances continue to encourage violent acts on the part of ethnic challengers. Put differently, violent state actions mounted in defense often have the unanticipated effect of polarizing and energizing challenger groups.

We uncover several differences in the findings in this chapter compared to those presented earlier, regarding the effects of world system variables in Table 9.2. Recall that in previous chapters, violence and protest were positively and significantly related to membership in greater numbers of INGOs. Indeed, in almost all of these analyses of events prior to 1985, embeddedness in the world system had the effect of raising the rate of ethnic violence. Yet when analyzing the most recent period in models specifying endogeneity, no such impact of embeddedness in the world system shows up.

In Table 9.2, we find that there is no significant effect of a high level of participation in a global non-governmental organizations network, apart from the effects of world system status. The effects of world system status follow previous findings: semi-periphery countries are significantly less likely to experience high rates of violent ethnic movements, while core countries, those most central and dominant in the world system, experience more ethnic violence. This last finding continues to run counter to most theories of ethnic violence, which expect more violence in peripheral or weaker states (Gurr 2000).

Earlier chapters also reviewed a number of important theories linking democratic regimes to lower levels of ethnic violence. These theories reflect a number of important social movement and collective action perspectives suggesting that states with regularized avenues of access for large proportions of the citizenry would be able to defuse violent movements, whose grievances could be channeled into more institutionalized party politics and through regularized participation in civil society. Table 9.2 shows no significant effect of using Sambanis's (2001) modified "democratic regime" scheme, which takes into account countries in transition in terms of previous levels of democracy and autocracy and creates a single scale that ranges from

−10 to 10. Thus, although some scholars would like to believe that democratic regimes undercut the motivation for violence by providing alternative means for the expression of dissent, there is no evidence for this optimistic view of state democracies in this analysis. However, there is no negative effect of democratic regimes, suggesting that authoritarian regimes are neither more nor less likely to experience ethnic violence than other types of regimes. This, too, runs counter to a number of theories that would predict that authoritarian regimes are less open to challenge because of high levels of repression and surveillance (Rasler 1996). Evidently, taking into account prior state violence against minority groups diminishes any effect of measures of the openness and competitiveness of a regime.

Why would this modified democracy–autocracy scale fail to show that democracy undercuts ethnic violence? While democratic polity arguments have a long tradition in political science and seem highly plausible, they ignore the global aspect of social movement mobilization, in which groups borrow information, tactics, and organizational forms of challenge to state authority from across national borders. Such global perspectives have begun to challenge previous assumptions that grievance movements—and movements that are ethnically based—are related solely to internal factors.

The significant and positive effect of core status in the world system on the rate of ethnic violence makes sense in this context. The fact that core states are more (not less) likely to experience ethnic violence is consistent with the notion that core nations are first and foremost the most affected by all patterns of diffusion and activity, over and above internal factors such as GDP per capita and ethnic diversity. Thus, core nations are not exempt from ethnic violence—far from it. Rather, they are significantly more likely than non-core nations to experience ethnic challenges within the relatively short period of time examined (1984–95).[1]

---

[1] Efforts to examine outlier nations within the core proved interesting. Specifically, the positive effect of core position on the rate of ethnic violence seen in the far-right column of Table 9.2 did not disappear when specific countries such as the United States or the United Kingdom were omitted from the model, and efforts to dampen this effect by adding a number of regional dummy variables did not influence it either. Nor were any of the regional effects (e.g., including a dummy variable for Middle East, Africa, Europe, former U.S.S.R. countries, countries in the Warsaw Pact, Asia, etc.) significant, as others have found in analyses of civil war prevalence (Elbadawi and Sambanis 2002).

BOOTSTRAPPING TECHNIQUES

One additional exploration of these effects that was conducted with these data deserves mention. As is well known, estimates of standard errors from two-stage least squares are not necessarily accurate, and a number of technical transformations are usually necessary to provide more precise estimates of standard errors. This is particularly true in this case, where there are unbalanced panel waves (related to the fact that many countries dissolved and others have come into existence over this period). Rather than restrict ourselves to some small number of countries that have been remarkably stable over time, it made more sense to incorporate the messy reality of these histories that include both deaths and births of many countries. This means that panel estimates are likely to be affected by these lopsided conditions, where countries such as France contribute information for all eleven years of observation, whereas Germany (as a single entity) contributes information beginning only in 1990, and East and West Germany observations end in 1989. All of these issues are likely to affect the validity of standard errors in these complicated two-stage least squares models. To begin to examine the extent of problems with standard errors, I used a number of bootstrap methods (Efron and Tibshirani 1993).

Because bootstrapping techniques are not yet available for the unbalanced panel models reported in Table 9.2, I chose another closely aligned panel generalized least squares (GLS) model that incorporates the effects of heteroskedasticity and autocorrelated errors. Table 9.2 is essentially the same model shown in Table 9.1, with the application of instrumental variables method of estimation. This pooled cross-sectional time series model is not precisely the same as the classic instrumental variables panel model, however, because several of the measures in Table 9.2 do not vary over time. Thus, for measures that do not vary over time (e.g., world system position, ethnic and religious fractionalization) the results in Table 9.2 regarding bias in the standard errors will not be informative.

I next compared this analysis to a bootstrapping model that estimates bootstrap standard errors over 1000 repetitions. What do the bootstrapping methods tell us about the estimates of the standard errors in Table 9.2? As stated above, because the bootstrap method of estimation reflects a different parameterization than the method used in Table 9.2, the coefficients for all covariates are not the same, and thus I cannot simply replace the original standard errors in Table 9.2 with the bootstrap standard errors as "corrections." However, by comparing the pattern of results, I can examine the coefficients from the same (non-bootstrap) runs and compare the coefficients and standard errors when using cross-sectional and times series models and applying bootstrap techniques to these models. In every single case, all of the parameter estimates were significant and in the same direction for all three examinations: instrumental variable model (Table 9.1), pooled cross section and times series panel model (Table 9.2), and bootstrap techniques applied to the pooled cross section and times series models (not shown). Furthermore, in all cases the standard errors were only slightly higher in the bootstrap technique, and the bias measures were extremely low (often .0001 or lower). Moreover, differences between bootstrap estimates and non-bootstrap estimates of the effects in the pooled cross section and times series model were exactly as expected: none of the measures that were constant over time were significant using bootstrap techniques.

ENDOGENOUS EFFECTS OF ECONOMIC WELL-BEING AND VIOLENCE

There are good reasons to suspect that a country's economic viability is deeply affected by domestic turmoil. Not only are local businesses, employment, and productivity patterns interrupted by unrest, but a loss of external sources of investment and trade can curtail subsequent growth and sustained economic activity (Moaddel 1994; Sambanis 2001). Indeed, in the case of South Africa, the international sanctions applied to that country's trade operations have often been used as an explanation for major economic crises in that country. Furthermore, some scholars of politics in South Africa have maintained that this economic threat eventually gave rise to the conditions leading to the demise of the apartheid regime (Lapping 1989).

This argument also suggests that there is two-way (perhaps nearly simultaneous) causation between economic growth and ethnic violence. Efforts to untangle these effects have generally relied on lagged panel designs, which build in lagged effects that may or may not reflect the correct time lag of the actual effects. Furthermore, models that include lagged measures of ethnic violence along with lagged measures of GDP per capita only exacerbate the problem of endogeneity, and this effect is more problematic if there is a relationship between economic conditions and ethnic violence. In order to untangle this second endogeneity problem, it seems important to explore economic well-being in terms of endogeneity effects as well.

I conducted the same two-stage least squares diagnostics with GDP per capita, using the residuals from an equation predicting GDP per capita from lagged GDP per capita, per capita exports, and population size. Using the residual measure, I found no evidence of endogeneity for this measure, unlike the state violence equations. I also performed a number of bootstrap operations using the cross section and times series models, and found evidence of very little bias. An analysis conducted over the short run (1984–95) found little evidence that GDP per capita is endogenous to the process of ethnic violence. As Elbadawi and Sambanis (2002) warn, however, this does not mean that such endogeneity does not exist—it means only that using these methods and an admittedly restricted number of instrumental variables, we have been unable to find evidence that endogeneity has affected the results.

Endogeneity of State Repression and Nonviolent Ethnic Protest

Theories of collective action and rebellion generally assume that violence not only follows a different trajectory from nonviolent forms of protest, but that nonviolence will diminish more rapidly than violence in response to state repression. On the other hand, it seems clear from earlier reviews of the literature (in Chapters 1 and 2) that ethnic violence may be preceded or punctuated by nonviolent protest—that the two forms may complement each other. For just one scenario, consider how the South African state attempted to apply alternating forms of repression and reforms as a means for keeping the anti-apartheid movement at bay (Olzak et al. 2003). However, as we know, the combination of reward and punishment strategies was ultimately ineffective in the effort to crush the protest movement. This second view would hold that ethnic violence and nonviolence might be causally related, and that both may be stimulated by a variety of state actions, including acts of state repression.

Given this debate, it seems reasonable to proceed by analyzing ethnic nonviolence in a set of runs parallel to those conducted on ethnic violence. I undertook initial explorations of the effects of the residuals obtained from the same equation as used in Table 9.1, to obtain a residualized state violence measure. It was statistically significant, indicating the presence of endogeneity with state violence and nonviolent protest. So I conducted a parallel two-stage least squares analysis, and present the results in Table 9.3.

TABLE 9.3
Effects of State Violence on Nonviolent Ethnic Protest, 1984–1995,
Two-Stage Least Squares Panel Estimates (standard errors in parentheses)

	(1)	(2)	(3)
Lagged count of state violence	7.86***	7.42***	6.57***
	(1.50)	(1.42)	(1.40)
Ln lagged population size in millions	.011	.010	.009
	(.006)	(.006)	(.006)
Ln lagged GDP per capita	.347	.424	.138
	(.845)	(.797)	(.766)
Ethnic fractionalization index (Fearon 2002)	9.93**	9.17***	8.86***
	(3.42)	(3.28)	(3.20)
Religious fractionalization index (Reynal-Querol 2002)	−.070	−.080*	−.067*
	(.001)	(.037)	(.034)
Resettlement of minority population during 1980s (MAR)	1.25	1.23	2.24**
	(.775)	(.741)	(.718)
Televisions per capita 1990	25.4**	25.20**	19.23**
	(8.92)	(8.22)	(7.93)
Time trend	−1.20	−1.13	.747
	(1.10)	(1.04)	(1.02)
Lagged number of INGO memberships (Hironaka 2000)	−.001	.002	−.002
	(.003)	(.003)	(.002)
Periphery status	.281		
	(2.29)		
Semi-periphery status		−4.09*	
		(1.66)	
Core status			6.21*
			(2.54)
Lagged democratic regime index (scale −10 to 10)(Sambanis 2002)	−.174	.177	−.148
	(.172)	(.164)	(.159)
Constant	2375.8	2227.9	1481.9
	(2192.9)	(2073.7)	(2020.6)
Chi-square	67.7	148.2	168.9
Number of observations	974	974	974
Between group R-square	.49	.54	.56

NOTE: Instrumented variable: Lagged count of state violence. First-stage instruments: Lagged proportion of labor force in military, military expenditures as percent of central government expenditures (World Bank Time-Series Indicators). F-tests of significance for first-stage regressions (regressions on group means) significant below .001 level of significance (xtivreg in STATA, StataCorp 2001). Two-tailed tests of significance reported. * $p < .05$, ** $p < .01$, *** $p < .001$.

Given the analyses in earlier chapters documenting the differences between forms of ethnic violence and nonviolence, comparison of Tables 9.2 and 9.3 reveals surprising similarities. There are a few differences that stand out. First, state violence mobilizes both violence and nonviolence, but the effect of state violence on ethnic nonviolence is steeper. As the count of state violence rises from nil to one standard deviation above its mean level, the rate of ethnic violence more than triples. However, the coefficient of 7.86 in Table 9.3 suggests that a one-standard-deviation rise in state violence would increase nonviolent protest fourteen-fold. Most theories of collective action and repression would expect that state violence would dampen the likelihood of mild forms of protest, and yet, for ethnic protest, the opposite appears true. Indeed, the results suggest that state repression of ethnic activity fuels both types of protest and violence by ethnic groups.

We see in Table 9.3 that many of the same factors that produce surges in ethnic violence also elevate nonviolent ethnic protest, especially levels of state repression and ethnic fractionalization. This finding runs counter to some prior research on ethnic civil war (analyzed as a separate category in Sambanis 2001; Fearon and Laitin 2003). I suggest that several reasons for this discrepancy are plausible. First, recall that the present analyses in Tables 9.2 and 9.3 include very diverse forms of ethnic activity, including legal demonstrations, peaceful protest, conflict among differing ethnic groups, and ethnic civil war. Not only is ethnic civil war a subset of ethnic activity, but civil wars constitute a very small proportion of all of the ethnic events analyzed here.

The next step in the analysis compares nonviolent ethnic protest with violent ethnic activity, and the results reveal one key difference. This is the result showing a positive and significant impact of the media (measured by the number of television sets per capita) on protest but not on violence. As Table 9.3 shows, the prevalence of television sets, presumably an indirect measure of media access in a country, raises the rate of nonviolent protest significantly. This finding suggests an important qualification for many media-driven theories of contagion and diffusion: that ethnic nonviolence is much more susceptible to diffusion effects than are violent forms of ethnic activity.

Why would this effect of the media be asymmetric for ethnic violence and nonviolence? Perhaps one explanation lies embedded in the contradictory effects of violence—it is more dramatic and more likely to be televised by local media, and thus information about the tactics and amount of attention devoted to violence is more likely to spread rapidly, but violence also is more likely to turn public opinion against those who use it (Koopmans 1995). Research conducted in Western Europe suggests that the public's response to nonviolent protest is likely to be more accepting in democratic countries, because nonviolent tactics and threats are likely to be perceived as more legitimate (Koopmans 1995; Kriesi et al. 1995). Thus, according to this view, televised events of nonviolence present pictures of relatively straightforward political tactics and demands, while violence by protesters carries strong negative connotations with much of the public, and the use of violence can backfire. Moreover, if bystanders or victims are killed or injured during the course of a protest, or if significant damage to property occurs, public support for protest tactics and issues declines sharply (Koopmans 1995). In contrast, nonviolent protest has a greater potential for raising support for protester demands, because nonviolent methods are more likely to resonate with greater numbers of the public. Seen in this light, nonviolent protest has a higher instrumental value, without incurring the costs of personal injury or arrest. This would be especially true in democratic countries, where protest has gained political legitimacy, and where access to media is greatest.[2]

Finally, for both ethnic violence and nonviolence, core countries are significantly more likely to engage in ethnic mobilization, while semi-peripheral countries are less likely to engage in ethnic mobilization over this period. This pattern is consistent with the argument that embeddedness in the world system matters. However, this result does not fit the exact prediction offered at the outset of this book. In Chapter 1, I argued that core countries would have more nonviolence, but that peripheral (and perhaps also semi-peripheral countries) that were more linked into the system of international non-governmental organizations would be more likely to exhibit violent ethnic activity. This hypothesis is not supported at all in the period 1984–95, and this brings into question the notion that peripheral countries (or even countries that are poor) have more grievances and thus nothing to lose by engaging in violence. Indeed, it appears as though dominant countries engender significantly more violence, independent of country wealth.

Conclusion

What lessons have we learned from this analysis of the endogenous effects of state repression and ethnic mobilization? It seems reasonable that at least two conclusions can be drawn. First, it appears that state repression is

[2]An alternative view would hold that the number of television sets per capita is just a proxy for national wealth or development, and thus conflates issues of media spread with income. However, the effect of this indicator holds even when the effects of GDP per capita, core status, and other measures of relative inequality and wealth are included in models (not all shown in Table 9.3).

intricately linked to ethnic mobilization efforts, both violent and nonviolent, but repression does not always dampen ethnic mobilization, as some theories might have expected. Indeed, state repression appears to have raised rates of ethnic mobilization over this 1984–95 period. Second, when models that attempt to parse out the effects of feedback loops of repression on ethnic mobilization are taken into account, many earlier findings hold up under scrutiny, despite evidence of two-way causation.

In particular, in these models we retain confidence in two earlier findings that reported that ethnic fractionalization produces higher rates of ethnic violence and protest, while religious fractionalization lowers these rates. Recall that the analysis in this chapter (and in earlier chapters) followed the lead of Reynal-Querol (2002) in including her measure of religious fractionalization; this had important payoffs, and the results suggest that investigation of the potential of cross-cutting cleavages might be worthwhile. The results here point to the fact that religious fractionalization provides an alternative source of loyalty, identity, and mobilization, one that can cross-cut ethnic movements (which perhaps are no less violent, once they are mobilized and organized movements themselves).

Several other results show consistency across all of the chapters on ethnic violence. Contrary to a number of dire predictions about the demise of the nation-state and the turmoil of ethnic movements everywhere in the world, ethnic violence appears to be on the decline overall. It appears that the early 1990s witnessed a peak in ethnic movements, and that there has been a gradual reduction in their incidence since that time.

Why has ethnic violence declined? This chapter has provided some answers to this question based on the externalities of the world system and on countries' levels of embeddedness in networks of world trade, diplomacy, and information. Earlier chapters argued that states that are more embedded in the world system are more likely to see episodes of ethnic mobilization, and that core and periphery nations are more and less likely, respectively, to experience higher rates of ethnic activity, based upon the interconnectedness with acts of violence in other states. States closest to each other are more likely to be affected by the trajectories of each other's ethnic movements. Thus, it might be expected that ethnic activity first increases at a rapid rate, then gradually declines. The empirical patterns in the analysis reflect this cycle.

A number of important theories in political science and economics about the ways that democracy and economic stability undermine the motivation and resources for ethnic violence meet with criticism here. In particular, there is little evidence over the 1984–95 period that richer or more democratic nations had significantly lower rates of ethnic violence. Indeed, core nations were significantly more likely to experience ethnic violence.

Finally, this chapter has explored a number of techniques for dealing with problems of endogeneity, which cause trouble when we try to produce structural models of cause and effect in social science. I explored several diagnostic techniques and methods for using instrumental variables to estimate the effect of endogenous variables. While the scarcity of good data still hampers the study of cross-national politics, these results show that by taking into account the potential problems associated with two-way causation, much can be learned about the dynamics of the process. Thus, many of the findings from the dyadic interaction studies of stimulus-response in politics have been supported with panel data from a number of countries, while controlling for a number of economic and political variables.

CHAPTER TEN

Conclusions and Future Considerations

What causes variation across countries in ethnic mobilization? To begin to consider this question, this book has explored the argument that there is a causal link between ethnic mobilization and processes associated with globalization. In particular, I argued that as countries with different resource bases have become more interdependent, economic, cultural, and social status differences that persist among groups within and across countries have become magnified.

The political and economic connections among states, regions, and people have produced two apparently contradictory trends. On one hand, states and their actions are increasingly linked across territories, as political events, economic crises, and natural disasters in one setting have consequences in many distant countries. We do not know, but we suspect, that this phenomenon might be relatively recent, fueled by modern communications and media links and economic interdependencies that have created dense networks of actions and reactions. On the other hand, there is evidence that local ethnic identities have generated a surge in social movement activities in recent decades (Gurr 1993). My aim has been to ask if these two processes can be understood by using a global perspective that builds a connection among forces of international integration, incorporation, inequality, and group mobilization.

My research is based on theories suggesting that the impact of globalization across the world is likely to be uneven, depending upon a state's centrality and dominance in world economic, trade, and diplomatic networks, its resource base, and its previous history of political stability, confrontation, and conflict. Key arguments predict that core states will have more ethnic mobilization that is less violent, while countries more embedded in a world system of non-governmental organizations will experience more ethnic activity of all kinds. I also used world polity and social movement perspectives, which suggest that the rapid diffusion of a global human rights ideology has provided a legitimate platform for making claims for redress of ethnic injustices, inequalities, and discrimination based upon ethnic or racial identities (J. Meyer et al. 1997; Keck and Sikkink 1998). This process implies that countries most embedded in this international system, countries with more diverse populations, and countries with widespread poverty would be most likely to experience ethnic mobilization.

To bolster this argument, I have followed a number of scholars in political science and sociology who offer the insight that nationalism, diffusion, social movements, and ethnic collective action share fundamental characteristics.[1] According to these views, the number and density of ties to international organizations have become conduits of various social movement concerns. Most notably, these scholars offer the argument that international organizations legitimate and diffuse claims for expansion of civil liberties and human rights. Moreover, these links have built dense information and resource networks among members and leaders, producing isomorphism in organizational forms, tactics, and rhetoric (Soysal 1994; J. Smith 1995, 2004; Tarrow 2005). While this emerging social movement tradition has had a distinctly global perspective, it has not yet considered the links between globalization processes and protest movements, outbreaks of conflict, ethnic rebellion, and civil war.

This challenge is picked up and extended in this book in a number of ways. I have tried to provide a cohesive argument that links measures of inequality at the global and country levels of analysis in ways that make sense. For instance, a number of theories suggest that closer contact among different units—whether countries, state officials, social movement activists, or individuals facing new refugees and/or guest workers—unleashes forces of competition and conflict. Yet few scholars have explained how processes of competition might be extended to a global level of analysis.

To address these issues, I used two different data sets that provide information on ethnic mobilization over the last four decades. The analysis

---

[1]For examples, see J. Meyer et al. (1997), Brubaker (1996), Boli and Thomas (1999), Hechter (2000, 2004), della Porta and Tarrow (2005), Sikkink (2005), and Tarrow (2005).

generated a number of findings that have implications for theories of ethnic mobilization. The results were generally consistent with the overall argument that global patterns of integration and diffusion were relevant to ethnic movements. In particular, I found that core/periphery distinctions among countries in the world system do matter, as anticipated by my argument. Before the end of the Cold War, periphery countries and countries with more inequality had higher rates of ethnic violence, while core countries experienced moderate forms of ethnic nonviolence. After the end of the Cold War in 1989, both core and periphery countries had more ethnic violence than countries in the semi-periphery.

My argument regarding the impact of global diffusion of human rights ideology found supporting evidence that exclusion of minorities increased the level and seriousness of ethnic violence. Rather unsurprisingly, I found that when ethnic groups have competing interests and goals, as is the case when there is direct competition for land or over policies that explicitly exclude some minorities and favor others, ethnic violence rises. The results also suggest a general diffusion of group conflict across types of wars. As anticipated, ethnic violence and civil war are mutually reinforcing, but ethnic violence also ignites conflict between countries, as in the case of international war (which involves third parties). All of these findings are relevant to my basic theoretical perspective regarding the importance of identifying global processes that produce ethnic resistance movements at the local level. The next section highlights the relevance of each of these findings to the theories of ethnic and racial social movements.

Effects of Integration into the World System

My argument rests on the assumption that forces of integration into the world economic and political network produce variation in local responses to globalization. This global integration approach has two components. First, I offer the argument that world system status shapes the frequency and forms of ethnic activity. In particular, I argue that when ethnic rights have gained institutional legitimacy in core countries, ethnic movements adopt nonviolent tactics and make claims for the expansion of civil rights. Over time, claims of ethnic sovereignty gradually diffuse to peripheral regions of the world. Where ethnic claims are resisted (or repressed), such movements are likely to turn violent, creating higher rates of ethnic violence in peripheral countries as a result. Thus, given the internal dynamics of peripheral countries, and the number and type of international constraints confronted by them, I argue that core and periphery states ought to experience quite different forms of ethnic mobilization. Second, I argue that countries with greater numbers of memberships in international non-governmental organizations (INGOs) ought to have higher rates of ethnic mobilization. I speculated that such organizations raise levels of ethnic awareness and facilitate mobilization because they provide information, resources, and organizational strategies that link local organizations and residents in participating countries to ethnic rights issues and campaigns. Following a number of scholars investigating "transnational social movements," I argue that by clarifying the interaction between local-level characteristics and global factors of integration we may learn more about the mechanisms that have made ethnic movements commonplace. In this way, I expected that a number of internal features of states (especially poverty and repression) would magnify (or suppress) the impact of globalization at the local level.

PERIPHERAL STATUS IN THE WORLD SYSTEM OF STATES

Drawing on world system theory, I predicted that core countries would experience more nonviolent ethnic protest that is channeled by democratic institutions and other routine access to political elites. I noted that globalization disproportionately benefits dominant countries economically and politically, and argued that the resulting declines in relative poverty and political stability imply that core countries would experience less ethnic violence compared to less dominant countries. Conversely, I argued that peripheral countries (experiencing fewer benefits from globalization), will show increases in poverty, more political instability, and repressive regimes, and that they will have more rebellions and greater magnitudes of ethnic violence. Results from the empirical chapters using indices of ethnic conflict and rebellion show support for these hypotheses. The analysis shows that peripheral countries have significantly higher magnitudes of ethnic violence.[2] However, peripheral countries do not show a greater incidence of ethnic violence when this is measured by annual event counts of violence (using the PANDA data set).

[2]For specific results, see Chapter 5 for analysis of the 1965–69 and 1985–89 periods, and Chapter 7 for analysis of the 1995–98 period, using the *Minorities at Risk* index of ethnic violence and rebellion.

Analysis using more recent data (1995–98) on the magnitude of ethnic violence (from the MAR data set) shows that peripheral status provokes more serious forms of rebellion, but not necessarily more events. Indeed, I found that, following the end of the Cold War in 1989, core countries were more likely to experience higher counts of ethnic violence than were other types of states, which suggests that centrality in the world system does not inoculate countries against outbreaks of ethnic conflict, as I had anticipated. While this finding was unexpected, it is consistent with the view that social movement activity, including violence, diffuses from the core to other parts of the world. Altogether there is powerful evidence that the post–Cold War period experienced a shift in the locus and magnitude of ethnic social movements that has not been recognized previously in the literature.

INTERNATIONAL NON-GOVERNMENTAL ORGANIZATIONS

A second component of my integration argument concerns the impact of international non-governmental organizations on local outbreaks of ethnic conflict. While a variety of case studies report that international human rights associations and other non-governmental organizations have assisted policymakers and fostered transnational social movements, examination of the impact of INGOs on ethnic mobilization reveals a more complicated picture. Some studies have documented a positive brokerage role for international organizations, which are able to settle disputes and negotiate truces among disputants (Brown 1996; Tarrow and McAdam 2005). Indeed, based on case studies, scholars discussing solutions to ethnic conflict often recommend expanding the role of such third-party interventions as a solution to ethnic strife (Brown 1996; Räikkä 1996; Rotberg 1996; Ghai 2001; Horowitz 2001).

Such optimism, however well-meaning, finds little support across all periods in the analyses (see also Regan 2002). Other scholars have also noticed that INGOs have played active roles in attempting to subdue conflict; however, many of these studies are based upon successful stories of intervention and peaceful outcomes. Moreover, the evidence suggests that international organizations have not been successful in preventing escalation of serious internal wars and conflict (Keck and Sikkink 1998; O'Brien et al. 2000, Sikkink 2005). International organizations are key actors in the dissemination of information about the potential for ethnic conflict (and this may be especially true when organizations strive to be apolitical or nonpartisan). Because of their outsider role among the grassroots organizations of a society, some see a potentially significant brokerage role for them in reporting "early warning" signs of conflict to other international agencies and governments (Gurr and Lichbach 1986; Gurr and Harff 1996; Rotberg 1996; Gurr 2000). As Jentelson points out (1998: 306), by sending early warning signals to governments or warring factions, INGOs risk becoming associated with one or another side to a dispute, resulting in escalation of the conflict. With ethnic conflict, prior coalitions and alliances play a role in determining expectations of alliances, which further challenge claims that third parties are truly disinterested (see also Hironaka 2005). If this argument holds, then countries that have more INGO memberships should have significantly higher levels of ethnic mobilization.

The rather sobering results found in this book support the hypothesis that interaction with non-governmental organizations raises the likelihood of ethnic mobilization. The findings suggest that while INGOs engage in human rights, rural development, education, health, and other fields, these organizations also indirectly endorse principles of sovereignty and ethnic rights. To the extent that these global ideologies become relevant to local realities, intergroup conflict, protest, or anti-state activity occurs. Whether or not an ethnic group's demands are seen as justified depends on the observer's political alliances, historical coalitions, treaties, and a number of other patterns related to prior interactions among states, regions, and groups. Thus, ethnic conflict (and protest) can be analyzed as a function of trends that affect regions and states differentially, but it also appears that international organizations, states, and regional associations determined to subdue or repress conflict do not always succeed in doing so.

As might be expected, the effect of memberships in INGOs has varied over time. In general, throughout the earlier of the periods examined, rates of violence are generally higher in the periphery. After the end of the Cold War in 1989, both core and peripheral countries with higher numbers of memberships in INGOs had higher levels of ethnic rebellion (especially in the 1995–98 interval). Indeed, analyses of data from the more recent decades find that increased numbers of INGO memberships raise the likelihood that a country's violence will be more intense.[3] When analyzing either the prevalence of ethnic activity (measured and analyzed as event counts over the 1984–95 period, using the PANDA data set of newswire-reported events) or

---

[3] See Table 6.3 for rebellion over the 1990–94 period, Table 7.2 for the 1995 period, and Tables 7.3 and 8.1 for analysis of the counts of ethnic violence over the 1989–95 period.

as the magnitude of ethnic rebellions (using the MAR data, especially for the 1990–98 period), I found a systematic and positive influence of INGO memberships on ethnic violence.

The findings regarding international non-governmental organizations are impressive. In both data sets, countries with large numbers of INGO memberships have higher levels and rates of ethnic violence.[4] Furthermore, the number of countries differs between the data sets, in part because inclusion rules for the MAR sample required that minority groups in a country meet some threshold of either prior mobilization or experience with previous economic or political discrimination (Gurr 1993: 6). Put differently, because the MAR sample was chosen partly on the basis of prior ethnic activity, it would not be surprising to most scholars if levels of ethnic rebellion in the sample were high.[5] The addition of analysis of event counts using the PANDA data provides a more rounded picture of ethnic movements because the sample was not chosen on the basis of prior ethnic activity. The results of international association links across these two data sets tell a similar story, lending support to the globalization thesis that a country's embeddedness in a network of international non-governmental associations is likely to escalate ethnic violence (especially since the end of the Cold War).

However, the findings do not imply that all efforts by international organizations are counterproductive. Indeed, my results show that a country's membership in large numbers of INGOs strengthens protest capacities of underrepresented groups. Open displays of protest strengthen civil liberties and democracy in those settings, to the extent that protest is not immediately extinguished and repressed. Furthermore, under a variety of conditions, human rights organizations have intervened in ways that have attenuated violence (Regan 2002). For instance, by gaining support and legitimacy through regional associations that offer military or refugee aid, international non-governmental organizations could act in concert with local ones to

---

[4]The MAR data set measures levels of intensity in protest and violence aggregated over five-periods, but the data do not indicate the amount of ethnic activity, nor its duration. The PANDA data set consists of annual information on the count of events of ethnic activity, but these counts do not take into account the relative intensity of events.

[5]However, in any given five-year interval, there was a substantially large number of countries in this "at risk" set that had no reported ethnic activity. This variation in ethnic activity makes this data set worth exploring.

provide cease-fire inducements to the warring parties in regional conflicts. Such international efforts have not been analyzed systematically, however, and few studies have explored the long-term outcomes of such programs. From a policy standpoint, varying the conditions under which organizational interventions have produced undesirable results is worth pursuing (see, e.g., Cederman 2004).

My analytical results cast doubt on the conventional wisdom that characterizes all forms of ethnic mobilization as inherently destructive. A more benign aspect of ethnic movements can be found in my analysis of nonviolent ethnic protest. Nonviolent ethnic protest is a function of expansion of civil liberties, income levels, and democratic politics. These findings run counter to mainstream studies in ethnic politics and international relations that often have taken the position that all forms of ethnic mobilization constitute a serious threat to international order. Most studies in this field tend to approach ethnic social movements from the standpoint of the existing state system, thus regional and ethnic conflict movements threaten the order of a system organized around viable state actors.

An alternative perspective on ethnic social movements considers the ways in which ethnic diversity, immigration, and inclusionary politics have the capacity to strengthen democracies (by encouraging diversity, inclusion, and tolerance) in a number of ways not usually considered by most of the literature on ethnic conflict. Ethnic protest is a form of interest-group politics that threatens the comfortable status quo, yet ethnic protest carries the potential for bringing civil liberties and rights to greater numbers of people. One has only to compare the contemporary South African regime with that country's past regimes to see how inclusionary policies increase the strength of a nation's political and moral assets (internally and internationally). The findings regarding the association between civil liberties and protest also raise important questions about the trade-offs between domestic stability and expanding economic opportunities.

It is equally important to consider an alternative explanation for my findings regarding the effect on ethnic conflict of embeddedness in world organizations. This alternative hypothesis would suggest that the causal relationship between participation in INGOs and ethnic conflict is actually the reverse of what I have proposed. In this view, international organizations interested in furthering peace efforts would be motivated to establish outposts in countries with substantial histories of violence and ethnic conflict

(Rotberg 1996).[6] I explored several time series analyses of the effect of violence on membership rates; however, the results did not show any relationship in this direction, net of the effects of GDP per capita. Indeed, no significant effects of ethnic protest nor conflict on the counts of membership in INGOs were found. Thus, although the anecdotal evidence seems to support the story that INGOs rush to various ethnic outbreaks (and many undoubtedly do so), the systematic evidence reported here does not support this view for the time period studied.

What lessons can we draw from these findings? First, it seems clear that since the end of the Cold War, core countries have had more ethnic activity, both violent and nonviolent. This finding is consistent with the world system perspective, which indicates that core regions provide fertile ground for social movements, cultural forms, and organizational templates that become modular forms of protest adopted in other settings (J. Smith 2004). Does this mean that ethnic activity has necessarily diffused from the core to semi-periphery and periphery nations? To answer this question, we need to turn to the role of internal features of inequality and ethnic inclusion, to see how those factors shape local reactions to globalization.

EFFECTS OF GLOBAL INTEGRATION ON POVERTY AND INEQUALITY

A second and related argument suggests the ways that global integration affects economic equality. It builds on the notion that as a global ideology that views group inequality as unjust and unfair diffuses, it provides moral grounding to social movements at the regional and local levels. The moral principle that everyone deserves basic human and civil rights has become an especially powerful ideological framework in recent decades, underlying the rhetoric of most identity politics worldwide (Keck and Sikkink 1998; Tarrow 2001).

[6] For the purposes of discussion, this alternative argument seems quite reasonable. However, it is important to note that the types of INGOs analyzed here are not solely concerned with ethnic minorities, group conflict, or international peace. The majority of them are concerned with environmental issues, labor conditions, animal rights, children's rights, women's rights, hunger and poverty, health organizations and health care, etc. (see Keck and Sikkink 1998; Boli and Thomas 1999; and della Porta and Tarrow 2005). Future research might concentrate on participation in international minority rights organizations, in an effort to tease out the implications of this argument. Unfortunately, information on the goals of these INGOs was not available in the data set I used.

The globalization of human rights ideologies of justice, sovereignty, and rights to self-determination means that these messages resonate more potently where inequality and poverty are greatest. To the extent that particular ethnic identities can be linked to patterns of economic inequality, such demands carry more weight than they would otherwise. Thus, ethnic groups regularly make demands for resource redistribution based upon a human rights ideology that has been endorsed by many states, social movement organizations, and international organizations (Coicaud et al. 2003; Ghai 2001; Schofer and Fourcade-Gourinchas 2001). Moreover, the claim that group-based inequality is unjust has coincided with the expansion of communications networks, media, and other sources that spread awareness about existing gaps in equality.

Under what conditions will poverty generate ethnic movements? A variety of scholars have suggested that the answer lies in understanding the differences between ethnic identification, solidarity, and the activation of ethnic identity (Bonacich 1972; Hechter 1975; Olzak 1992). Where there are discrete differences in economic stratification between ethnic groups, identification, cohesion, and solidarity are likely to be stronger among members of these groups than is the case in more economically homogeneous systems (Hechter 1975, 2004). However, the empirical evidence suggests that group solidarity is not inevitably transformed into social movements. Rather, a wide variety of ethnic networks, self-help organizations, communities, and cultural activities might also result from ethnic solidarity. In other words, the overlap of ethnic and class identities is a necessary but not sufficient condition for ethnic mobilization.[7]

Inequality activates ethnic identity when it becomes linked to an ideology of sovereignty and national self-determination of a "people," a "race," or a "region." This link is necessary because it provides a key emotional spark that drives the process of collective action, especially in the case of ethnic conflict (Petersen 2002; Kalyvas 2003). Because claims about nationalism and sovereignty commonly rest upon ethnic distinctions, the rhetorical demands for redistribution of income (and wealth) have become increasingly ethnic or racial in character. Groups that perceive that they are not receiving their fair share of the world's resources are likely to become increasingly aware of

---

[7] See also Wilkinson (2004) and Varshney (2002) for similar conclusions drawn from the case of India.

existing discrepancies, as communication and information about standards of living in other countries has become more commonplace. At the outset, I hypothesized that poverty would be a major driving force underlying ethnic mobilization.

The results reported here generally support the argument that economic well-being lowers rates of ethnic violence. Across most analyses, GDP per capita decreases the magnitude of violence. In many cases, measures of greater inequality within countries also are associated with increased rates of ethnic violence. Such findings are consistent with past research that has documented powerful effects of poverty on civil war, ethnic war, and ethnic tensions (Sambanis 2001; Collier and Sambanis 2002; Fearon and Laitin 2002).

Despite the consistency of these results with some prior results on ethnic conflict, a number of important questions about the quality of measures and sampling procedures used to gain information on economic inequality still linger. Analysis of the impact of GDP per capita in countries has been controversial for a number of reasons, both theoretical and methodological (K. Gleditsch 2002). First, for many countries, despite heroic efforts by the World Bank, there is missing information on per capita GDP and income inequality. There are good reasons to suspect that the countries with missing data are systematically different (politically and economically) from those that do report this information. Second, the quality of economic data is likely to be uneven because the capacity to collect comprehensive information and data collection techniques both vary across countries. Income distributions have been sampled at different intervals in different countries, making it difficult to identify the source of variation in GDP per capita.

I consider several specifications of models with two-way causation in Chapter 9. This issue, common to most macropolitical studies, concerns the issue of endogeneity of economic and political measures of regime stability and economic health (or poverty). It is likely that countries experiencing more ethnic unrest will also experience economic upheaval, suggesting that the forces of unrest hinder economic development. According to this view, results that indicate that economic instability produces ethnic unrest might change once the reverse causal argument has been investigated. Thus, although the results generally support the contention that poorer countries are more vulnerable to ethnic violence, there are good reasons to be skeptical about the direction of causation.

Recent increases in the availability of inequality indices have allowed researchers to distinguish the impact of inequality from that of overall poverty levels. Thus, in analyses of ethnic rebellion over the 1965–69 period (reported in Chapter 5) I found that countries with more income inequality experienced significantly lower levels of ethnic rebellion (as measured in the MAR data), which runs counter to most expectations. Unfortunately, the income inequality (Gini index) measures are not time-varying, and thus the data cannot address arguments suggesting that changing levels of inequality matters most.

A key empirical part of the world integration argument holds that, as an ideology of human rights and liberty comes to be accepted worldwide, economic inequality among ethnic groups will become the basis of demands by these groups to redress the inequities. The temporal pattern of my results supports this argument. So, while analysis of the pre-1989 period showed mixed effects of inequality, when income inequality was analyzed for a later period (1989–95, in Chapter 7), it was associated with increased rates of violent activity (conflicts and rebellion) based upon ethnicity. This is precisely the pattern that my world integration argument would predict.

Effects of economic inequality measured at the group level were much weaker in the analysis than were country-level measures. I found no significant effect on ethnic conflict of severity of economic disadvantage experienced by a group (MAR data set). This is all the more surprising given the country-level findings regarding poverty and ethnic rebellion, and given the large body of literature suggesting that economic grievances based upon gaps in inequality motivate and sustain insurgent activity. Why would poverty affect ethnic rebellion at the national level, but show no systematic effect regarding disadvantaged minorities?

Several collective action theories, reviewed in Chapter 1, provide explanations for these results by pointing to the *positive relationship between improved economic conditions and increased mobilization*. Thus, despite overall poverty, groups that experience improvement in economic well-being are subsequently more likely to mobilize. A large body of evidence suggests that sustained collective action, in the form of enduring social movements, occurs not when a group is most downtrodden, but instead when new opportunities and resources raise a group's standard of living.

Unfortunately, measures of income inequality are not available over time for a large number of cases (and indeed, reliable cross-sectional indicators of inequality have become available for a large number of countries only recently). Another important goal for the next stage of this line of research will be to gather more precise and reliable information on changes in levels of ethnic income inequality and ethnic mobilization.

EFFECTS OF WORLD INTEGRATION ON DEMOCRATIC AND AUTOCRATIC
POLITIES

My world integration argument suggests that there are strong cultural pressures on states to expand citizenship rights, implement inclusionary policies, and provide the institutional means for citizens to express demands to political elites, regardless of ethnicity, religion, or gender. Because democratic regimes have institutionalized nonviolent protest tactics and organizations, we would expect more nonviolent ethnic protest to occur where these rights are upheld most clearly. In this view, authoritarian regimes that are characterized by policies of ethnic exclusion, segregation, or repression will inspire more violent reactions from minority ethnic groups. Thus, another implication of the world integration argument is that more ethnic violence will occur under authoritarian than in democratic regimes. However, the evidence uncovered here did not support this assertion, and in some cases the opposite relationship held.

Many conventional explanations of violence have also proposed that violence is concentrated in underdeveloped countries, where democratic policies are rare and authoritarian regimes repress minorities. International relations perspectives have suggested that political shifts among contenders in multiparty systems play an influential role in shaping ethnic conflict. The findings presented in this book show that core countries experienced more ethnic protest (as expected) during the 1965–89 period and more ethnic violence (which was not anticipated) in the most recent period analyzed, 1995–98. Evidently, ethnic violence is not restrained by democratic polities, even when measures of media access, income levels, and other measures are included in the analysis. The findings for core countries remain potent, even when specific outliers (e.g., the United States and the United Kingdom) are taken out of the analysis, and even when per capita numbers of television sets (or radios, or newspapers) are included in the models.

Perhaps even more interesting are the findings that show that media-access measures are generally insignificant in models of ethnic nonviolence. However, the analyses presented here found some evidence that widespread access to the media increases the rate of ethnic violence. This finding suggests that violence is more easily diffused in countries with a strong television presence (holding constant income, income inequality, and prior unrest).

EFFECTS OF WORLD INTEGRATION ON ETHNIC COMPETITION

My world integration argument suggests that as the political and economic consequences of events in different countries become more intertwined, and as cultural patterns diffuse across regions, ethnic mobilization based on local concerns commands attention on an increasingly international platform. Because actions in one country affect other countries in the same network of economic, diplomatic, and organizational ties, local ethnic tensions can become cause for international concern and intervention. If this argument is correct, then, as ethnic competition theory suggests, we would expect to find that competition between ethnically distinct populations over agricultural or pastoral land or other scarce resources will escalate levels of inter-ethnic conflict. What did our analysis show in the way of support for these competition theories? Interestingly, competition for land substantially raised the likelihood of more serious levels of ethnic violence, while similar competition for land decreased large-scale protest. However, geographic concentration of ethnic populations had no effect on violence.[8] Nor did measures of group solidarity have any discernible effect on either ethnic protest or ethnic violence.

However, geographic concentration of groups may not always be due to high levels of solidarity—they may have been forced to settle in various "homelands" or "reservations." Thus, it could be difficult to isolate the effects of state repression and of geographic concentration on ethnic violence. To parse these effects, I included a measure of duration of residence by a group in a single area, and this had no effect on violence or protest. Indeed, the analysis that attempted to adjudicate between these explanations showed that prior repression had more consistently positive and significant effects on ethnic violence, when compared to the reverse causal argument.

Previous confrontations among groups over land substantially raise the likelihood of ethnic violence. Since this indicator concerns competition over

[8] But see Fearon and Laitin (2002) for evidence that group concentration increased the magnitude of ethnic rebellions in 1960. In this study, Fearon and Laitin used a revised measure of group concentration, but did not control for all of the variables included in this book's analysis.

land (rather than government appointments, political representation, wages, jobs, or something else), this measure might be considered a proxy for agricultural economies, in which land disputes would be most intense. However, I found no independent effects of level of urbanization (or its inverse). Thus, the majority of results suggest that a group's experience with competition over territory provokes more ethnic violence (see also Toft 2003). An alternative explanation of this finding is that repressive colonialist regimes incite territorial rebellion, which generates subsequent rebellions (Sambanis 2004). However, I found no effect of colonial histories in this analysis, suggesting that it is current competition that incites violence.

It is also important to notice that the analyses suggest that competition over land might be escalating. The results show that competition over land had instigated more serious ethnic rebellions since the end of the Cold War than before then. Competition for land has an escalating effect on the magnitude and count of annual violent events, when the results from 1995–98 are compared to earlier periods. In all periods, inclusion of this measure of land competition raised rates of ethnic violence.

Interestingly, competition for land did not affect civil wars, interstate wars, or international wars. Stepping back from the details, it seems reasonable that ethnic competition would raise rates of violence among ethnic groups; however, some will find it surprising that land competition within states did not spill over to incite violence among state actors, once other factors are taken into account.

EFFECTS OF WORLD INTEGRATION ON STATE REPRESSION

One of the most consistent findings throughout this book concerns state actions designed to isolate and segregate ethnic populations—internal resettlement policies by states consistently contributed to the magnitude and incidence of ethnic protest and sustained ethnic movements throughout the period. In the event count analysis, the impact of resettlement policies directed against minorities consistently and significantly raised rates of ethnic violence and protest during the 1989–95 period (see Chapter 8). When analyses considered resettlement policies in the 1980s (see Chapter 6) and again in the 1990s (Chapter 8), the results remained equally potent for each period. Contrary to what state authorities may have wished, efforts to resettle and isolate minority groups served to increase the potential for rebellion that challenged these states. The world integration argument provides an explanation for these findings that rests on the diffusion of human rights ideology, which increasingly de-legitimates repression of minorities by state authorities. As a consequence, victimized groups mobilize against state authorities that have attempted to subdue them.

Other measures of state repression were explored, but were found wanting for a number of reasons. Because lagged measures of the dependent variable were included in the same models with (lagged) measures of repression, autocorrelation of error terms across panel waves might be hindering the analysis. Thus, an alternative hypothesis suggested was that state repression is endogenous to the process being examined. In this view, state repression is likely to be a function of prior strength of mobilization by challengers. For this reason, I explicitly modeled the cross-effects of state violence on ethnic violence (see Chapter 9).

The results were revealing, and suggest there is a mutually reinforcing pattern of state-sponsored violence and ethnic violence. Similar to the "tit-for-tat" perspective, my two-stage least squares analysis of state violence and ethnic violence showed potent effects, when a variety of other measures were included in the model. Moreover, prior state violence (measured by the count of violent events instigated by state authorities) significantly increased the number of incidents of ethnic violence. State violence also increased ethnic protest, net of the effects of other measures (including resettlement policies instigated by states).[9] Moreover, there is strong evidence that state violence escalates both violent and nonviolent activity, which suggests that state violence has a powerful mobilizing effect on minority groups.

Taken together, the findings on state repressive activity specifically directed against ethnic minorities show that such state actions are far from effective. My results are consistent with other findings showing that repression increases group solidarity and escalates the magnitude of ethnic movements. Contrary to many expectations, the evidence suggests that the presence of democratic institutions in a state does not moderate this effect of state violence. Moreover, state violence escalates ethnic mobilization in both violent and nonviolent forms even in democratic states. The lesson learned here is a significant one for understanding the effects of policies designed to undercut ethnic demands. The results shown here suggest that state violence and

---

[9] Recall that state repression includes activities directed against ethnic or racial groups by state armies, police, and other agents, in which arrests, violence, and mob attacks were sanctioned by internal state authorities.

geographical segregation of groups had the effect of raising rates of ethnic activity, not lowering them.

Cultural Distinctions and Group Mobilization

Do forces of internationalization promote different outcomes for ethnicity when more and less homogeneous states are compared? There are many reasons to suspect that internal divisions matter to mobilization. This perspective rests on a long-standing belief that the extent of cultural differences creates a potential for fissures and conflict among groups, which makes it more difficult to integrate a nation or region, and creates the potential for mobilization against centralized authority (Williams 1994). Moreover, the literature on nation-building and ethnic movements has indicated that diversity (when combined with geographic concentration) dampens integrative capacities of states and encourages nationalism, civil war, and ethnic-regional resistance movements.[10] By these arguments, ethnic diversity should increase the capacity of ethnic groups to mobilize against other groups and against state authorities, net of the effects of world-level forces.

Recent work has challenged these notions, arguing (among other things) that political mobilization creates and sustains cultural differences, not vice versa. Few researchers have found effects of linguistic fractionalization on ethnic mobilization, and the effects of cultural differences or distinctiveness on social movements are a matter of considerable debate (Cornell and Hartmann 1998). Up until recently, few studies have included measures of international organizational memberships and ethnic diversity in their analyses of these phenomena.

Though many theories would expect otherwise, in the models analyzed in this book indicators of language distinctions and ethnic heterogeneity were poor predictors of ethnic violence (see also Fearon and Laitin 2003).[11]

---

[10]See Eisenstadt and Rokkan (1975), Fearon and Laitin (2003), Toft (2003).

[11]I found some evidence that the relevance of ethnic diversity varied over time. For instance, for the 1965–69 period I found that the ethnic fractionalization index (Fearon 2002) was significantly related to higher magnitudes of ethnic protest and violence. However, for the period after 1975, I found no effect of ethnic fractionalization on the magnitude of ethnic rebellion. I also, in similar analyses to those presented here, explored Fearon's (2002) measure of cultural fractionalization, and found no systematic effects of the measure.

Thus, although many have argued that linguistic population distinctions matter to group solidarity and mobilization, I found almost no evidence supporting this claim. Nevertheless, it is difficult to dismiss the emotional and mobilizing power of ethnic distinctions. Clearly, it seems plausible that homogeneous settings have different kinds of interaction dynamics and lower potentials for conflict compared to settings that are becoming increasingly heterogeneous. Social psychologists tell us that interaction networks made up of self-identifying communities are the heart of any recruitment campaign, whether aimed at integration or disintegration of a state, religious salvation, or anti-war objectives. Ethnic movements are bounded by particular self-identifying features such as language and customs, which serve as interaction barriers. Furthermore, because most of the literature examining linguistic differences has focused on internal war more generally, the relationship of linguistic differences and ethnic war has remained obscure (but see Sambanis 2001, 2004).

I also explored a combined index of "cultural differentials" (provided by the MAR data set), which represents the degree of differences in religion, language, cultural beliefs, and norms of a given group with respect to the majority/official ethnic population in a country. In the analysis of nonviolent protest over the 1980–94 period, this index of cultural distinctiveness had a significant and positive effect on levels of ethnic nonviolent activity (see Chapter 6), but it did not affect violent rebellion. Nevertheless, it is difficult to ascertain from these findings which comes first: cultural differences or mobilization. In other words, cultural distinctions might be a function of prior mobilization, which reinforces group boundaries.

The fluidity of identity politics in various settings has intrigued researchers in the areas of social movements, anti-foreigner politics, the new social movements literature, and collective violence. While the findings reported here suggest that some kinds of identity markers (notably ethnic ones) enhance nonviolent ethnic politics, other types of identities (here religious ones) undercut ethnic movements. Several provocative lines of research have suggested that it will be useful to examine *how collective action forms identities,* as, under some conditions, these identities come to take on a life of their own (Gould 1999; McAdam et al. 2001; Tilly 2003). These mutually reinforcing processes will be especially important to understand when trying to sort out and isolate the roles of cultural, linguistic, and religious differences in producing animosity and ethnic tensions.

I found that religious fractionalization subdues ethnic conflict and protest over most of the periods analyzed. Religious fractionalization also subdues the potential for civil wars of all kinds (this result is significant in most, but not all, cases). The powerful negative effect of religious diversity on ethnic violence suggests that we should revisit some of the classic treatments of cross-cutting cleavages in theories of nation-building and conflict (e.g., Eisenstadt and Rokkan 1975), and suggests some advantages to studying religious, cultural, and ethnic identities simultaneously. The results showing that religious fractionalization undercuts ethnic violence suggest the importance of understanding the conditions under which identities will lead to violence, and those under which other identities provide cross-currents that undermine this process. Because few if any researchers have considered the role of religion and ethnicity at the same time, our understanding of the relationship between identities and mobilization has been limited (but see Reynal-Querol 2002). The findings reported here provide some insights on how various cultural identities can alternately encourage either social integration or disintegration, under specific conditions.

Effects of Ethnic Conflict on Civil and International War

To understand the relationship of ethnic mobilization to other types of conflict situations, I analyzed a data set containing annual counts of internal, interstate, and international war. I follow the lead of Gleditsch et al. (2001), Sambanis (2001, 2004), Fearon and Laitin (2002, 2003), and others, who have turned scholarly attention to both the similarities and the differences between ethnic wars and other types of major conflict. I found a significant relationship between prior ethnic violence and internal wars, but also found that ethnic wars were significantly associated with the outbreak of international wars. Using newly available data on the outbreak of different types of wars, I found that the pattern of effects for these types of non-ethnic wars was significantly different from the patterns associated with ethnic violence. There is one exception to this finding: lower income levels were associated with most types of war.

While ethnic fractionalization had no effect on ethnic violence in my analysis, the examination of forms of civil and international war tells a different story, one that is more consistent with the argument that ethnic fractionalization generates animosity. I found that ethnic fractionalization consistently and significantly raised the likelihood of international war. Ethnic fractionalization is related more generally to interstate conflict, but not related to group conflict within states (especially in recent years), which is intriguing because it is somewhat counterintuitive. As others have found, intense ethnic conflicts do not coincide with boundaries indicating extremes in cultural difference.

I explored the impact of a number of political indicators on international, interstate, and civil wars, in an attempt to examine theories of democratic structure, regularized access to politics, and restrictions on civil rights. Grievance models would suggest that states that restrict civil rights and states without regular access to expression of political demands would be significantly more likely to experience civil wars of various kinds, including intervention of international war. While restrictions on civil rights seemed to have a significant effect on the level of internal war, the presence of a democratic regime did not affect internal, interstate, or international war. The positive effect of restrictions on internal war is consistent with the world polity argument (supported in several chapters) that exclusionary laws reinforce ethnic identities and render existing discriminatory patterns unacceptable.[12]

There are strong spillover effects of violence influencing the outbreak of interstate war.[13] As Elbadawi and Sambanis (2002) argue, living in a "dangerous neighborhood" apparently raises the likelihood that interstate violence will occur, as might be expected. This book also reports evidence suggesting that transnational support from ethnic kindred groups strongly influenced the pattern of ethnic violence in the 1995–98 period. Thus, both indicators suggest that having ethnically similar friends in nearby regions influences the trajectory of violent social movements based upon ethnicity.

Factors related to ethnic violence were often unrelated to civil wars. For example, resettlement policies and embeddedness in the world system were not significant determinants of non-ethnic civil wars, and countries with larger populations were less vulnerable to international war and ethnic violence (but these countries were likely to have interstate wars). Contrary to what many might have expected, peripheral status of a country significantly

---

[12] These results also support grievance models of collective action. Without direct measures of changes in grievance levels (or subjective perceptions of discrimination), it is difficult to adjudicate between these two explanations, given the limitations of my measures.

[13] Recall that interstate war is defined here as war between two states.

decreased the rates of international war, independent of prior ethnic violence in a state.

As Collier and Sambanis (2002) and others have found, internal wars are often fueled by poverty. I found that measure of GDP per capita consistently perform better than other indicators, and that the effect of higher per capita GDP is to decrease violence of all types. Investigation of primary trade exports and oil exports (often used as proxy measures of warring faction "greed") did not show any significant effects, net of the effect of GDP per capita. Thus, as many have warned, poverty breeds discontent of various types, leading to a variety of wars, including ethnic ones.

Future Considerations

Mobilization based on ethnic and racial identity is not new. However, what might be novel about the contemporary period is the notion that ethnic movements constitute a threat to world stability (Barber 1996; Gurr 1993). This book questions this claim on a number of grounds, including evidence that the amount of ethnic protest and violence seems to be declining. This same conclusion cannot be drawn from the evidence on the magnitude of serious ethnic rebellion. Thus, when the trends in more violent forms of ethnic mobilization are examined, the evidence that ethnicity is declining in importance is more ambiguous. The data show that while the number of events involving ethnic claims has declined in recent years, the remaining ethnic movements seem more entrenched and intractable. We see a downward trajectory in counts of ethnic events, but this downward trend is concentrated in wealthier countries and countries that have mitigating religious cleavages. If the trends continue, these patterns raise some fundamental questions about the persistence of group mobilization, identity politics, and violence.

Taken together, the results suggest that poverty and embeddedness in a world system of organizations has led to a concentration of violent ethnic activity in a few vulnerable regions. Although democratic and wealthier countries are not immune to ethnic mobilization and conflict, sustained ethnic rebellions are significantly more likely in regions that have more poverty and fewer natural resources.[14] Whether or not these trends continue remains an open empirical question.

[14]For evidence on trends in income inequality, see Goesling (2001) and Firebaugh and Goesling (2004).

Although the absolute number of violent acts on behalf of ethnic or racial identity may have declined, violent ethnic movements continue, and other types of terrorist activity (such as suicide bombings) seem to have increased in frequency. Outbreaks of terrorism and violence in recent decades have led some to suggest that a serious transformation in forms of ethnic violence has occurred. Although not all of the evidence is in, contemporary violence appears to be less centralized (or harder to trace directly to state authorities), more sporadic, and more transnational in character, in terms of both participants and location of violence. Indeed, it has become almost commonplace to argue that violence is international. Only a few scholars have taken this observation to the next step and asked if the kinds of globalization processes analyzed in this book escalate other forms of group violence, including war (e.g., Tarrow 2001, 2005; Bremer et al. 2003).

Without solid historical evidence showing increases in other forms of violence generated by globalization, it is difficult to answer this question with certainty. Ongoing communal violence in the Middle East, Afghanistan, Iraq, Saudi Arabia, Iran, Sudan, the Congo, and elsewhere does not support an optimistic prediction for peace in these regions. The world system arguments offered here provide some important insights about the politico-geographical location of challenges to state authority, suggesting that peripheral regions are isolated from a number of international links that might moderate such movements. Policymakers might benefit from this global perspective, especially when considering aid to poor or developing countries.

The results presented here suggest that some caution should be taken in assuming that dire consequences result from the awakening of ethnic identity. The assumption that ethnic mobilization poses a threat to world stability ignores a more important historical lesson about the dynamics of ethnicity and politics. In democratic nations, ethnic politics have long played a role in building diversity within political machines at the local level, increasing the ability of newcomers to participate in political decision-making. As a democratizing element, ethnic protest has often strengthened (not weakened) civil society in most Western societies. The same process may hold for nondemocratic countries, as ethnic protest diffuses from core to peripheral countries, and as groups make demands for inclusionary rather than exclusionary politics. Thus, fears about the destructive aspects of ethnic politics should be tempered by the understanding that ethnic politics also open opportunities and broaden democracy.

Another implication of the findings is that comparisons across types of group conflicts (comparing factors related to civil war, ethnic mobilization, and international war) allow us to assess the relative effects of international processes and national processes on mobilization. In particular, it appears that some ethnic movements remain local and challenge existing national regimes, while other types of wars seem more likely to mobilize along some other line of cleavage and gradually gain influence in nearby countries, and still other movements emanate from several national origins simultaneously. The global nature of social movements has only just begun to be examined, and much more study of cross-border flows of goals, techniques, tactics, funding, and personnel is needed.

While the difficulties of studying cross-border movements are substantial, the payoffs to such study are enormous. More macro-level theories will be required to understand the mechanisms behind the increasingly global scope of many movements, including a variety of human rights, anti-globalization, peace, environmental, and religious revival movements. This book has employed versions of world system and world polity theories as potentially useful paradigms for beginning to look at the broad range of macro-level processes that encourage mobilization based upon ethnicity. I have linked several global perspectives from nationalism theories and theories of collective action in order to begin understanding the conditions under which integration into the world system leads to different forms of ethnic mobilization.

The challenge for future research will be to specify more precisely the implications of these claims by expanding theories about the nature of ethnicity, identity, and other social movements that both challenge and support existing institutions and state authority. The ambiguous and fluid nature of ethnic, racial, religious, and national boundaries has provoked contentious and lively debates about the sources of group conflict. This trend is likely to continue, as groups and individuals voice contesting and contradictory claims for expanded rights based on ethnic identity. This is both the beauty and the frustration of studying the fluctuation in ethnic mobilization as it continuously transforms and reshapes itself over time and place.

Countries in the Analysis in Chapters 4–6

1 Afghanistan	27 Egypt
2 Albania	28 El Salvador
3 Algeria	29 Ethiopia
4 Angola	30 France
5 Argentina	31 Germany(fr 1990)
6 Australia	32 Ghana
7 Bahrain	33 Greece
8 Bhutan	34 Guatemala
9 Bolivia	35 Guinea
10 Botswana	36 Guyana
11 Brazil	37 Honduras
12 Bulgaria	38 Hungary
13 Burma	39 India
14 Burundi	40 Indonesia
15 Cameroon	41 Iran
16 Canada	42 Iraq
17 Chad	43 Israel
18 Chile	44 Italy
19 China	45 Ivory Coast
20 Colombia	46 Japan
21 Costa Rica	47 Jordan
22 Cyprus	48 Kampuchia
23 Czechoslovakia	49 Kenya
24 Dominican Republic	50 Laos
25 East Germany (until 1990)	51 Lebanon
26 Ecuador	52 Liberia

53 Madagascar

54 Malasia

55 Mali

56 Mauritania

57 Mexico

58 Morocco

59 Namibia

60 New Zealand

61 Nicaragua

62 Niger

63 Nigeria

64 North Vietnam (until 1972)

65 Pakistan

66 Panama

67 Papua New Guinea

68 Paraguay

69 Peru

70 Philippines

71 Republic of Congo

72 Romania

73 Rwanda

74 Saudi Arabia

75 Senegal

76 Sierra Leone

77 Singapore

78 Somalia

79 South Africa

80 South Korea

81 South Vietnam (until 1973)

82 Spain

83 Sri Lanka

84 Sudan

85 Switzerland

86 Syria

87 Taiwan

88 Tanzania

89 Thailand

90 Togo

91 Turkey

92 United Kingdom

93 United States

94 United Soviet Socialist Rep.
   (until 1990)

95 Uganda

96 Venezuela

97 Vietnam (fr 1973)

98 West Germany (until 1990)

99 Yugoslavia (until 1994)

100 Zaire

101 Zambia

102 Zimbabwe

Countries in the Analysis in Chapters 7–9

1 Afghanistan
2 Albania
3 Angola
4 Argentina
5 Australia
6 Austria
7 Bahrain
8 Bangladesh
9 Belgium
10 Belize
11 Benin
12 Bhutan
13 Bolivia
14 Bosnia (after 1993)
15 Bulgaria
16 Burma
17 Burundi
18 Cameroon
19 Canada
20 Cape Verde
21 Central African Rep.
22 Chad
23 Chile
24 China
25 Colombia
26 Costa Rica

25 Croatia (fr 1993)
26 Cuba
27 Cyprus
28 Czechoslovakia
    (until 1993)
29 Czech Republic (fr 1993)
30 Denmark
31 Djibouti
32 Dominican Republic
33 Ecuador
34 East Germany (until 1990)
35 Egypt
36 El Salvador
37 Eritrea (after 1991)
38 Ethiopia
39 Fiji
40 Finland
41 France
38 Gabon
39 Gambia
40 Germany (fr 1990)
41 Georgia (fr 1990)
42 Ghana
43 Greece
44 Guatemala
45 Guinea

46 Guinea-Bissau

47 Guyana

48 Haiti

49 Honduras

50 Hungary

51 Iceland

52 India

53 Indonesia

54 Iran

55 Iraq

56 Ireland

57 Israel

58 Italy

59 Ivory Coast

60 Jamaica

61 Japan

62 Jordan

63 Kampuchia

64 Kazhakhstan (fr 1992)

65 Kenya

66 Korea (S)

67 Korea (N)

68 Kuwait

69 Kyrgyzstan (fr 1992)

70 Laos

71 Latvia (fr 1992)

72 Lebanon

73 Lesotho

74 Liberia

75 Lithuania

76 Macedonia

77 Madagascar

78 Malaysia

79 Mali

80 Mauritania

81 Mautitius

82 Mexico

83 Moldova (fr 1992)

84 Morocco

85 Mozambique

86 Namibia

87 Nepal

88 Netherlands

89 New Zealand

90 Nicaragua

91 Niger

92 Nigeria

93 Norway

94 Pakistan

95 Panama

96 Papua New Guinea

97 Paraguay

98 Peru

99 Philippines

100 Poland

101 Portugal

102 Qatar

103 Republic of Congo

104 Romania

105 Rwanda

106 Saudia Arabia

107 Senegal

108 Sierra Leone

109 Singapore

110 Slovakia (fr 1993)

111 Somalia

112 South Africa

113 Spain

114 Sri Lanka

115 Sudan

116 Suriname

117 Swaziland

118 Sweden

119 Switzerland

120 Syria

121 Taiwan

122 Tajikistan (fr 1991)

123 Tanzania

124 Thailand

125 Tunisia

126 Turkey

127 Turkmenistan (fr 1991)

128 United Arab Ermirates

129 United Kingdom

130 United States

131 Uganda

132 Ukraine (fr 1991)

133 Uruguay

134 Uzbekistan (fr 1991)

135 Venezuela

136 Vietnam (fr 1973)

137 West Germany (until 1990)

138 Yemen (fr 1991)

139 Yugoslavia (until 1994)

140 Zaire

141 Zambia

142 Zimbabwe

Akbar, Ahmed S. 1995. "'Ethnic Cleansing': A Metaphor for Our Time?" *Ethnic and Racial Studies* 18: 3–25.

Alderson, Arthur S., and François Nielsen. 2002. "Globalization and the Great U-Turn: Income Inequality Trends in 16 OECD Countries." *American Journal of Sociology* 107: 1244–99.

Anderson, Benedict O'Gorman. 1991. *Imagined Communities*. London: Verso.

Appadurai, Arjun. 1996. *Modernity at Large: Cultural Dimensions of Globalization*. Minneapolis: University of Minnesota Press.

Arrighi, Giovanni, and Beverly J. Silver. 1999. *Chaos and Governance in the Modern World System*. Minneapolis: University of Minnesota Press.

Atlas Narodov Mira [Atlas of Peoples of the World]. 1964. Moscow: Glavnoe Upravlenie Geodezii i Kartografii.

Baldassare, Mark. 1994. *The Los Angeles Riots: Lessons for the Urban Future*. Boulder, CO: Westview.

Baltagi, Bani H. 1995. *Econometric Analysis of Panel Data*. New York: Wiley.

Baltagi, Bani H., and Y. Chang. 2000. "Simultaneous Equations with Incomplete Panels." *Econometric Theory* 16: 269–79.

Banks, Arthur S. 1990. *Cross-National Time-Series Data Archive*. Binghamton, NY: Center for Comparative Political Research.

Banton, Michael. 1983. *Racial and Ethnic Competition*. Cambridge: Cambridge University Press.

Barber, Benjamin. 1996. *Jihad vs. McWorld: How Globalization and Tribalism Are Reshaping the World*. New York: Ballantine.

Barron, David N. 1990. "Analysis of Event Counts: Over-Dispersion and Autocorrelation." M.A. thesis, Cornell University.

———. 1992. "The Analysis of Count Data: Overdispersion and Autocorrelation." Pp. 179–220 in Peter V. Marsden (ed.), *Sociological Methodology*, vol. 22. Oxford: Blackwell.

Barron, David N., and Michael T. Hannan. 1991. "Autocorrelation and Density Dependence in Organizational Founding Rates: Quasi-likelihood Estimation." *Sociological Methods and Research* 20: 218–41.

Barth, Fredrik. 1956. "Ecologic Relationships of Ethnic Groups in Swat, North Pakistan." *American Anthropologist* 58: 1079–89

—— (ed.). 1969. "Introduction." Pp. 1–38 in *Ethnic Groups and Boundaries*. Boston: Little, Brown.

Beissinger, Mark. 2002. *Nationalist Mobilization and the Collapse of the Soviet State*. New York: Cambridge University Press.

Berkowitz, Nitza. 1999. *From Motherhood to Citizenship: Women's Rights and International Organizations*. Baltimore, MD: Johns Hopkins University Press.

Bennett, Scott Jr., and Christian Davenport. 2005. *MARGene: Minorities at Risk Data Generation and Management Program v1.05, Documentation*. www.cidcm.umd.edu/inscr/mar/margene.asp (accessed August 28, 2005).

Bhavnani, Ravi, and David Backer. 2000. "Localized Ethnic Conflict and Genocide." *Journal of Conflict Resolution* 44: 283–306.

Blalock, Hubert M. 1967. *Toward a Theory of Minority Group Relations*. New York: Wiley.

Blau, Peter. 1977. *Inequality and Heterogeneity*. New York: Free Press.

Blomberg, S. Brock, and Gregory D. Hess. 2002. "The Temporal Links Between Conflict and Economic Activity." *Journal of Conflict Resolution* 46: 74–90.

Boli, John. 2001. "Sovereignty from a World Polity Perspective." Pp. 53–82 in Krasner, *Problematic Sovereignty*.

Boli, John, and George M. Thomas. 1999. *Constructing World Culture*. Stanford, CA: Stanford University Press.

Bollen, Kenneth. 1989. "Democracy, Stability, and Dichotomies." *American Sociological Review* 54: 612–21.

Bonacich, Edna. 1972. "A Theory of Ethnic Antagonism: The Split Labor Market." *American Sociological Review* 37: 547–59.

Bookman, Milica Z. 2002. *Ethnic Groups in Motion: Economic Competition and Migration in Multiethnic States*. London: Frank Cass.

Bornschier, Volker, and Christopher Chase-Dunn. 1985. *Transnational Corporations and Underdevelopment*. New York: Praeger.

Borstelmann, Thomas. 2001. *The Cold War and the Color Line*. Cambridge, MA: Harvard University Press.

Boskin, Joseph. 1976. *Urban Racial Violence in the Twentieth Century*. Beverly Hills, CA: Glencoe.

Boswell, Terry. 1986. "A Split Labor Market Analysis of Discrimination Against Chinese Immigrants." *American Sociological Review* 51: 352–71.

Boswell, Terry, and William J. Dixon. 1990. "Dependency and Rebellion: A Cross-National Analysis." *American Sociological Review* 55: 540–59.

Box-Steffensmeir, Janet, Dan Reiter, and Christopher Zorn. 2003. "Nonproportional Hazards and Event History Analysis in International Relations." *Journal of Conflict Resolution* 47: 33–53.

Brass, Paul R. 1991. *Ethnicity and Nationalism: Theory and Comparison*. Newbury Park, CA: Sage.

———. 1997. *Theft of an Idol: Text and Context in the Representation of Collective Violence*. Princeton, NJ: Princeton University Press.

Bremer, Stuart A., Patrick Regan, and David H. Clark. 2003. "Building a Science of World Politics: Emerging Methodologies and the Study of Conflict." *Journal of Conflict Resolution* 47: 3–12.

Brown, Michael E. (ed.). 1996. *The International Dimensions of Internal Conflict*. Cambridge, MA: MIT Press.

Brubaker, Rogers. 1996. *Nationalism Reframed: Nationhood and the National Question*. Cambridge: Cambridge University Press.

Brubaker, Rogers, and David D. Laitin. 1998. "Ethnic and Nationalist Violence." *Annual Review of Sociology* 24: 423–52.

Calhoun, Craig. 1993. "Nationalism and Ethnicity." *Annual Review of Sociology* 19: 211–39.

Cameron, A. Colin, and Pravin K. Trivedi. 1986. "Econometric Models Based on Count Data." *Journal of Applied Econometrics* 1: 29–53.

———. 2003. *Regression Analysis of Count Data*. Cambridge: Cambridge University Press.

Caniglia, Beth Schaefer. 2002. "Elite Alliances and Transnational Environmental Movement Organizations." Pp. 153–69 in J. Smith and Johnston, *Globalization and Resistance*.

Carment, David, and Patrick James. 1995. "International Constraints and Interstate Ethnic Conflict." *Journal of Conflict Resolution* 39: 82–109.

Cederman, Lars-Erik. 2004. "Articulating the Geo-Cultural Logic of Nationalist Insurgency." Version 2.0. Paper presented at the Joint Session of Workshops, ECPR, Uppsala Sweden, April 2004, and at the conference "Order, Conflict, and Violence," Department of Political Science, Yale University, May 2004.

Clinton, Joshua, Simon Jackman, and Douglas Rivers. 2004. "The Statistical Analysis of Roll Call Data." *American Political Science Review* 98: 355–70.

Coicaud, Jean-Marc, Michael W. Doyle, and Anne-Marie Gardner. 2003. *The Globalization of Human Rights*. Tokyo, Paris, New York: United Nations Press.

Collier, Paul. 2000. "Economic Causes of Civil Conflict and Their Implications for Policy." Washington, DC: World Bank, Development Research Group.

Collier, Paul, and Anke Hoeffler. 2004. "Greed and Grievance in Civil War." Oxford Economic Papers 56: 563–95 (http://oep.oxfordjournals.org/cgi/content/abstract/56/4/563).

Collier, Paul, Anke Hoeffler, and Mans Söderbom. 2001. "On the Duration of Civil War." *Journal of Peace Research* 41: 253–73.

Collier, Paul, and Nicholas Sambanis. 2002. "Understanding Civil War." *Journal of Conflict Resolution* 46: 3–12.

Connor, Walker. 1973. "The Politics of Ethnonationalism." *Journal of International Affairs* 27: 1–21

——. 1978. "A Nation Is a Nation, Is a State, is an Ethnic Group. . ." *Ethnic and Racial Studies* 1: 377–400.

Cornell, Stephen, and Douglas Hartmann. 1998. *Ethnicity and Race: Making Identities in a Changing World.* Thousand Oaks, CA: Pine Forge.

Davenport, Christian. 1995. "Multidimensional Threat Perception and State Repression: An Inquiry into Why States Apply Negative Sanctions." *American Journal of Political Science* 38: 683–713.

Deininger, Klaus, and Lyn Squire. 1996. "A New Data Set Measuring Income Inequality." *World Bank Economic Review* 10: 565–91.

della Porta, Donatella, and Sidney Tarrow (eds.). 2005. *Transnational Protest and Global Activism.* Lanham, MD: Rowman and Littlefield.

Deutsch, Karl. 1953. *Nationalism and Social Communication.* Boston: MIT Press.

Earl, Jennifer. 2003. "Tanks, Tear Gas, and Taxes: Toward a Theory of Movement Repression." *Sociological Theory* 21: 44–68.

Efron, Brad, and Rob Tibshirani. 1993. *An Introduction to the Bootstrap.* New York: Chapman and Hall.

Eisenstadt, S. N., and Stein Rokkan (eds.). 1975. *Building States and Nations.* Vol. 2. Beverly Hills, CA: Sage.

Elbadawi, Ibrahim, and Nicholas Sambanis. 2000. "Why Are There So Many Civil Wars in Africa? Understanding and Preventing Violent Conflict." *Journal of African Economics* 9: 244–69.

——. 2002. "How Much War Will We See?" *Journal of Conflict Resolution* 46: 307–34.

Emerson, Rupert. 1964. *Malaysia: A Study in Direct and Indirect Rule.* Kuala Lumpur: University of Malaya Press.

Enloe, Cynthia. 1973. *Ethnic Conflict and Political Development.* Boston: Little, Brown.

——. 1980. *Ethnic Soldiers* Athens: University of Georgia Press.

Esman, Milton J. 1995. *International Organizations and Ethnic Conflict.* Ithaca, NY: Cornell University Press.

Fearon, James D. 1998. "Commitment Problems and the Spread of Ethnic Conflict." Pp. 107–26 in Lake and Rothchild, *The International Spread of Ethnic Conflict.*

——. 2002. "Ethnic Structure and Cultural Diversity Around the World: A Cross-National Data Set on Ethnic Groups." Paper presented at the annual meeting of the American Political Science Association, Boston, Aug. 2002.

——. 2004. "Why Do Some Civil Wars Last So Much Longer Than Others?" *Journal of Peace Research* 41: 275–302.

——. 2005. "Primary Commodity Exports and Civil War." *Journal of Conflict Resolution* 49: 483–507.

Fearon, James D., and David D. Laitin. 1996. "Explaining Interethnic Cooperation." *American Political Science Review* 90: 715–35.

——. 1997. "A Cross-Sectional Study of Large-Scale Ethnic Violence in the Postwar Period." Unpublished manuscript, Department of Political Science, University of Chicago.

——. 1999. "Weak States, Rough Terrain, and Large-Scale Ethnic Violence." Paper presented at the annual meeting of the American Political Science Association, Atlanta, Sept. 1999.

——. 2002. "Group Concentration and Civil War." Paper presented at the annual meeting of the American Political Science Association, Boston, Aug. 2002.

——. 2003. "Ethnicity, Insurgency, and Civil War." *American Political Science Review* 97: 75–90.

Firebaugh, Glenn, and Brian Goesling. 2004. "Accounting for the Recent Decline in Global Inequality." *American Journal of Sociology* 110: 283–312.

Fox, Jonathan. 2002. *Ethnoreligious Conflict in the Late Twentieth Century.* Oxford: Lexington Books.

Francisco, Ronald A. 1995. "The Relationship Between Coercion and Protest: An Empirical Evaluation in Three Coercive States." *Journal of Conflict Resolution* 39: 263–82.

Frank, David John, Ann Hironaka, and Evan Schofer. 2000. "The Nation-State and the Natural Environment over the Twentieth Century." *American Sociological Review* 65: 96–116.

Frank, David John, and Elizabeth H. McEneaney. 1999. "The Individualization of Society and the Liberalization of State Policies on Same-Sex Sexual Relations, 1984–1995." *Social Forces* 77: 911–43

Fredrickson, George M. 1995. *Black Liberation: A Comparative History of Black Ideologies in the United States and South Africa.* New York: Oxford University Press.

Freedom House. 1972–73 to 2001–02. *Freedom in the World: The Annual Survey of Political Rights and Civil Liberties.* www.freedomhouse.org/research.

Gamson, William A. 1975. *The Strategy of Social Protest.* Homewood, IL: Dorsey.

Gamson, William A., and David Meyer. 1996. "Framing Political Opportunities." Pp. 275–90 in Doug McAdam, John McCarthy, and Mayer Zald (eds.), *Current Perspectives on Social Movements.* New York: Cambridge University Press.

Gastil, Raymond D. 1973–2002 (annual vols.). *Freedom in the World: Political Rights and Civil Liberties.* New York: Freedom House..

Gellner, Ernest. 1983. *Nations and Nationalism.* Ithaca, NY: Cornell University Press.

Ghai, Yash. 2001. *Public Participation and Minorities.* London: Minority Rights International.

Gleditsch, Kristian Skrede. 2002. "Expanded Trade and GDP Data." *Journal of Conflict Resolution* 46: 712–24.

——. 2003. "Transnational Dimensions of Civil War." Unpublished Manuscript, Department of Political Science, University of California, San Diego, and

Centre for the Study of Civil War, International Peace Research Institute, Oslo, Norway.

Gleditsch, Nils Petter, Håvard Strand, Mikael Eriksson, Margareta Solleberg, and Peter Wallensteen. 2001. "Armed Conflict 1946–99: A New Dataset." Paper presented at the conference "Identifying Wars: Systematic Conflict Research and Its Utility in Conflict Resolution and Prevention," co-sponsored by the International Peace Research Institute, Oslo, the Department of Peace and Conflict Research, Uppsala University, and the World Bank, Development Economics Research Group, Uppsala, Sweden, June 2001.

Glick Schiller, Nina, Linda Basch, and Cristina Blanc-Szanton (eds.). 1992. *Towards a Transnational Perspective on Migration: Race, Class, Ethnicity and Nationalism Reconsidered.* New York: New York Academy of Sciences.

Glick Schiller, Nina, and Andreas Wimmer. 2003. "Methodological Nationalism, the Social Sciences, and the Study of Migration: An Essay in Historical Epistemology." *International Migration Review* 37: 576–610.

Goesling, Brian. 2001. "Changing Income Inequalities Within and Between Nations: New Evidence." *American Sociological Review* 66: 745–61.

Goldstone, Jack A., Ted Robert Gurr, Barbara Harff, Marc A. Levy, Monty G. Marshall, Robert H. Bates, David L. Epstein, Colin H. Kahl, Pamela T. Surko, John C. Ulfelder Jr., and Alan N. Unger. 2000. *State Failure Task Force Report: Phase III Findings.* McLean, VA: Science Applications International Corporation, 30 September. See also www.cidcm.umd.edu/inscr/stfail/.

Gould, Roger. 1999. "Collective Violence and Group Solidarity: Evidence from a Feuding Society." *American Sociological Review* 64: 356–80.

Green, Donald P., Jack Glaser, and Andrew Rich. 1998. "From Lynching to Gay Bashing: The Elusive Connection Between Economic Conditions and Hate Crime." *Journal of Personality and Social Psychology* 75: 82–92.

Green, Donald P., Janelle S. Wong, and Dara Z. Strolovitch. 1998. "Defended Neighborhoods, Integration, and Racially Motivated Crime." *American Journal of Sociology* 104: 372–403.

Gupta, Dipak K., Harinder Singh, and Tom Sprague. 1993. "Government Coercion of Dissidents: Deterrence or Provocation?" *Journal of Conflict Resolution* 37: 301–39.

Gurowitz, Amy. 1999. "Mobilizing International Norms: Domestic Actors, Immigrants, and the Japanese State." *World Politics* 51: 413–45.

Gurr, Ted Robert. 1990. *Polity II: Polity Structures and Regime Change, 1800–1986.* Ann Arbor, MI: Inter-University Consortium on Political and Social Research.

——. 1993. *Minorities at Risk: A Global View of Ethnopolitical Conflicts.* Washington, DC: United States Institute of Peace Press.

——. 1996. *Minorities at Risk Phase III Dataset*, User's Manual. College Park, MD: Center for International Development and Conflict Management, University of Maryland.

——. 1999. *Minorities At Risk Dataset Users Manual MARDS.899*. College
    Park, MD: Center for International Development and Conflict Management,
    University of Maryland. www.cidcm.umd.edu (accessed January
    2001).

——. 2000. *Peoples Versus States: Minorities at Risk in the New Century*.
    Washington, DC: United States Institute of Peace Press.

——. 2003. MARGene. Minorities at Risk Data Generation and Management
    Program. College Park, MD: Center for International Development and
    Conflict Management, University of Maryland.
    www.cidcm.umd.edu/inscr/mar/data.asp (accessed July 2004).

Gurr, Ted Robert, and Barbara Harff. 1996. *Early Warnings of Communal Conflict
    and Genocide: Linking Empirical Research to International Responses*. Tokyo:
    United Nations University Press.

Gurr, Ted Robert, and Mark Irving Lichbach. 1986. "Forecasting Internal Conflict:
    A Competitive Evaluation of Empirical Theories." *Comparative Political
    Studies* 19: 3–38.

Gurr, Ted Robert, and Will H. Moore. 1997. "Ethnopolitical Rebellion: A Cross-
    Sectional Analysis of the 1980s with Risk Assessments for the 1990s."
    American Journal of Political Science 41: 1079–1103.

Gurr, Ted Robert, and James R. Scarritt. 1989. "Minorities at Risk: A Global
    Survey." *Human Rights Quarterly* 11: 375–405.

Halperin, Sandra. 1998. "The Spread of Ethnic Conflict in Europe: Some
    Comparative-Historical Reflections." Pp. 151–84 in Lake and Rothchild, *The
    International Spread of Ethnic Conflict*.

Hannan, Michael T. 1979. "The Dynamics of Ethnic Boundaries in Modern
    States." Pp. 253–75 in Meyer and Hannan, *National Development and the
    World System*.

Hechter, Michael. 1975. *Internal Colonialism*. Berkeley: University of California
    Press.

——. 1987a. *Principles of Group Solidarity*. Berkeley: University of California
    Press.

——. 1987b. "Nationalism as Group Solidarity." *Ethnic and Racial Studies* 10:
    415–26.

——. 1992. "The Dynamics of Secession." *Acta Sociologica* 35: 267–83.

——. 2000. *Containing Nationalism*. Oxford: Oxford University Press.

——. 2004. "From Class to Culture." *American Journal of Sociology* 110:
    400–445.

Hechter, Michael, and Margaret Levi. 1979. "A Comparative Analysis of
    Ethno-Regional Movements." *Ethnic and Racial Studies* 2: 260–74.

Hegre, Håvard, Ranveig Gissinger, and Nils Petter Gleditsch. 2003. "Globalization
    and Internal Conflict." Pp. 251–75 in Gerald Schneider, Katherine Barbieri,
    and Nils Petter Gleditsch (eds.), *Globalization and Armed Conflict*. Lanham,
    MD: Rowman and Littlefield.

Henderson, Errol A. 1997. "Culture of Contiguity: Ethnic Conflict, the Similarity of States, and the Onset of War, 1820–89." *Journal of Conflict Resolution* 41: 649–68.

Henderson, Errol A., and J. D. Singer. 2000. "Civil War in the Post-Colonial World, 1946–92." *Journal of Peace Research* 37: 275–99.

Hill, Stuart, Donald Rothchild, and Colin Cameron. 1998. "Tactical Information and the Diffusion of Peaceful Protests." Pp. 61–88 in Lake and Rothchild, *The International Spread of Ethnic Conflict*.

Hironaka, Ann. 2005. *Neverending Wars: Weak States, the International Community, and the Perpetuation of Civil War*. Cambridge, MA: Harvard University Press.

Horowitz, Donald L. 1985. *Ethnic Groups in Conflict*. Berkeley: University of California Press.

———. 2001. *The Deadly Ethnic Riot*. Berkeley: University of California Press.

Hug, Simon, and Dominique Wisler. 1998. "Multiple Sources in the Collection of Data on Political Conflict." *Mobilization: An International Journal* 3: 141–61.

Huntington, Samuel P. 1996. *The Clash of Civilizations and the Remaking of the World Order*. New York: Simon and Schuster.

———. 2000. "Try Again: A Reply to Russett, Oneal and Cox." *Journal of Peace Research* 37: 609–10.

———. 2004. *Who Are We? The Challenges to America's National Identity*. New York: Simon and Schuster.

Isaacs, Harold. 1975. *Idols of the Tribe*. Cambridge, MA: Harvard University Press.

Jalali, Rita, and Seymour Martin Lipset. 1992–93. "Racial and Ethnic Conflicts: A Global Perspective." *Political Science Quarterly* 107: 585–606.

Jenkins, J. Craig, and Doug Bond. 2001. "Conflict Carrying Capacity, Political Crisis and Reconstruction." *Journal of Conflict Resolution* 45: 3–31.

Jenkins, J. Craig, and Susanne Schmeidl. 1995. "Flight from Violence: The Origins and Implications of the World Refugee Crisis." *Sociological Focus* 28: 63–82.

Jenness, Valerie, and Rykken Grattet. 2001. *Making Hate a Crime*. New York: Russell Sage Foundation.

Jentelson, Bruce W. 1998. "Preventive Diplomacy and Ethnic Conflict: Possible, Difficult, Necessary." Pp. 293–316 in Lake and Rothchild, *The International Spread of Ethnic Conflict*.

Jepperson, Ronald L. 1992. "National Scripts: Varying Construction of Individualism and Opinion Across Modern Nation-States." Ph.D. diss., Yale University.

———. 2000. "Institutional Logics: On the Constitutive Dimension of the Modern Nation-State Polities." Working Paper 2000/36, Robert Schuman Centre for Advanced Studies, European University Institute, Florence, Italy.

———. 2002. "Political Modernities: Disentangling Two Underlying Dimensions of Institutional Differentiation." *Sociological Theory* 20: 61–85.

Kaldor, Mary. 1999. *New and Old Wars: Organized Violence in a Global Era.* Stanford, CA: Stanford University Press.

Kalyvas, Stathis. 2003. "The Ontology of 'Political Violence': Action and Identity in Civil Wars." *Perspectives on Politics* 1: 475–94.

Keck, Margaret E., and Kathryn Sikkink. 1998. *Activists Beyond Borders*. Ithaca, NY: Cornell University Press.

Keohane, Robert O., and Helen V. Milner (eds.). 1996. *Internationalization and Domestic Politics*. Cambridge: Cambridge University Press.

Keohane, Robert O., and Joseph Nye, Jr. (eds.). 1972. *Transnational Relations and World Politics*. Cambridge, MA: Harvard University Press.

Khagram, Sanjeev. 2004. *Dams and Development: Transnational Struggles for Water and Power*. Ithaca, NY: Cornell University Press.

Khagram, Sanjeev, James V. Riker, and Kathryn Sikkink (eds.). 2002. *Transnational Restructuring: Social Movements, Networks, and World Politics*. Minneapolis: University of Minnesota Press.

King, Gary. 1989. "Variance Specification in Event Count Models: From Restrictive Assumptions to a Generalized Estimator." *American Journal of Political Science* 33: 762–84.

Kiser, Edgar, and Michael Hechter. 1991. "The Role of General Theory in Comparative-Historical Sociology." *American Journal of Sociology* 97: 1–30.

Klandermans, Bert, and Suzanne Staggenborg. 2002. *Methods of Social Movement Research*. Minneapolis: University of Minnesota Press.

Koopmans, Ruud. 1993 "The Dynamics of Protest Waves: West Germany, 1965 to 1989." *American Sociological Review* 58: 637–58.

——. 1995. *Democracy from Below*. Boulder, CO: Westview.

——. 1996. "New Social Movements and Changes in Political Participation in Western Europe." *Western European Politics* 19: 28–50.

Koopmans, Ruud, and Susan Olzak. 2004. "Discursive Opportunities and the Evolution of Right-Wing Violence in Germany." *American Journal of Sociology* 110: 198–230.

Koopmans, Ruud, and Paul Statham. 1999. "Challenging the Liberal Nation-State? Postnationalism, Multiculturalism, and the Collective Claims Making of Migrant and Ethnic Minorities in Britain and Germany." *American Journal of Sociology* 105: 652–96.

—— (eds). 2000. *Challenging Immigration and Ethnic Relations Politics: Comparative European Perspectives*. Cambridge: Cambridge University Press.

Krain, Matthew. 1997. "State-Sponsored Mass Murder: The Onset and Severity of Genocides and Politicides." *Journal of Conflict Resolution* 41: 331–60.

Krasner, Stephen (ed.). 2001. *Problematic Sovereignty: Contested Rules and Political Possibilities*. New York: Columbia University Press.

Kriesi, Hanspeter. 1995. "The Political Opportunity Structure of New Social Movements: Its Impact on Their Mobilization." Pp. 167–98 in J. Craig Jenkins and Bert Klandermans (eds), *The Politics of Social Protest*. Minneapolis: University of Minnesota Press

Kriesi, Hanspeter, Ruud Koopmans, Jan Willem Duyvendak, and Marco G. Guigni. 1995. *New Social Movements in Western Europe*. Minneapolis: University of Minnesota Press.

Kuper, Leo, and M. G. Smith. 1969. *Pluralism in Africa*. Berkeley: University of California Press.

Laitin, David D. 1995. "National Revivals and Violence." *Archives Européennes de Sociologie* 36: 3–43.

———. 1998. *Identity in Formation: The Russian-Speaking Populations in the Near Abroad*. Ithaca, NY: Cornell University Press.

———. 2000. "What Is a Language Community?" *American Journal of Political Science* 44: 142–55.

Lake, David A., and Donald S. Rothchild (eds.). 1998. *The International Spread of Ethnic Conflict*. Princeton, NJ: Princeton University Press.

Lapping, Brian. 1989. *Apartheid: A History*. New York: George Braziller.

Levi, Margaret. 1997. *Consent, Dissent, and Patriotism*. Cambridge: Cambridge University Press.

Levine, Alicia. 1996. "Political Accommodation and the Prevention of Secessionist Violence." Pp. 311–41 in Brown, *International Dimensions of Internal Conflict*.

Levitt, Peggy. 2001. *The Transnational Villagers*. Berkeley: University of California Press.

Levitt, Peggy, and Rafael de la Dehesa. 2003. "Transnational Migration and the Redefinition of the State: Variation and Explanations." *Ethnic and Racial Studies* 26: 587–611.

Lichbach, Mark Irving. 1987. "Deterrence or Escalation?" *Journal of Conflict Resolution* 31: 266–97.

———. 1995. *The Rebel's Dilemma*. Ann Arbor: University of Michigan Press.

Lieberson, Stanley. 1991. "Small N's and Big Conclusions: An Examination of the Reasoning in Comparative Studies Based on a Small Number of Cases." *Social Forces* 70: 307–20.

———. 1994. "More on the Uneasy Case for Using Mill-Type Methods in Small-N Comparative Studies." *Social Forces* 72: 1225–37.

Lijphardt, Arend. 1977. *Democracy in Plural Societies*. New Haven, CT: Yale University Press.

Long, J. Scott, and Jeremy Freese. 2001. *Regression Models for Categorical and Limited Dependent Variables with Stata*. College Station, TX: Stata Press.

Marsh, Kristin. 2001. "Compromise in South Africa: Class Relations, Political Opportunities, and the Contextual 'Ripe Moment' for Resolution." *Research in Social Movements, Conflict and Change* 23: 37–68.

Marshall, Monty G., and Keith Jaggers (principle investigators). 2005. *Polity IV Data Archive*. College Park, MD: Center for International Development and

Conflict Management, University of Maryland. www.cidcm.umd.edu/ inscr/polity.

Marx, Anthony. 1998. *Making Race and Nation: A Comparison of the United States, South Africa, and Brazil.* Cambridge: Cambridge University Press.

Mazrui, Ali A. 2000. "Transnational Ethnicity and Subnational Religion in Africa's Political Experience." Pp. 37–63 in Kjell Goldmann, Ulf Hannerz, and Charles Westin (eds.), *Nationalism and Internationalism in the Post–Cold War Era.* London: Routledge.

McAdam, Doug. 1982. *Political Process and the Development of Black Insurgency.* Chicago: University of Chicago Press.

———. 1983. "Tactical Innovation and the Pace of Insurgency." *American Sociological Review* 48: 735–54.

———. 1995. "'Initiator' and 'Spin-Off' Movements: Diffusion Processes in Protest Cycles." Pp. 217–39 in Mark Traugott (ed.), *Repertoires and Cycles of Collective Action.* Durham, NC: Duke University Press.

McAdam, Doug, John D. McCarthy, and Mayer Zald. 1988. "Social Movements." Pp. 695–738 in Neil J. Smelser (ed.), *Handbook of Sociology.* Newbury Park, CA: Sage.

McAdam, Doug, Sidney Tarrow, and Charles Tilly. 2001. *Dynamics of Contention.* Cambridge: Cambridge University Press.

McCarthy, John D., Clark McPhail, and Jackie Smith. 1996. "Images of Protest: Dimensions of Selection Bias in Media Coverage of Washington Demonstrations, 1982 and 1991." *American Sociological Review* 61: 478–99.

McCarthy, John D., and Mayer Zald. 1977. "Resource Mobilization and Social Movements: A Partial Theory." *American Journal of Sociology* 82: 1212–41.

McMichael, Phillip. 2004. *Development and Social Change: A Global Perspective.* 3rd edition. Thousand Oaks, CA: Pine Forge.

McPhail, Clark, and Ronald Wohlstein. 1983. "Individual and Collective Behaviors Within Gatherings, Demonstrations, and Riots." *Annual Review of Sociology* 9: 579–600.

Medrano, Juan Diez. 1994. "The Effects of Ethnic Segregation and Ethnic Competition on Political Mobilization in the Basque Country." *American Sociological Review* 59: 873–89.

Meyer, David S., and Sidney Tarrow (eds.). 1998. *The Social Movement Society.* Lanham, MD: Rowman and Littlefied.

Meyer, John W., John Boli, George Thomas, and Francisco Ramirez. 1997. "World Society and the Nation-State." *American Journal of Sociology* 103: 144–81.

Meyer, John W., and Michael T. Hannan (eds.). 1979. *National Development and the World System: Educational, Economic, and Political Change.* Chicago: University of Chicago Press.

Meyer, John W., and Ronald L. Jepperson. 2000. "The 'Actors' of Modern Society: The Cultural Construction of Social Agency." *Sociological Theory* 18: 100–120.

Mitchell, Sara McLaughlin, Scott Gates, and Håvard Hegre. 1999. "Evolution in Democracy-War Dynamics." *Journal of Conflict Resolution* 43: 771–92.

Moaddel, Mansoor. 1994. "Political Conflict in the World Economy: A Cross-national Analysis of Modernization and World-System Theories." *American Sociological Review* 59: 276–303.

Moore, Will. 1995. "Action-Reaction or Rational Expectations?" *Journal of Conflict Resolution* 39: 129–67.

——. 1998. "Repression and Dissent: Substitution, Context, and Timing." *American Journal of Political Science* 42: 851–73.

——. 2000. "The Repression of Dissent: Substitution, Context, and Timing." *Journal of Conflict Resolution* 44: 624–51.

Morris, Aldon. 1984. *The Origins of the Civil-Rights Movement*. New York: Free Press.

Morrison, Donald, Robert Mitchell, and John Paden. 1989. *Black Africa: A Comparative Handbook*. 2nd edition. New York: Paragon.

Muller, Edward, and Mitchell Seligson. 1987. "Inequality and Insurgency." *American Political Science Review* 81: 425–49.

Muller, Edward, and Eric Weede. 1990. "Cross-National Variation in Political Violence." *Journal of Conflict Resolution* 34: 624–51.

Myers, Daniel J. 1997. "Racial Rioting in the 1960s: An Event History Analysis of Local Conditions." *American Sociological Review* 62: 94–112.

——. 2000. "The Diffusion of Collective Violence: Infectiousness, Susceptibility, and Mass Media Networks." *American Journal of Sociology* 106: 173–208.

Myers, Daniel J., and Beth Schaefer Caniglia. 2004. "All the Rioting That's Fit to Print: Selection Effects in National Newspaper Coverage of Civil Disorders, 1968–1969." *American Sociological Review* 69: 519–43.

Nagel, Joane. 1980 "The Conditions of Ethnic Separatism: The Kurds in Turkey, Iran, and Iraq." *Ethnicity* 27: 279–97.

——. 1995. "American Indian Ethnic Renewal: Politics and the Resurgence of Identity." *American Sociological Review* 60: 947–65.

Nagel, Joane, and Susan Olzak. 1982. "Ethnic Mobilization in New and Old States: An Extension of the Competition Model." *Social Problems* 30: 127–43.

Nielsen, François. 1980 "The Flemish Movement in Belgium after World War II: A Dynamic Analysis." *American Sociological Review* 45: 76–94.

——. 1985. "Ethnic Solidarity in Modern Societies." *American Sociological Review* 50: 133–45.

O'Brien, Robert, Anne Marie Goetz, Jan Aart Scholte, and Marc Williams. 2000. *Contesting Global Governance: Multilateral Economic Institutions and Global Social Movements*. Cambridge: Cambridge University Press.

Olivier, Johan L. 1989. "Collective Violence in South Africa: A Study of Ethnic Collective Action in the Pretoria-Wiswatersrand-Vaal Triangle Area." Ph.D. Diss., Cornell University.

——. 1990. "Causes of Ethnic Collective Action in the Pretoria-Witwatersrand-Vaal Triangle." *South African Sociological Review* 2: 89–108.

Olzak, Susan. 1982. "Ethnic Mobilization in Quebec." *Ethnic and Racial Studies* 5: 253–75.

——. 1983. "Contemporary Ethnic Mobilization." *Annual Review of Sociology* 9: 355–74.

——. 1989 "Analysis of Events in the Study of Collective Action." *Annual Review of Sociology* 15: 119–41

——. 1992. *The Dynamics of Ethnic Competition and Conflict*. Stanford, CA: Stanford University Press.

——. 1998. "Ethnic Protest in Core and Periphery States." *Ethnic and Racial Studies* 21: 187–217.

——. 2004. "Ethnic and Nationalist Social Movements." Pp. 666–93 in Snow, Soule, and Kriesi, *The Blackwell Companion to Social Movements*.

Olzak, Susan, Maya Beasley, and Johan L. Olivier. 2003. "The Impact of State Reforms on Anti-Apartheid Protest in South Africa." 2003. *Mobilization: An International Journal* 8: 26–50.

Olzak, Susan, and Joane Nagel (eds.). 1986. *Competitive Ethnic Relations*. Orlando, FL: Academic Press.

Olzak, Susan, and Johan L. Olivier. 1998. "Racial Protest and Conflict in the U.S. and South Africa." *European Sociological Review* 14: 255–78.

——. 1999. "Comparative Event Analysis: Black Civil Rights Protest in South Africa and the United States." Pp. 253–83 in Dieter Rucht, Ruud Koopmans, and Friedhelm Neidhardt (eds.), *Acts of Dissent*. Lanham, MD: Rowman and Littlefield.

Olzak, Susan, and Suzanne Shanahan. 1996. "Deprivation and Race Riots: An Extension of Spilerman's Analysis" *Social Forces* 74: 931–61.

——. 2003. "Racial Policy and Racial Conflict in the Urban United States, 1869–1924." *Social Forces* 82: 481–517.

Olzak Susan, Suzanne Shanahan, and Elizabeth H. McEneaney. 1996. "Poverty, Segregation, and Race Riots, 1960–1993." *American Sociological Review* 61: 590–613.

Olzak, Susan, Suzanne Shanahan, and Elizabeth West. 1994. "School Desegregation, Interracial Exposure, and Antibusing Activity in Contemporary Urban America." *American Journal of Sociology* 100: 196–214.

Olzak, Susan, and Kiyoteru Tsutsui. 1998. "Status in the World System and Ethnic Mobilization." *Journal of Conflict Resolution* 42: 691–720.

Oneal, John R., and Bruce M. Russett. 1997. "The Classic Liberals Were Right: Democracy, Interdependence, and Conflict, 1950–1985." *International Studies Quarterly* 41: 267–94.

——. 2000. "A Response to Huntington." *Journal of Peace Research* 37: 611–12.

Opp, Karl-Dieter. 1994. "Repression and Revolutionary Action: In 1989." *Rationality and Society* 6: 101–38.

Paige, Jeffrey M. 1975. *Agrarian Revolution.* New York: Free Press.

Petersen, Roger D. 2002. *Understanding Ethnic Violence: Fear, Hatred, and Resentment in Twentieth-Century Eastern Europe.* Cambridge: Cambridge University Press.

Posner, Daniel. 2003. "The Political Salience of Cultural Difference: Why Chewas and Tumbukas Are Allies in Zambia and Adversaries in Malawi." Paper presented at the Laboratory in Comparative Ethnic Processes (LiCep) Conference, Yale University, May 2003.

Prazniak, Roxann, and Arif Dirlik (eds.) 2001. *Places and Politics in an Age of Globalization.* Lanham, MD: Rowman and Littlefield.

Quinn, Kevin, Michael Hechter, and Erik Wibbels. 2003. "Ethnicity, Insurgency, and Civil War Revisited." Paper presented at the Laboratory in Comparative Ethnic Processes (LiCep) Conference, Yale University, May 2003.

Räikkä, Juha. 1996. *Do We Need Minority Rights?* The Hague: Kluwer Law International.

Ramirez, Francisco, Yasemin Soysal, and Suzanne Shanahan. 1997. "The Changing Logic of Political Citizenship: The Cross-national Acquisition of Female Suffrage, 1850–1990." *American Sociological Review* 62: 735–45.

Rasler, Karen. 1996. "Concessions, Repression, and Political Protest in the Iranian Revolution." *American Sociological Review* 61: 132–52.

Regan, Patrick M. 2002. "Third-Party Interventions and the Duration of Intrastate Conflicts." *Journal of Conflict Resolution* 46: 55–73.

Regan, Patrick M., and M. Roadwan Abouharb. 2002. "Interventions and Civil Conflicts." *World Affairs* Summer 2002: 42–54.

Reilly, Benjamin. 2000. *Shades of Citizenship.* Stanford, CA: Stanford University Press.

Reynal-Querol, Marta. 2002. "Ethnicity, Political Systems, and Civil Wars." *Journal of Conflict Resolution* 46: 29–54.

Risse, Thomas, Stephen C. Ropp, and Kathryn Sikkink (eds.). 1999. *The Power of Human Rights.* Cambridge: Cambridge University Press.

Risse-Kappen, Thomas (ed.). 1995. *Bringing Transnational Relations Back In.* Cambridge: Cambridge University Press.

Roeder, Philip G. 1991. "Soviet Federalism and Ethnic Mobilization." *World Politics* 43: 196–232.

——. 2001. "Ethnolinguistic Fractionalization (ELF) Indices, 1961 and 1985." http://weber.ucsd.edu/

Rokkan, Stein. 1970. *Citizens, Elections, Parties.* New York: McKay.

Rotberg, Robert I. (ed.). 1996. *Vigilance and Vengeance: NGOs Preventing Ethnic Conflict in Divided Societies.* Washington DC: Brookings Institution.

Roy, Beth. 1994. *Some Trouble with Cows: Making Sense of Social Conflict.* Berkeley, CA: University of California Press.

Russett, Bruce M., John R. Oneal, and Michaelene Cox. 2000. "Clash of Civilizations or Realism and Liberalism Deju Vu? Some Evidence." *Journal of Peace Research* 37: 583–608.

Sambanis, Nicholas. 2001. "Do Ethnic and Nonethnic Civil Wars Have the Same Causes?" *Journal of Conflict Resolution* 45: 259–82.

——. 2004. "What Is Civil War? Conceptual and Empirical Complexities of an Operational Definition." *Journal of Conflict Resolution* 48: 814–58.

Scarritt, James R., and Shaheen Mozaffar. 1999. "The Specification of Ethnic Cleavages and Ethnopolitical Groups for the Analysis of Democratic Competition in Africa." *Nationalism and Ethnic Politics* 5: 82–117.

Schock, Kurt. 1996. "A Conjunctural Model of Political Conflict." *Journal of Conflict Resolution* 40: 98–133.

Schofer, Evan, and Marion Fourcade-Gourinchas. 2001. "The Structural Contexts of Civic Engagement: Voluntary Association Membership in Comparative Perspective." *American Sociological Review* 66: 806–28.

Sikkink, Kathryn. 2005. "Patterns of Dynamic Multilevel Governance and the Insider-Outsider Coalition." Pp. 151–73 in della Porta and Tarrow, *Transnational Protest and Global Activism.*

Singer, J. David, and Melvin Small. 1994. *Correlates of War: International and Civil War Data, 1816–1992.* Originally distributed by ICPSR (Inter-University Consortium for Political and Social Research), Ann Arbor, MI. See also www.correlatesofwar.org/.

Skocpol, Theda, and Margaret Sommers. 1980. "The Uses of Comparative History in Macrosocial Inquiry." *Comparative Studies in Society and History* 22: 174–97.

Skrentny, John D. 2002. *The Minority Rights Revolution.* Cambridge, MA: Harvard University Press.

Smith, Anthony D. 1979. "Towards a Theory of Ethnic Separatism." *Ethnic and Racial Studies* 2: 21–35.

——. 1981. *The Ethnic Revival in the Modern World.* Cambridge: Cambridge University Press.

——. 1984. "National Identity and Myths of Ethnic Descent." *Research in Social Movements, Conflict and Change* 7: 95–130.

——. 1986. *The Ethnic Origins of Nations.* Oxford: Blackwell.

——. 1991. *National Identity: Ethnonationalism in a Comparative Perspective.* Reno: University of Nevada Press.

——. 2000. *The Nation in History.* Hanover, NH: University Press of New England.

Smith, Jackie. 1995. "Transnational Political Processes and the Human Rights Movement." *Research on Social Movements, Conflict and Change* 18: 185–220.

——. 2004. "Transnational Processes and Movements." Pp. 311–35 in Snow, Soule, and Kriesi, *The Blackwell Companion to Social Movements.*

Smith, Jackie, Charles Chatfield, and Ron Pagnucco. 1997. "Social Movements and Global Politics: A Theoretical Framework." Pp. 59–80 in Jackie Smith, Charles Chatfield, and Ron Pagnucco (eds.), *Transnational Social Movements and Global Politics: Solidarity Beyond the State.* Syracuse, NY: Syracuse University Press.

Smith, Jackie, and Hank Johnston (eds.). 2002. *Globalization and Resistance.* Lanham, MD: Rowman and Littlefield.

Snow, David A. 2004. "Framing Processes, Ideology, and Discursive Fields." Pp. 380–413 in Snow, Soule, and Kriesi, *The Blackwell Companion to Social Movements.*

Snow, David A., and Susan E. Marshall. 1984. "Cultural Imperialism, Social Movements, and the Islamic Revival." *Research in Social Movements, Conflicts and Change* 7: 131–52.

Snow, David A., R. Burke Rochford Jr., Steven K. Worden, and Robert D. Benford. 1986. "Frame Alignment Processes, Micromobilization, and Movement Participation." *American Sociological Review* 51: 464–81.

Snow, David A., Sarah A. Soule, and Hanspeter Kriesi (eds.). 2004. *The Blackwell Companion to Social Movements.* Malden, MA: Blackwell.

Snyder, David, and Edward L. Kick. 1979. "Structural Position in the World System and Economic Growth, 1955–1970." *American Sociological Review* 84: 1096–1126.

Snyder, David, and Charles Tilly. 1972. "Hardship and Collective Violence in France, 1830–1960." *American Sociological Review* 37: 105–23.

Soule, Sarah A. 1997. "The Student Divestment Movement in the United States and the Shantytown: Diffusion of a Protest Tactic." *Social Forces* 75: 855–82.

——. 2004. "Diffusion Processes Within and Across Movements." Pp. 294–310 in Snow, Soule, and Kriesi, *The Blackwell Companion to Social Movements.*

Soysal, Yasemin. 1994. *Limits of Citizenship: Migrants and Postnational Membership in Europe.* Chicago: University of Chicago Press.

Spilerman, Seymour. 1970a. "The Causes of Racial Disturbances: A Comparison of Alternative Explanations." *American Sociological Review* 35: 627–49.

——. 1970b. "Comment on Wanderer's Article on Riot Severity and Its Correlates." *American Journal of Sociology* 75: 556–59.

——. 1971. "The Causes of Racial Disturbances: Test of an Explanation." *American Sociological Review* 35: 427–42.

——. 1976. "Structural Characteristics of Cities and the Severity of Racial Disorders." *American Sociological Review* 41: 771–93.

StataCorp. 2001. Stata Statistical Software: Release 8.0 SE. College Station, TX: StataCorp.

Strand, Håvard, Joachim Carlsen, Nils Petter Gleditsch, Håvard Hegre, Christin Ormgaug, and Laws Wilhelmsen. 2003, 2005. *Armed Conflict Dataset Codebook.* Uppsala, Norway: Department of Peace and Conflict Research, Uppsala University, and Department of Sociology and Political Science, Norwegian University of Science and Technology. For current updates, see www.prio.no/cwp/armedconflict/(accessed December 26, 2005).

Strang, David. 1990. "From Dependency to Sovereignty: An Event-History Analysis of Decolonialization." *American Sociological Review* 55: 846–60.

Strang, David, and John Meyer. 1993. "Institutional Conditions for Diffusion." *Theory and Society* 22: 487–511.

Strang, David, and Sarah A. Soule. 1998. "Diffusion in Organizations and Social Movements: From Hybrid Corn to Poison Pills." *Annual Review of Sociology* 24: 265–90.

Strang, David, and Nancy Brandon Tuma. 1993. "Spatial and Temporal Heterogeneity in Diffusion, " *American Journal of Sociology* 99: 614–39.

Strange, Susan. 1996. *The Retreat of the State: The Diffusion of Power in the World Economy*. Cambridge: Cambridge University Press.

Tarrow, Sidney. 1998. *Power in Movement: Social Movements and Contentious Politics*. 2nd edition. Cambridge: Cambridge University Press.

——. 2001. "Transnational Politics: Contentions and Institutions in International Politics." *Annual Review of Political Science* 4: 1–20.

——. 2005. *The New Transnational Activism*. New York: Cambridge University Press.

Tarrow, Sidney, and Donatella della Porta. 2005. "'Globalization,' Complex Internationalism, and Transnational Contention." Pp. 227–46 in della Porta and Tarrow, *Transnational Protest and Global Activism*.

Tarrow, Sidney, and Doug McAdam. 2005. "Scale Shift in Transnational Contention." Pp. 121–47 in della Porta and Tarrow, *Transnational Protest and Global Activism*.

Taylor, Charles Lewis, and Michael Lewis Hudson. 1972. *World Handbook of Political and Social Indicators*. 2nd edition. New Haven, CT: Yale University Press.

Taylor, Charles Lewis, and David A. Jodice. 1983. *World Handbook of Political and Social Indicators*. 3rd edition. New Haven, CT: Yale University Press.

Thernstrom, Stephan (ed.). 1980. *Harvard Encyclopedia of American Ethnic Groups*. Cambridge, MA: Belknap.

Tilly, Charles. 1975. "Reflections on the History of European State-Making." pp. 3–83 in Charles Tilly (ed.), *The Formation of States in Western Europe*. Princeton: Princeton University Press.

——. 1978. *From Mobilization to Revolution*. Reading, MA: Addison-Wesley.

——. 1993. *European Revolutions, 1492–1992*. New York: Blackwell.

——. 2000. "Violent and Nonviolent Trajectories in Contentious Politics." Paper presented at the symposium "States in Transition and the Challenge of Ethnic Conflict," Russian Academy of Sciences US National Academy of Sciences, Moscow, December 2000.

——. 2003. *The Politics of Collective Violence*. Cambridge: Cambridge University Press.

Toft, Monica Duffy. 2003. *The Geography of Ethnic Violence*. Princeton, NJ: Princeton University Press.

Tolnay, Stewart E., and E. M. Beck. 1995. *A Festival of Violence: An Analysis of Lynching of Blacks in the American South*. Urbana: University of Illinois Press.

Tsutsui, Kiyoteru. 2004. "Global Civil Society and Ethnic Social Movements in the Contemporary World." *Sociological Forum* 19: 63–87.

Ulfelder, Jay. 1997. "Ethnic and Nationalist Protest in the Baltic Republics, 1987–1991: Causes, Dynamics, and Consequences." Ph.D. diss., Stanford University.

———. 2004. "Baltic Protest in the Gorbachev Era: Movement Content and Dynamics." *The Global Review of Ethnopolitics* 3: 23–43.

Union of International Associations. 1966, 1977, 1982. *Yearbook of International Organizations*. Munich: K.G. Saur.

van den Berghe, Pierre L. 1967. *Race and Racism: A Comparative Perspective*. New York: Wiley.

Vanhanen, Tatu. 1999. "Domestic Ethnic Conflict and Ethnic Nepotism: A Comparative Analysis." *Journal of Peace Research* 36: 55–73.

———. 2001. "Domestic Peace and Ethnic Violence." Paper presented at the Fourth Pan-European International Relations Conference, ECPR Standing Group on International Relations, Canterbury, Sept. 2001.

Varshney, Ashutosh. 2001. "Ethnic Conflict and Civil Society." *World Politics* 53: 362–98.

———. 2002. *Ethnic Conflict and Civil Life: Hindus and Muslims in India*. New Haven, CT: Yale University Press.

———. 2003. "Nationalism, Ethnic Conflict and Rationality." *Political Perspectives* 1: 85–99.

Villarreal, Andrés. 2004. "The Social Ecology of Rural Violence: Land Scarcity, the Organization of Agricultural Production, and the Presence of the State." *American Journal of Sociology* 110: 313–48.

Wallerstein, Immanuel. 1976. *The Modern World-System: Capitalist Agriculture and the Origins of the European World-Economy in the Sixteenth Century*. New York: Academic Press.

Weingast, Barry R. 1998. "Constructing Trust: The Politics and Economics of Ethnic and Regional Conflict." Pp. 163–200 in Karol Soltan, Eric, M. Uslaner, and Virginia Haufler (eds.), *Institutions and Social Order*. Ann Arbor: University of Michigan Press.

Welsh, Jennifer M. 1996. *Humanitarian Intervention and International Relations*. Oxford and New York: Oxford University Press.

Wilkes, Rima, and Dina G. Okamoto. 2002. "Ethnic Competition and Mobilization by Minorities at Risk." *Nationalism and Ethnic Politics* 8: 1–23.

Wilkinson, Steven I. 2004. *Electoral Competition and Ethnic Violence in India*. Cambridge: Cambridge University Press.

Williams, Robin M., Jr. 1994. "The Sociology of Ethnic Conflicts: Comparative International Perspectives." *Annual Review of Sociology* 20: 49–79.

Wilson, William Julius. 1978. *The Declining Significance of Race*. Chicago: University of Chicago Press.

Wimmer, Andreas. 2002. *Nationalist Exclusion and Ethnic Conflict: Shadows of Modernity*. Cambridge: Cambridge University Press.

Winant, Howard. 1994. *Racial Conditions: Politics, Theory, Comparisons*. Minneapolis: University of Minnesota Press.

World Bank. 1980. *World Development Report 1980*. New York: Oxford University Press.

———. 1985. *World Development Report 1985*. New York: Oxford University Press.

———. 1997. *World Development Indicators 1997*. Washington, DC: World Bank.

Yashar, Deborah J. 1999. "Democracy, Indigenous Movements, and the Postliberal Challenge in Latin America." *World Politics* 52: 76–104.

———. 2001. "Globalization and Collective Action." *Comparative Politics* 34: 355.

Young, Crawford. 2002. "Deciphering Disorder in Africa: Is Identity the Key?" *World Politics* 54: 532–57.

Zafarullah, Habib, and Mohammed Habibur Rahman. 2002. "Human Rights, Civil Society, and Nongovernmental Organizations: The Nexus in Bangladesh." *Human Rights Quarterly* 24: 1011–24.

Zald, Mayer, and John D. McCarthy (eds.). 1987. *Social Movements in an Organizational Society*. New Brunswick, NJ: Transaction Books.